The Political Impossibility
of Modern Counterinsurgency

Columbia Studies in Terrorism and Irregular Warfare

Columbia Studies in Terrorism and Irregular Warfare

BRUCE HOFFMAN, SERIES EDITOR

This series seeks to fill a conspicuous gap in the burgeoning literature on terrorism, guerrilla warfare, and insurgency. The series adheres to the highest standards of scholarship and discourse and publishes books that elucidate the strategy, operations, means, motivations, and effects posed by terrorist, guerrilla, and insurgent organizations and movements. It thereby provides a solid and increasingly expanding foundation of knowledge on these subjects for students, established scholars, and informed reading audiences alike.

Ami Pedahzur, *The Israeli Secret Services and the Struggle Against Terrorism*

Ami Pedahzur and Arie Perliger, *Jewish Terrorism in Israel*

Lorenzo Vidino, *The New Muslim Brotherhood in the West*

Erica Chenoweth and Maria J. Stephan, *Why Civil Resistance Works: The Strategic Logic of Nonviolent Resistance*

William C. Banks, *New Battlefields/Old Laws: Critical Debates on Asymmetric Warfare*

Blake W. Mobley, *Terrorism and Counterintelligence: How Terrorist Groups Elude Detection*

Michael W. S. Ryan, *The Deep Battle: Decoding Al-Qaeda's Strategy: The Deep Battle Against America*

David H. Ucko and Robert Egnell, *Counterinsurgency in Crisis: Britain and the Challenges of Modern Warfare*

Bruce Hoffman and Fernando Reinares, editors, *The Evolution of the Global Terrorist Threat: From 9/11 to Osama bin Luden's Death*

Boaz Ganor, *Global Warning: The Rationality of Modern Islamist Terrorism and the Challenge to the Liberal Democratic World*

The Political Impossibility of Modern Counterinsurgency

Strategic Problems, Puzzles, and Paradoxes

M.L.R. SMITH
and DAVID MARTIN JONES

Columbia
University
Press
New York

Columbia University Press
Publishers Since 1893
New York   Chichester, West Sussex
cup.columbia.edu
Copyright © 2015 Columbia University Press
All rights reserved

Library of Congress Cataloging-in-Publication Data
Smith, M. L. R. (Michael Lawrence Rowan), 1963–
   The political impossibility of modern counterinsurgency : strategic problems,
   puzzles, and paradoxes / M. L. R. Smith and David Martin Jones.
      pages cm. — (Columbia studies in terrorism and irregular warfare)
   Includes bibliographical references and index.
   ISBN 978-0-231-17000-0 (cloth : alk. paper) — ISBN 978-0-231-53912-8 (e-book)
   1. Counterinsurgency—History—21st century. 2. Terrorism—History—21st century.
   I. Jones, David Martin, 1950– II. Title.
   U241.S64   2015
   355.02'18—dc23
                                                      2014025193

Columbia University Press books are printed on permanent and durable
   acid-free paper.
This book is printed on paper with recycled content.
Printed in the United States of America

c 10 9 8 7 6 5 4 3 2 1

COVER DESIGN: Fifth Letter
COVER ART: The Noun Project, Creative Commons

References to websites (URLs) were accurate at the time of writing. Neither
   the author nor Columbia University Press is responsible for URLs that
   may have expired or changed since the manuscript was prepared.

Contents

Acknowledgments

In many ways, this book represents the culmination of work on the relationship between strategy and violent nonstate actors stretching back the best part of three decades. The content of the chapters that have come to compose this volume has passed through many iterations, both verbal and written, over many years, beginning with doctoral research in the mid-1980s and extending to the teaching of courses on strategy and counterinsurgency, first at the National University of Singapore in the early 1990s, then at the Royal Naval College in the mid-1990s, and finally at King's College London from the early 2000s. David Martin Jones and I thank the editors and reviewers of the following journals and periodicals for being receptive to our work throughout these years: *International Affairs, Review of International Studies, Journal of Strategic Studies, Small Wars and Insurgencies, Studies in Conflict and Terrorism, Cambridge Review of International Affairs, The World Today,* and *World Defence Systems.* We are very grateful for their support. Likewise, we extend grateful appreciation to our friends and colleagues Celeste Ward Gventer and John Stone. Celeste provided acute insights into the U.S. policymaking world that would come to elevate counterinsurgency to a position of explicit importance in military and defense circles. From her skeptical and questioning approach, based on hard experience of the most troubled times during the Coalition occupation of Iraq, we learned much. John is a fine strategic theorist, and he undoubtedly helped refine many points of our thinking, thus enhancing the quality of the analysis in the following pages. We are very appreciative of all the excellent work that Anne Routon, Whitney Johnson, and the staff of Columbia University Press have put into commissioning the volume and bringing the manuscript to publication. We are particularly grateful to the anonymous readers who reviewed both the initial proposal and final manuscript for their many helpful insights and recommendations. Finally, we owe much thanks to Bruce Hoffman, the editor of the series in which this study appears, for his always pluralistic, openhanded approach to academic inquiry and his constant encouragement in supporting the publication of this volume.

MLRS
London

Introduction

"I still thought we had a good chance of turning things round merely by adjusting our counter-insurgency tactics, reflecting lessons learned in Malaya, Algeria, Vietnam or Northern Ireland," Sherard Cowper-Coles, the former British ambassador to Afghanistan, lamented.[1] The memoir of his time as the United Kingdom's man in Kabul charts his mounting disenchantment. Yet Cowper-Coles began his posting believing in the efficacy of counter-insurgency—or COIN, as it popularly known. However, after sitting through one too many PowerPoint presentations, replete with abstruse graphics and flow charts on COIN metrics, listening to the "hopeful vocabulary of stabilization," and experiencing the "eager-earnest syntax over counter-insurgency," Cowper-Coles felt his faith fading.[2] Although he started from the premise that counterinsurgency was a logical, historically proven set of understandings that confronted violent challenges to established authority and stabilized volatile regions, his experiences led him to recognize the constituting ambiguities in the notion of COIN, which once seemed to represent a magic panacea for the conduct of complex interventions in faraway places.

This volume explores the ambiguities and dissonances—the puzzles and enigmas—in the contemporary appreciation and practices of counterinsurgency: an idea that in the first decade of the twenty-first century assumed a prominent position in Western military and strategic thought.[3] Cowper-Coles's journey from belief to doubt is only one account of how a generation of diplomats, advisers, aid workers, soldiers, and scholars who once believed in the seductive blandishments of COIN became disillusioned.[4] The story of how a community of thinkers and practitioners in Western nations came to believe in the transformative power of counterinsurgency is not, however, the central theme of this book. That story is interesting, and it is necessary to state its background, but it need not detain us long, for its lineaments are increasingly well documented.[5]

The Rise of COIN

The rise of modern counterinsurgency thinking begins with the events of September 11, 2001 (9/11), when members of the al-Qaeda jihadist network hijacked four airliners. The loss of nearly three thousand lives when two of the planes commandeered as weapons flew into the Twin Towers of the World Trade Center in New York City, while the third struck the Pentagon in Alexandria, Virginia, and the fourth crashed into a Pennsylvania field, defined the political contours of Western foreign policy for the succeeding decade. It was the events of the "9/11 era" that saw counterinsurgency evolve as the seemingly logical response to this "asymmetric" threat.

In the wake of 9/11, analytical attention at first focused on al-Qaeda's capacity to mount indiscriminate suicide assaults. The events of 9/11 were followed by further al-Qaeda-linked conspiracies and bombings in Western cities as well as in other targets in Southeast Asia, the Middle East, and Africa. "Home-grown" or fifth-column jihadists perpetrated many of these attacks. As a consequence, Western state attention focused on how to deter these threats through legal and intelligence measures as well as through strengthening internal resilience through greater social cohesion, mutual cooperation among threatened states, and programs that aimed to "deradicalize" either actual or potential jihadist operatives.[6] Although not recognized as such at the time, the practical effort in the years immediately after 9/11 might be described as the first wave of counterinsurgency thinking, concerned as it was to understand and confront transnational jihadist attempts to disturb the modern secular democratic West through a program of violent subversion.[7]

This "counterjihadist" or counterradicalization phase was the mise-en-scène to a new era of counterinsurgency thinking that took shape among Western militaries after 2004. The overtly COIN era evidently responded to the events of 9/11. Yet, somewhat paradoxically, its leading theorists drew inspiration and doctrinal insight from historic—often colonial era—cases of counterinsurgency, such as those Cowper-Coles alludes to in Malaya, Algeria, Vietnam, and Northern Ireland, rather than from 9/11 itself.[8] The new COIN era, or second counterinsurgency wave, originates in the events that followed the 9/11 attacks. It began when Western coalition forces invaded Afghanistan to rid the country of the hard-line Taliban regime that had provided a safe haven for the core leadership of al-Qaeda. A combined effort, involving Western Special Forces in conjunction with the indigenous resistance of the Northern Alliance, swiftly overthrew the Taliban.

Western forces subsequently occupied Afghanistan in an increasingly uneasy alliance with the government of Hamid Karzai, whose authority suffered almost constant armed challenge from the remnants of the Taliban, particularly in the Pashtun heartlands of Helmand and Kandahar Provinces. The difficulty coalition forces encountered in stabilizing a weak and ethnically fragmented Afghan parastate that had suffered historically from factionalism and an absence of civic institutions and in supporting the increasingly corrupt Karzai government represented a classical counterinsurgency dilemma—namely, how to win popular support for the government cause and secure the country against subversion.[9]

The decade after 9/11 saw the Taliban insurgency draw Western forces into an increasingly problematic conflict that progressively disheartened those who had once supported this just war. However, it was President George W. Bush's decision to invade Iraq in March 2003 that justified the new military thinking that gave rise to the counterinsurgency era. The optimism that initially accompanied the fall of Saddam Hussein's regime in 2003 quickly gave way to despondency as the occupation forces confronted the violent collapse and fragmentation of Iraqi society. The combination of Saddam's fall, the Coalition

Provisional Authority's decision to remove officials and army personnel tainted by previous Baathist connections, overoptimistic assessments of a return to stability, and a lack of security on the ground saw Iraq degenerate into anarchy.[10] Fierce sectarian violence erupted between the Shiite majority and the once politically dominant Sunni minority population, while jihadist elements, now functioning under the all-purpose umbrella of "al-Qaeda in Iraq," exploited the political vacuum and launched indiscriminate attacks on government targets, Coalition troops, and their mainly Shiite religious opponents.

As Iraq disintegrated, the Provisional Authority appeared reluctant to confront the reality that it faced a concerted insurrection. Convinced that al-Qaeda activists from outside Iraq were responsible for the escalating violence, Coalition military operations focused—so it was frequently alleged—on hard "kinetic" encounters intended to eliminate pockets of militant resistance. These conventional force-on-force concentrations paid little attention to the wider effects of such violence in populated areas, in particular the collateral damage and noncombatant casualties. The Coalition reluctantly accepted that it faced a protracted "insurgency," thus setting the scene for the counterinsurgency narrative to insert itself in the political discourse.

According to the evolving narrative, after 2006 the U.S. administration replaced too "conventionally" minded generals with apparently more progressive and flexible commanders equipped with both service experience in Iraq and new ways of thinking about war among the people.[11] This new cadre, the COIN narrative held, took the necessary steps to address the Iraq crisis. Drawing inspiration, in part, from a range of classical writings on COIN dating from the British and French experience of decolonization in the 1950s and 1960s, this new soldier-scholar elite and their advisers in the military, academe, and nongovernmental think tanks developed the new COIN paradigm. Utilizing concepts of population-centric war and deep cultural knowledge of the enemy, these officers, advisers, commentators, and planners brought fresh thinking to the challenge of insurgency. A "surge" in U.S. troops, which effectively doubled the number of U.S. soldiers in Iraq, provided the necessary security on the ground to apply the new tactics. New techniques of understanding the adversary's value systems and motivations enabled the Coalition to prize tribal chieftains away from al-Qaeda's embrace in a "Sunni awakening." Winning the battle for hearts and minds further entailed reconstruction projects, while more precise intelligence-led operations eliminated the militants responsible for the violence destabilizing Iraqi society. As a result, violence declined dramatically, enabling Iraq to progress to elections and self-government.

The apparent success of the application of COIN technique in Iraq between 2006 and 2009 facilitated a storyline that presented events as proceeding in a dialectical fashion of challenge, response, setback, adaption, and ultimate triumph. It was a teleological tale of manifest destiny, culminating in the victory of Western—or, more precisely, American—values of freedom and modernity in the face of the violent reactionary challenge from premodern tribalism. This three-act drama, then, told in the first act of the shock at the surprise attack of 9/11 on the American heartland and the swift retribution dealt al-Qaeda and its fellow travelers via the invasions of Afghanistan and Iraq. The second act witnessed the mishandling of the occupations of these fragile states and the promise of preemption undermined, while these broken states disintegrated. The intervention of dynamic, innovative leaders capable of bold, decisive action in the third act of the drama resolved the incipient tragedy of the second act (at least in the case of Iraq). Between 2007 and 2010, this account achieved quasi-official status. Counterinsurgency became the creed of choice in Western strategic thought: a militarily effective, politically efficacious, humane form of warfare. In an unusual twist, the military handbooks that codified the new counterinsurgency orthodoxy achieved much publicity, with popular media commentary widely extolling its virtues.[12] COIN advocates subsequently advanced its practice as the template for addressing the likely form of future war.[13]

COIN Puzzles, Problems, and Paradoxes

Presenting COIN as a reproducible "way of war" is at best ambitious, at worst hubristic.[14] It assumes that future war will take the form of civil war—that is, "low-intensity" conflicts occurring within states rather than greater-intensity conflicts between states. As such, it is not a new assumption. Commentators have proclaimed the demise of classic interstate war and the rise of intrastate conflict ever since the end of the Cold War.[15] What changed in the decade after 9/11 was the understanding that confronting the challenge presented by violent nonstate and often transnational actors required specialized military knowledge and related techniques: in other words, the thought and practice of counterinsurgency principles.

The political legacy of Western involvement in Iraq and Afghanistan has led in time, however, to some revision to the COIN mantra. This revisionism has been especially evident in the problematic case of Western engagement in Afghanistan.[16] The assumption in some sections of the armed forces and their defense bureaucracies that COIN represented a ubiquitous tool set transferable from Iraq to Afghanistan came into question.[17] After a decade of steady losses in personnel and mounting financial costs in defending the regime in Kabul, individuals such as Cowper-Coles began to view COIN not as a panacea but as a program of continuous commitment that imbricated Western democracies in protracted conflicts without any evident political endgame. "As always," Cowper-Coles observed skeptically after enduring another discourse on counterinsurgency, "the theme was that we were making progress, but that challenges remained."[18] Progress without end, the future promise of success without any solution in sight, epitomized the false promise of counterinsurgency.

Thus, although since 2011 COIN no longer exerts the influence it once did in Washington and elsewhere, the outcome of these "low-intensity conflicts" remains problematically undetermined. There is now an evolving debate about whether the focus on small wars will continue to influence Western strategic thought or a concern with larger conflict will supersede it. This debate notwithstanding, it would seem propitious to step back from current debates about future war to evaluate the theory and practice of what some commentators have termed "large-scale, third-party COIN" and to draw attention to its puzzling incoherence and the way it came to exert influence over Western strategic thinking during the first decade of this century.[19]

It was in the course of the 1990s that the new small-war security environment began to assert itself. The growing literature on the subject presented the rediscovery of COIN as a self-contained and self-evident set of understandings and practices derived mainly from British and French experiences in the period of decolonization in the 1950s and 1960s. As a consequence, COIN came to be seen as a relatively coherent military and political solution to the internal wars that the United States and its North Atlantic Treaty Organization (NATO) and Coalition partners now confronted. This was somewhat ironic, given that the internal wars of the 1990s had evolved the capacity to extend their influence far beyond their territorial boundaries in the durably disordered world that globalization had, as if by an invisible hand, conjured into being.

In this context, a military-intellectual complex promoted COIN as a "way of war" that appeared logical, efficient, and democratically palatable to those regimes that confronted the challenge of low-intensity internal wars, which also had the capacity to manifest as external threats in an interconnected but by no means integrated global order. The transnational dimension of many of these struggles (for example, the Afghan insurgency's wider impact on both Western relations with Pakistan and the broader geostrategic balance in South Asia) meant that these wars were inexorably something more than internal. The books and articles published in this initial phase of thinking about globally interconnected conflict witnessed the reemergence of COIN within American strategic thinking as a discrete, technical set of practices that addressed the problem of "insurgency" with a countervailing technique of "counterinsurgency." More particularly, it was believed that when a knowledgeable soldiery under the guidance of an expert elite applied these techniques, they would successfully address these polymorphous threats.

Although after 2005 some critical commentators began to question the historical premises informing modern counterinsurgency advocacy, few studies have asked the simple but still puzzling question: What precisely is COIN? Is COIN a strategy, a doctrine, a theory, a military practice, or something else? In this respect, this analysis presents COIN as a set of intellectual puzzles that require both unpacking and skeptical deconstruction. This is the principal objective of this volume: to uncover the hidden thinking that obscures the contemporary understanding of COIN.

[handwritten margin notes: Disconnect between theory + practice. Coin taught evangelically but not executed at all by ground units. Token efforts only]

[handwritten bottom note: for Coy - 'Doing' full-spectrum COIN.]

[handwritten annotation: COIN was a framework for talking about the campaign. In practice, it was only used on briefing slides or by specialist units.]

The Structure of the Book

The chapters in this book thus evaluate the notion of COIN from first principles, exploring the relationship between counterinsurgency and war. The first enigma concerns COIN's relationship to established understandings of the character of war. Chapter 1 explores whether COIN possesses any unique attributes, as its advocates maintain, that distinguish it from war as classically understood. This chapter dissects the meaning of the term *insurgency* in order to reach an understanding of its analytic utility. It examines the notion of insurgency through a Clausewitzian lens. The question of what exactly constitutes insurgency leads to a curious puzzle because, as chapter 1 shows, classifying insurgency as a separate category or subcategories of war leads to an intellectually limiting and ultimately self-defeating set of policy prescriptions. Identifying insurgency as a discrete phenomenon and detaching it from a broader understanding of war leads, we argue, to five category mistakes: first, it exceptionalizes a certain form of war; second, it denies the intellectual study of war; third, it decontextualizes instances of war; fourth, it leads to overprescription in war; and, finally, it leads to the destrategization of war. The fundamental enigma then is: Does counterinsurgency possess any idea of what it is actually meant to be countering?

The second chapter evaluates the enigma of what COIN is from a practical military standpoint. Does it constitute a set of techniques that may be applied irrespective of time and place, or is it more contingent in its application to discrete conflicts? Despite becoming a core concept driving military operations in Afghanistan and, before that, in Iraq, as well as constituting the dominant view influencing both military planning and the interventions of the major Western powers, COIN remains opaque in both theoretical and practical terms. Again, this ambiguity raises a question: What is COIN exactly? Chapter 2 questions the assumption and relevance of the thinking behind contemporary counterinsurgency and explores whether it comprises a military doctrine or strategy. We demonstrate that the ultimate effect of much COIN thinking is to reduce the highly contingent nature of war to a series of techniques, the application of which are deemed viable whenever a state confronts a conflict that may be broadly defined as an "insurgency." Such assumptions, we shall contend, preempt necessary though by their nature difficult judgments about the construction and implementation of strategies that ensure that the ends sought are proportional to the means employed.

The third and fourth chapters turn to the puzzle of what COIN represents for contemporary strategic theory. These chapters investigate the various policy agendas that COIN seeks to address. Chapter 3 traces the resurgence of contemporary thinking about COIN. The focus of this chapter is COIN's renaissance, especially in the U.S. military, even though it was traditionally regarded as a secondary activity in military thinking and practice. It argues that COIN's reemergence can be subsumed into two distinct schools of thought: a neoclassical school and a global insurgency school (examined further in chapter 4). Chapter 3 suggests that modernization theory, revived in the 1990s under the auspices of an end-of-history ideology that assumed liberal democratic convergence, expressly informed the thinking of the neoclassical school. Neoclassicism saw U.S. policy as a means of transforming traditional societies into modern, market-friendly, pluralist democracies. This project permeated COIN thinking, leading to a nation-building emphasis that sought, through both military and civilian measures, to convert broken or failing autocracies into fledgling democracies. The chapter analyzes the connection between the reinvention of COIN after 2001 and the U.S. preoccupation with a modernization agenda that dated from the Cold War and the policy misadventures that often informed it.

Chapter 4 builds on this analysis of the neoclassical turn by examining the emergence of a revisionist global insurgency school that developed alongside the neoclassical school but that eventually contested the neoclassical formulation of counterinsurgency as unnecessarily restrictive both in theory and in its policy prescriptions. The rise of the global COIN school linked the growth of asymmetric challenges to Western power after 2001 with broader globalizing trends that, in its adherents' view, widened the character of the threat and, in turn, required solutions that ranged from sensitive policing to human security and humanitarian intervention that responsibly protected afflicted populations as a putative Arab Spring engulfed the Middle East and destabilized authoritarian regimes from Tunisia to Syria. This school appeared to evince a more sophisticated and critically aware appreciation of current security problems. However, a close examination of this school's thought and practice, we contend, leaves an incomplete understanding of the phenomenon of violent nonstate challenges and the policies and strategies necessary to combat them.

Chapter 5 turns to the question of the historical assumptions informing current COIN thinking, which draws much of its inspiration largely from British experiences during the period of decolonization. It addresses the puzzle of whether the British armed forces ever promulgated a coherent understanding of counterinsurgency. In recent years, a number of commentators have contended that the British reputation for conducting small wars has suffered in the wake of recent setbacks in Iraq and Afghanistan. The argument in this chapter questions whether such a tradition ever existed. A close examination of this tradition and of the myths associated with it reveals the claim to COIN expertise to be of recent ideological fashioning. In fact, the British armed forces have rarely advanced an explicit facility for counterinsurgency or small war, and, to the extent that they have, it has often been deeply contradictory. Invariably, as we suggest, it has been commentators external to the British armed forces and often outside the United Kingdom who have ascribed this tradition to the British. Most notably, as demonstrated, commentators in the United States keen to prescribe practices of minimum force or rapid institutional learning for U.S. forces largely created the legend of British COIN expertise. A more critical group of scholars subsequently questioned this narrative, arguing that the British conduct of small wars was often based on coercion. Ultimately, what this myth reveals is that political will, not an all-purpose template for fighting insurgencies, has determined whatever success Britain has had in so-called small war.

Chapter 6 returns the discussion to the concept of counterinsurgency and the final question: If COIN is, as its adherents argue, a qualitatively distinct form of warfare, how does the escalation process (which governs actions and outcomes in war) differ, if at all, from so-called conventional war? If insurgency and COIN frame a distinct kind of war, the escalation process would surely differ. Escalation is both the practical and theoretical key to unlock the course and eventual resolution of all violent clashes. Yet if all violence is intended to achieve political outcomes, what is distinctive about escalation in insurgent–counterinsurgent clashes? To answer this question, the chapter applies the principles of strategic theory. The assessment demonstrates how the escalation process in conditions of insurgency and counterinsurgency might be reconceptualized and illustrates how certain broad observations may be verified. In the final analysis, the argument emphasizes that the process of escalation can never follow a predetermined pattern, given that all wars are unique to their time and place and will be affected in their conduct by the contingent forces of passion, chance, and reason.

The conclusion of this study seeks to tie the various strands of the analysis together and draw out a number of durable themes that fall out from the previous chapters. The finale points to the underlying problem surrounding the elusive nature of the concept of insurgency, which is inordinately difficult to define with clarity. This lack of exactitude contains corresponding implications for the comprehension of counterinsurgency, rendering the notion of COIN malleable. We maintain that counterinsurgency all too easily ends up not as a robust theory, but as a faux narrative preoccupied with technique and "lessons" to be learned. In other words, the contemporary advocacy of COIN stakes its credibility on identifying a timeless and almost scientifically predictable pattern to certain tactical practices in war, yet this emphasis on exploring the technical grammar of conduct comes at the expense of understanding the contingent political factors that make all war exclusive to its time and place and thus unpredictable. Ultimately, we conclude, the COIN narrative's attempt to scientize the complexity of war illustrates a fallacy within much Western social inquiry, which seeks to impose a meaning and structure on events in the past even though that meaning was not actually present during the events themselves. The resulting capacity for self-delusion and ideologically induced policy mistakes inherent in the counterinsurgency paradigm is therefore profound. At the heart of the analysis contained in these chapters lies a warning of the dangers posed to effective foreign and military policy by the imposition of the theoretical blinkers that we suggest an obsession with COIN all too readily embodies.

Defining Strategic Theory

It should be evident already that this work questions the accepted precepts of counterinsurgency. At the same time, it differs from other critical assessments. It does not present a history of the problems associated with COIN.[20] Nor does it provide a critique of military tactics or of the broader difficulties that have afflicted interventions in Iraq, Afghanistan, and elsewhere.[21] And it does not seek to criticize the impact of COIN on any particular armed force or its institutions.[22] Instead, this study intends to interrogate COIN theory's conceptual underpinnings and to show how an inadequate appreciation of first-order assumptions leads to intellectual incoherence that ultimately manifests itself in bad policy outcomes. In other words, this volume identifies "politics"—the attempt to attain goals commensurate with the interests and values promulgated in democracies by elected representatives—as the neglected dimension in discussions of counterinsurgency.

The necessity of conducting military operations in pursuit of "clear political goals" was something that began to worry Western policy makers as the prolonged and intractable nature of the Afghan intervention became increasingly apparent after 2008.[23] Cowper-Coles's account of his growing pessimism noted that what he and his embassy team had not really appreciated was that counterinsurgency "was not really a strategy at all." In fact, he observed, COIN "amounts to little more than a technique or tactic for suppressing, locally and temporarily, the symptoms of an insurgency, rather than curing the underlying disease."[24] Here we can see diplomats and some military practitioners beginning to grasp the political dislocation at the heart of COIN thinking. It is this crucial strategic factor linking tactical conduct on the ground to political outcomes meant to achieve the higher goals of policy that constitutes the core of this study.[25]

Strategic theory thus forms the analytical framework to evaluate counterinsurgency. Put simply, strategy relates means to ends, or, as Michael Howard explained thirty years ago, it is the "use of available resources to gain any objective."[26] Here, the term *resources (means)* refers not simply to the tangible elements of power but also to the many intangible factors that might affect a decision maker—most notably the degree of will that an actor may mobilize in the pursuit of its goals. Strategic theory, in other words, concerns itself with the study of ends, ways, and means in social action.[27]

To talk of a "theory" in this context requires further clarification. Given the infinite variety of human conduct, strategic theory does not claim the status of a hard scientific understanding that achieves reproducible results across time and space. Strategic theory is thus no different from other branches of the humanities that cannot yield systematically reproducible data, despite styling themselves "sciences" of politics or sociology.[28] Human conduct does not lend itself to laboratory conditions. Strategic theory does offer, though, a theory in the sense that it advances a set of propositions that, if true, explain certain patterns of behavior and events. In this respect, strategic theory advances a series of purposive assumptions that guide analysis.[29] The theory, then, is parsimonious in setting limits that enable the generation of insights at the level of the unitary political actor. In analyzing ways, ends, and means, strategy encompasses the widest consideration of how to attain designated goals. Significantly, as the strategic approach has evolved in the study of social action, it has often considered military power as one of the more potent means of achieving given aims. Although this approach does not have to entail military means to have validity,[30] it is worth acknowledging that as a methodology it has often implied the study of the use or threat of use of organized armed force to achieve political outcomes. The Greek word *strategos*, the "art of the general," is the etymological root of the modern term *strategy*, but *strategic theory* applies, as classical strategic theorists such as Thomas Schelling have consistently demonstrated,[31] to all forms of human activity.

Notwithstanding the universal applicability of strategy, counterinsurgency evidently signifies, in understanding and application, elements of military practice and degrees of coercion. As a consequence, both COIN and insurgency fit logically within the strategic understanding of war as a rational, goal-orientated enterprise. To employ the often cited aphorism of Prussian philosopher of war Carl von Clausewitz, we can say that "war is a continuation of political intercourse, carried on with other means."[32] The "other means" in this context are the instruments of organized violence. War is, then, a rationally purposive exercise,[33] where the deed of violence itself constitutes *"an act of force to compel the enemy to do our will."*[34] War is thus intimately bound up in understandings of strategy as one possible set of means to attain desired goals. If war is a political act, then it follows that counterinsurgency as a mechanism of coercive pressure fits within the strategic postulate that it is one possible method to attain specific objectives.

Indeed, adhering to the precepts of strategic theory, all acts of violence, regardless of their character, are understood to fulfill a political purpose. In this respect, counterinsurgency (or insurgency) does not necessarily differ from any other set of tactical approaches in war. Contrary, therefore, to much prevailing academic and military commentary, which asserts a clear difference between counterinsurgency and counterterrorism,[35] our analysis does not distinguish between them. The two terms, *counterinsurgency* and *counterterrorism*, address the same phenomenon—namely, political actors using asymmetrically violent means to attain their political ends. This constitutes our broad working definition of insurgency. Conversely, our working definition of counterinsurgency denotes the endeavor to confound violent challenges to established authority. Should our argument subsequently identify dissimilarities in tactical and strategic practice, we explain and demonstrate them rather than simply assert them. Initially, however, we assume that the difference between counterinsurgency and counterterrorism are theoretically insignificant. They are distinctions without a difference.

Finally, a prerequisite of strategic theory is that it practices a value-neutral approach toward its object of inquiry. It lays to one side the observer's moral position regarding questions of means and ends. Academic disinterest here is particularly important in considering the role of violence in political conduct, which a study of counterinsurgency inevitably entails. Strategic theory analyzes situations within a framework that places social actors' conscious choices above any focus on the morality or causality of violence itself. As Thomas Schelling notes, strategic analysis is "usually about the situation, not the individuals—about the structure of incentives, of information and communication, the choices available, and the tactics that can be employed." Accordingly, strategic theory "deals with situations in which one party has to think about how the others are going to reach their decisions."[36] Because determining how others are likely to react to one's own decisions and actions is difficult and uncertain, strategic theory can be defined as the understanding of interdependent decision making under conditions of uncertainty.[37] As Harry Yarger succinctly explains, "Strategic theory opens the mind to all the possibilities and forces at play, prompting us to consider the costs and risks of our decisions and weigh the consequences of those of our adversaries, allies, and others."[38]

The Political Impossibility
of Modern Counterinsurgency

1

What Is Counterinsurgency Meant to Counter?

The Puzzle of Insurgency

In order to address the conceptual underpinnings of counterinsurgency, we must, as a first-order concern, consider whether the term *insurgency* possesses analytical utility. As the introduction outlined, we can see how COIN came to occupy a prominent place in Western military thought, arising as it did from the events of 9/11 and the occupations of Iraq and Afghanistan.[1] Comprehending what should be done at the tactical and operational levels in order to address what *The US Army/Marine Corps Counterinsurgency Field Manual* declares are "organized movement[s]" that aim to overthrow "constituted government through the use of subversion and armed conflict"[2] has preoccupied attention. However, as Lincoln Krause points out, "academics and practitioners tend to concentrate their analyses on the government's role in combating and defeating insurgencies."[3] The emphasis of much COIN thinking—focusing on what the authorities should be thinking and doing—often overlooks the need to define the nature of the intellectual phenomenon that is being engaged—namely, the idea of insurgency. In other words, this focus fails to ask what counterinsurgency in fact counters.

This chapter, therefore, examines the notion of insurgency as a conceptual tool. It argues that classifying insurgency as a separate category or subcategory of war is self-defeating. More particularly, the attempt to detach insurgency from a broader understanding of war commits five categorical errors: it exceptionalizes certain phenomena in war; it denigrates the philosophical study of war; it decontextualizes instances of war; it leads to overprescription in war; and, finally, it destrategizes the understanding of war. From these false premises, counterinsurgency establishes its case as a theory and practice. What is an insurgency? A broad understanding of the term *insurgency* would suggest that it denotes the attempt to violently overthrow established authority. Many definitions have been advanced, but most of the literature considers it the forceful challenge to wrest political control of the domestic political environment. The British Army's *Countering Insurgency* manual, for example, defines insurgency as "an organised, violent subversion used to effect or prevent political control, as a challenge to established authority."[4] This definition resembles that advanced in *The US Army/ Marine Corps Counterinsurgency Field Manual.* Such officially endorsed definitions mirror those of other observers. According to John Nagl, "Insurgency is an illegal attempt to overthrow a legitimate government or to change its policies through the use of military force."[5] For David Kilcullen, it is "a struggle to control a contested political space, between a state (or a group of states or occupying powers), and one or more popularly based, non-state challengers."[6]

These definitions are of recent vintage, but they echo those developed long before the post-9/11 era. Bard O'Neill asserted in 1990 that insurgency could be "defined as a struggle between a non-ruling group and the ruling authorities in which the non-ruling group consciously uses political resources (e.g. organizational expertise, propaganda, and demonstrations) and violence to destroy, reformulate, or sustain the basis of legitimacy of one or more aspects of politics."[7] Frank Kitson, even further back, in 1971, defined insurgency as "the use of armed force by a section of the people against the government for the purposes of overthrowing or changing the way they conduct [*sic*] business."[8]

There is, then, some common ground in the literature about how insurgency should be conceptualized. Yet extending these inferences to a concrete understanding of what the physical attributes of insurgency actually entail is more challenging. The academic and military study of insurgent activity has evolved over time. Attempts at systemizing a program of study saw the term *insurgency* grouped under a variety of headings: *irregular war, unconventional war, revolutionary war, guerrilla war, asymmetric war, bandit war, partisan war, insurrection*, and *low-intensity conflict*, to name but a few. The sheer number of names relating to or used as synonyms for essentially the same activity (to violently challenge or overthrow established authority) leads to considerable imprecision in the identification of a specific category of war called "insurgency": that is to say, a type of war imbued with its own distinctive character and practices. It is extremely difficult, in other words, to get beyond a broad statement that insurgency is the violent contestation for civil control.

The attempt to characterize insurgency as guerrilla warfare reflects this imprecision. Texts do not strictly define the practice of insurgency as guerrilla warfare but locate it within a tradition of warfare.[9] Insurgency or irregular war or guerrilla war, it is implied, constitutes a particular style of military practice that has been in evidence for centuries.[10] Implicit in much of the commentary is that this form of warfare involves a weaker side confronting a more powerful enemy,[11] an understanding sometimes rendered explicit via the term *asymmetric war*. The weaker side, in seeking to minimize its exposure to the more powerful adversary, functions by stealth, using hit-and-run tactics. The elision of terms and meanings thus gives rise to the assumption that the term *insurgency* denotes the presence of nonstate actors practicing guerrilla methods in conditions of civil war.[12] The existence of an insurgency is posited when these factors are deemed present.

This assumed tradition of warfare is, however, both impressionistic and falsifiable. It may, at first, seem a reasonable supposition that insurgencies signify the presence of a combatant inferior to its opponent fighting an asymmetric campaign. Yet this is a truism. War *always* takes place between unequal combatants in terms of the relative power among the contending actors. In theory and practice, therefore, all wars are "asymmetrical." All strategies adopted in war are likewise about exerting strengths and minimizing weakness. Nor are guerrilla tactics necessarily synonymous with insurgent campaigns. Methods associated with insurgencies can be employed by any type of belligerent in any set of circumstances, irrespective of whether the circumstances are those of an intrastate conflict.[13] Guerrilla actions in the form of hit-and-run operations, raids behind the lines, sabotage, ambushes, and so on are correspondingly likely to constitute features of "normal war."[14] The question then is, What is "normal war"?

Clausewitz's Chameleon

This question evokes Carl von Clausewitz's concept of war as a chameleon. The Prussian soldier-philosopher identified the lasting essence of war as a social phenomenon. War, in the classic Clausewitzian rendering, is a continuation of political dialogue through the means of violence, and the deed of war itself, he stated, is "an act of force to compel our enemy to do our will." War should therefore "never be thought of as something autonomous but always as an instrument of policy."[15] The social nature/structure of a particular belligerent and the wider environment in which the belligerent finds itself will form the values and interests it seeks to maintain. These factors will thus inform the policies the belligerent will wish to advance through war. The determination and skill with which the social actor pursues its goals through violence will always be conditioned, though, by the unique circumstances of time and place. "As a total phenomenon," Clausewitz observed, "[war's] dominant tendency always makes [it] a paradoxical trinity—composed of primordial violence, hatred, and enmity, which are to be regarded as a blind natural force; of the play of chance and probability within which the creative spirit is free to roam: and of its element of subordination, as an instrument of policy, which makes it subject to reason alone."[16]

Hence, if the very *nature* of war "is an act of policy," "a true political instrument, a continuation of political intercourse carried on by other means,"[17] the *character* of war will always differ in each case because of the interplay of popular passion, chance, and political reason. Clausewitz consequently averred: "These three tendencies are like three different codes of law, deep-rooted in their subject and yet variable in their relationship to one another." Accordingly, "wars must vary with the nature of their motives and the situation which gave rise to them."[18] Every instance of war is therefore exclusive and nonreproducible. The progression of each and every war will be different, influenced by why and how the combatants choose to fight. Ultimately, Clausewitz noted, war always "moves on its own goals with varying speed."[19]

For these reasons, Clausewitz considered war to be "more than a true chameleon that slightly adapts its characteristics to the given case."[20] The nature of the chameleon (the innate essence of war) remains the same, but its outer appearance (the individual character of each instance of war) always varies with historically and socially contingent circumstances. It follows that if all wars are unique in their character, then there can be no such thing as "normal" war. There is just war. But if wars are different in each and every case, how is it possible to subdivide war into so many apparent gradations and categories (guerrilla war, low-intensity war, revolutionary war)? Or how can one make distinctions between wars that may be deemed "conventional" and those that are supposedly "irregular," which is often held to characterize insurgent wars? Trying to divide war into something that is inherently indivisible makes no theoretical sense.

It may be held that differentiating certain forms of war does not question the existential fact of war but represents an attempt to map the characteristics of certain incidences of warfare. Accordingly, it might be argued, by such differentiation one is not questioning the intrinsic nature of the chameleon but merely identifying the different colorful variations the chameleon adopts. In this respect, as Colin Gray observes, the irresistible "urge to categorize and clarify" warfare reflects "the fashion of Victorian entomologists identifying new species of insects."[21] Even so, it must be recalled, if wars are always exceptional to their time and place, then they cannot possess any comparable characteristics with other wars beyond their shared essence—namely, to achieve goals of policy through violence. Individual incidences of war are inherently uncharacterizable. To put it simply, as Harry Summers suggests, "A war is a war is a war is a war."[22]

The "urge to categorize and identify" does, however, denote a fault line in war and strategic studies between essentialists who believe that differentiating analytical categories in war is futile[23] and those who assume distinctions can be made in the practice of war among certain types of combatants and who thereby maintain that "insurgencies, like other forms of armed conflict," can be "defined by their methodologies."[24] To put the case in simple terms, because "war moves on its own goals with varying speed," each war's relative power will affect its direction and duration, which, in turn, will influence how each combatant chooses to wage its campaign. Hence, in order to maximize its advantage at any given point in time, a combatant may decide to avoid or delay open battle and instead prosecute its campaign through less-direct confrontations, deploying guerrilla methods, hit-and-run operations, sabotage, and ambushes.

The attempt to evade direct battle creates the often unstated assumption that conceptual distinctions may be drawn between those conflicts in which outright force-on-force clashes take place on battlefronts and those in which they do not. The former are often labeled "conventional war," whereas the latter are considered "unconventional," "irregular," or "insurgent war." *Insurgent war* becomes a synonym for many other terms that categorize warfare without battles or battlefronts. It is from this assumption that many of the other suppositions about insurgencies follow: that they involve a nonstate actor confronting a more powerful controlling authority in conditions of intrastate war. Thus, it can be contended that categorizing does not lead to clarification because it contradicts the essentialist principle that there is only one category of war, and that is war itself.

Yet trying to divide the indivisible is exactly what counterinsurgency theory does. However, the urge to categorize and define a particular subset of war leads not to clarity, as it should, but to confusion. And conceptual confusion is the harbinger of poor thinking and ultimately policy mistakes. In particular, the effort to distinguish a specific category of war termed "insurgency" leads to the five categorical errors elaborated in the next five sections.

Exceptionalizing War

The analytical error in attempting to identify insurgency as a distinctive form of war is that it implies that it is a novel and ingenious method of war. Such an original method of war—so the thinking goes—requires novel and ingenious methods to counter it. The terms *irregular war* and *unconventional war* intimate that insurgency constitutes its own category of war. This thinking is logically flawed because objectively there is no such thing as "normal" war. Insurgency cannot therefore deviate from a norm. The problem with much writing on insurgency and counterinsurgency is that it seeks to exceptionalize something that cannot be exceptionalized. Logically speaking, this is the most serious analytical error from which the subsequent errors of categorization flow.

Exceptionalizing insurgency as something distinct in itself tempts writers to trace anachronistically a tradition of insurgency and counterinsurgency as a discrete style of war back through the centuries. However, the intellectual attempt to identify insurgency as a separate category of war has relatively recent origins. It was the war in French Indochina between 1945 and 1954—or, rather, French officers' deliberations about why France lost that war to the Communist-inspired rebellion of the Viet Minh—that generated the modern understanding of insurgency. Tracing this attempt to exceptionalize insurgency is instructive because it exerted an enduring influence on contemporary thinking about counterinsurgency.

Veteran French parachute officer Roger Trinquier argued in 1964 that the Indochina war was lost because "we hesitated to take the necessary measures or took them too late." The French Army's approach, he asserted, resembled "a pile driver attempting to crush a fly."[25] Trinquier believed that the Western powers faced a qualitatively new type of war that required fresh methods and doctrines. A period of intensive discussion inside the French Army took place on the reasons for its defeat. It was during this period of introspection that a novel theory of future war germinated known as *guerre révolutionnaire*—revolutionary war. Although this theory was never formally articulated as an official doctrine, it gained a wide following across sections of the French armed forces.[26]

Extrapolating from their experience fighting the Viet Minh, the French assumed that the character of warfare in the post–World War II epoch had fundamentally changed. As Raoul Girardet and Jean-Pierre Thomas argued, these officers had come to understand that Indochina had provided a "spectacular revelation of another intellectual and moral universe."[27] Advocates of *guerre révolutionnaire* maintained that the future would not witness interstate conflict between the two superpower blocs, the United States and the Soviet Union, confronting each other in mass battle along the lines of World War II, and would still less involve the mutually suicidal use of nuclear weapons. Instead, future war would see Communist-sponsored guerrilla movements mount challenges from *within* the state. For Commandant Jacques Hogard, this type of war represented "the war of revolution for the conquest of the world. This war has become permanent, universal, and truly global."[28] For adherents of this doctrine, *le troisiéme guerre mondiale*—the third world war—had already started.[29] Revolutionary war was the strategy by which the forces of global communism intended to win the Cold War without having to risk a costly, self-destructive war by "conventional" means.

The revolutionary aspect of this unique method of confrontation, pioneered by Communist revolutionaries from Vladimir Lenin to Mao Tse-tung, was that it was a war of the mind. French officers assiduously studied Communist theories as well as a range of thinking about crowd psychology, such as Serge Chakotine's *The Rape of the Masses.*[30] They concluded that Communist forces possessed major advantages over conventionally deployed military power: a very tight party organization and an intense ideological commitment. Through these means, Communist structures, it was held, could develop parallel systems of governance that would imbricate the people in shadow networks and hierarchies, facilitating their control and organizing them for guerrilla resistance against those in power.[31] Decisive battle would have no relevance in this new era. The principal "battle" would not be waged between mutually opposed armies or with the intention to gain territory. It would be a battle to win—or rather control—the minds of the population: as Trinquier stated, "We know that the *sine qua non* of *modern warfare* is the unconditional support of the population."[32] Seemingly, this form of war was indeed truly exceptional.

However, somewhat problematically for this thesis, the French Army in Indochina did not believe at the time that it faced a revolutionary new type of enemy. The war in French Indochina came to be regarded as the locus classicus of revolutionary war only in hindsight. What, we might wonder, was considered revolutionary about it? If we review the conduct of both the Viet Minh and the French, three determining features of the war suggest that it was far from exceptional. First, the Viet Minh's chief military strategist, General Võ Nguyên Giáp, conceived the Communist plan of action in fairly traditional terms, envisaging campaigns of defense, offense, maneuver, and positional warfare. Giáp mapped out for his political commissars in 1950 the phases through which the war would progress. The initial phase would involve the retreat of Viet Minh forces northward, ceding French control around Hanoi and the Gulf of Tonkin. The second phase would see the Viet Minh forces surround and destroy small French garrisons, thereby reducing the area of French control. The final phase would see the Viet Minh move toward a sustained offensive campaign of mobile warfare.[33]

This is indeed how the war progressed, with systematic Viet Minh military pressure eliminating French outposts, which gradually limited French control to the Red River delta region. The Viet Minh's Red River delta offensive in 1951 was entirely orthodox in orientation, involving frontal assaults against French defenses. Although the Viet Minh utilized guerrilla activities throughout the war, these activities did not constitute the main thrust of its military operations. Instead, they commonly supplemented main battle operations, and the Viet Minh's campaign followed this pattern. French columns and garrisons were ambushed. Regular Viet Minh infantry and artillery battalions often carried out these attacks.[34] Little of this activity diverges from accepted practices in war, and if we insist on calling these actions "guerrilla" or "insurgency" tactics, then there is little that is intrinsically revolutionary or, indeed, Communist about them.

To the extent that Giáp endorsed guerrilla operations to erode French morale and territory, he recognized that such tactics were secondary to set-piece offensives.[35] And this discloses the second notable feature of the war—namely, that the French *did* react to these tactics and with some effect. Commanders in the field innovated their own countertactics, such as the Groupes de commandos mixte aéroportés (Mixed Airborne Commando Group), which trained Montagnard and Vietnamese Catholic forces to operate behind Communist lines. Similarly, the 11éme Parachutistes de choc (Eleventh Shock Parachute Battalion) collaborated with the French intelligence service—the Service de documentation extérieure et de contre-éspionage—to conduct sabotage and counterguerrilla operations against Viet Minh units.

Further, to the degree that the French Army encountered enemy methods that might have been construed as unorthodox, it sought to respond with equally inventive countermeasures.[36] Meeting new tactics with countertactics is an entirely natural dynamic in war, as Clausewitz reminds us.[37] Indeed, this inventive French response questions the view of those such as Trinquier who argued that the French Army reacted like a pile driver trying to crush a fly. Perhaps the French armed forces adopted too late the more sophisticated measures to deal effectively with Viet Minh guerrilla forces that Trinquier, who was in fact a member of the Groupes de commandos mixte aéroportés in Indochina, advocated. But one wonders whether such advocacy is beside the point because it leads to the third feature of the war, which is whether the Viet Minh was really the metaphorical "fly" in the first place.

The assumption that Viet Minh forces were markedly inferior in either numbers or equipment to the French is in fact highly disputable. Estimates suggest that the total number of Viet Minh troops from 1950 on were in excess of 500,000.[38] Some 300,000 of them were arranged in regular army formations and composed Giáp's main battle forces, and the other 200,000 operated as guerrilla units or in other support roles. By contrast, French forces in Indochina stood at 400,000.[39] As well as regular French Army and Foreign Legion forces, this figure also included indigenous Vietnamese troops, who fought under the French flag along with troops from the French African colonies. Many of these troops, however, were tied down in defensive positions, and the French had no more than perhaps 150,000 troops available for offensive combat. Therefore, if we consider the relative strength of opposing forces, it seems apparent that the French were outnumbered. Not only did they lack adequate forces to prosecute antiguerrilla operations, but, more to the point, they also lacked the necessary forces to wage main battle operations as well. The asymmetry of forces ran against the French.

Indeed, from the onset of the Indochina war, a conservatively conceived and executed plan based on the application of numerical superiority at the theater level, rather than a new concept of revolutionary war, ultimately defeated the French. The first phase of Giáp's campaign saw the destruction of the northern French garrisons that protected the border and main routes from China. These posts were assaulted not by "guerrilla" forces, but by the Viet Minh's main infantry and artillery formations, which surrounded and pounded them into submission.[40] The elimination of these garrisons opened the border with China, allowing the further supply of the Viet Minh with heavy weaponry, notably artillery, mortars, and antiaircraft guns. The Communist forces' growing capability permitted Giáp to feel increasingly confident that he could take on the French in open warfare. Here, as some have noted, is a general thinking along highly orthodox lines.[41]

The Indochina war largely reflected the ebb and flow of traditional offensive and defensive battles. Effective French fortifications repulsed the Viet Minh's human-wave assault against the Red River delta in 1951. The defeat of the Viet Minh's forces in this instance encouraged the French to take the offensive, pursuing the retreating Communists to the North. The French, in turn, were subsequently beaten back as a result of overstretched supply lines and inferior troop numbers. These maneuvers were entirely consistent with expected patterns of war. The most telling proof of this was the decisive battle of Dien Bien Phu in 1954, which finally led to French withdrawal from Indochina. The battle was archetypal, involving two mutually opposing armies, with 50,000 Viet Minh combat soldiers grinding down with heavy artillery and infantry assaults the French base comprising 13,000 troops.[42]

If there was nothing revolutionary about the methods of war in Indochina, why did the French later see the conflict as emblematic of a new kind of war? The answer to this question lies not in the battlefields of northern Vietnam but in the way a traumatized French officer corps represented the war after the event. Defeat in Indochina came little more than a decade after the humiliating conquest of France by Germany in World War II, which, it must be remembered, had a devastating psychological impact on the French Army. Soldiers returning from the battles in Indochina subsequently retailed their bitter experiences of fighting an unforgiving enemy imbued with a fanatical political zeal. The Viet Minh's fervent, single-minded political and military focus contrasted dramatically with the vacillation and betrayal the French Army experienced at the hands of the Fourth Republic. From this perspective, successive French governments failed to invest the campaign against the Viet Minh with a political commitment equivalent to that of their Communist foes. Trinquier and others therefore felt an unprepared French Army had confronted

a unique enemy in the Viet Minh. Addressing their defeat consequently required a new counterdoctrine of equal potency. The resulting concept, *guerre révolutionnaire*, evolved into a set of techniques
and guidelines to deal with rural and urban guerrilla warfare, but it
principally embodied the *will* to defeat Communist-inspired subversion at any level it was encountered.

In effect, the anachronistic projection into the course of the Indochina war of a significance that in military terms it can scarcely have
possessed at the time follows an established pattern where traumatic
defeats are imbued with post hoc iconic, though misleading, significance. Similar patterns may be seen, for example, in the collapse of
Western Europe in the course of the German onslaught in World War
II between 1940 and 1941. The rapid fall of Norway, the Low Countries, and France itself seemed to intimate a wholly new type of war
and was given a specific name, *Blitzkrieg* (lightning war), even though
the Wehrmacht's armored assaults, if examined closely, reflected entirely conventional German–Prussian operational concepts of maneuver warfare.[43] In this regard, the characterizations of shock defeats
as something exceptional, bestowing them with labels such as *Blitzkrieg* or *revolutionary war*, ultimately functions as apologetics, excus-
ing why one side was outthought and outfought. It is always easier
to explain away the trauma of defeat by attributing it to something
remarkable, new, and unexpected.

In other words, the construction of the notion of revolutionary
war disguised an unremarkable truth: that a more skillful and disci-
plined opponent defeated a European-based imperial power. Deriving a new theory of revolutionary war from the Indochina war thus
offered the French armed forces a creedal motivation to fight for the
rest of France's colonial territories, notably Algeria between 1956 and
1962.[44] In this way, the idea of revolutionary war addressed two underlying concerns in the Cold War zeitgeist: first, that nonstate political actors could challenge Western nations, and, second, that these
actors were Communist in orientation. In an age of ideological division, this Cold War perspective ensured that such thinking found
a keen reception beyond France in the English-speaking world and
beyond. The translation of French military texts, in particular Trinquier's work, saw the precepts of *guerre révolutionnaire*—or "counter-

revolutionary war," as it was more popularly understood in English—influencing American Cold War strategic thinking at a time when the United States was escalating its effort against the Viet Cong in the second Indochina war.[45]

The term *revolutionary war*, then, failed to offer an accurate description of a distinctive facet of war. Instead, it served a Cold War ideological purpose. It chimed with the prevailing Western zeitgeist. European states faced a series of violent anticolonial nationalist uprisings while the world assumed a geopolitical division between two superpower-aligned blocs. It was as a result of these twin forces that the Western powers felt their global and regional interests uniquely vulnerable to Communist subversion. From the late 1950s on, the notion of insurgency as a distinctive category of war began, therefore, to take shape via the idea of revolutionary war. In particular, the U.S. military became increasingly obsessed with what Colin Gray terms "counterinsurgency faddism," the "cult of the guerrilla," and the "aura of Special Forces."[46]

The attempt to extrapolate particular understandings of military activity into the category "revolutionary war" facilitated the coinage of additional synonyms associated with insurgencies, such as *unconventional war*, which carried much the same implication—namely, a form of action undertaken by nonstate actors utilizing guerrilla methods. The question, of course, is that if there is nothing that is ultimately exceptional about this kind of activity, then how can it be regarded as unconventional? If we adhere to Clausewitzian precepts that all war is violence for a political purpose, then there can be no such thing as unconventional war. All war proceeds toward the attainment of political goals no matter who the actors and what the actions are.

Furthermore, if an action is assumed to defy a "convention," then what is that convention? A convention denotes the norm and relates to something that can be defined as the most common form of activity compared with other practices. As we have shown, however, when it comes to war, delineating what is "normal" is deeply problematic. If conventional war designates conflict that takes place among states, then the statistical evidence negates any claim that this is the normal form of war. Surveys of war since 1945 suggest that only 18 to 20 percent of wars can be accurately classed as interstate war, and more than

75 percent of the 164 cases of war since the end of World War II have involved armed conflict within states.[47]

Therefore, assessing the convention with reference to the incidence of interstate versus intrastate war would suggest that civil wars involving challenges to the ruling authority of the state—that is insurgencies—has been the *normal* form of conflict. It is "unconventional warfare" that represents *the convention*. It follows that exceptional categories to denote insurgency—"revolutionary war," "unconventional war," "irregular war"—reveal themselves as arbitrary, ideologically loaded expressions. During the Cold War, only those armed challenges to the interests of Western powers were termed unconventional. Meanwhile, the opposite of unconventional war—conventional or regular war—was an equally artificial construct designed to offload conflicts that did not involve state actors directly into a separate analytical sphere invariably because they were regarded as too complicated and messy to study.[48] Such conflicts were thus considered of lesser importance and therefore unconventional not because they defied any convention, but because, in Richard Betts's words, they did not involve or threaten "cataclysmic war among great powers."[49]

The Depreciation of the Philosophy of War

"I know of two types of warfare: mobile warfare and positional warfare. I have never heard of revolutionary warfare," remarked Charles de Gaulle, expressing his evident reservation about the French officer class's penchant for subdividing war into categories.[50] Superficially it might seem attractive to identify a distinctive insurgency style of warfare, permeated by a unique tactical and political character. However, the distinction undermines any comprehension of the philosophical essence of war and, as de Gaulle implied, obscures the core practices in war. In effect, exceptionalizing insurgency as a form of war and attributing to it epithets such as *unconventional, irregular*, and *revolutionary* render the understanding of tactical practice elusive and mysterious. There is, however, nothing mysterious or abnormal about the idea and methods associated with insurgency. Inferring that insurgency is an aberrant, irregular, unconventional form of war does not enhance the comprehension of war. On the contrary, it denigrates a coherent appreciation of war. It arbitrarily identifies a few tactical methods loosely connected to ideas of guerrilla warfare and combines them with a political context where these methods are enacted internally within the state in conditions of civil strife in order to establish a new category of conflict.

The denigration of a philosophical understanding of war is, therefore, the second serious analytical weakness arising from the consequences of categorical exceptionalism. Such depreciation forces an unnatural distinction between regular warfare and irregular war and, according to W. Alexander Vacca and Mark Davidson, "break[s] the link between war and politics." They argue: "Clausewitz is very clear that war is a political act with political objectives. Yet in irregular war, the political objectives are often forgotten as analysts focus on the tactical challenges."[51] In other words, those who make this distinction must necessarily claim that such "tactical challenges" exist outside the Clausewitzian paradigm of war. Indeed, asserting that the *normal, conventional*, and the *regular* occur only in conflict between more or less symmetrical (and probably state) actors and involve armed campaigns with highly organized forces introduces an abstract distinction that frames "irregular warfare in opposition to regular warfare."[52]

Once the distinction has been made, it is plausible to argue further that it is only within the framework of the *normal* and the *conventional* that war can be instrumental. Practices that deviate from this frame are perceived not only as distinct from regular war but as fundamentally irrational. As a consequence, the contention that wars are conducted to gain political objectives, as Clausewitz averred, is thereby discounted. Thus, in conflicts supposedly characterized as "unconventional" (that is where combatants employ guerrilla methods within the state), wars cease to be seen as instrumental in political terms. Instead, they are often considered the product of premodern urges that resist any rational comprehension of political action in war.[53] Wars that fall into the categories "insurgencies," "small wars," and "ethnic wars" (all of them problematic classifications) are regularly treated this way. The rise of ethnoreligious identity-based conflict in post–Cold War Europe and Central Asia reinforced this analytical tendency. In fact, the brutal wars of dissolution in the Balkans and

Transcaucasia that accompanied the breakup of the former Yugoslavia and Soviet Union in the 1990s led numerous commentators to dismiss the continuing relevance of the Clausewitzian paradigm. The "irregular" campaigns of ethnic particularity waged by various paramilitary groups are, in John Keegan's view, examples of "primitive war." Such conflicts, he maintained, "are fed by passions and rancours that do not yield to rational measures of persuasion or control: they are apolitical to a degree for which Clausewitz made little allowance."[54] Mary Kaldor, advancing her thesis that identity conflict constitutes a new type of war, pronounced, ex cathedra, that Clausewitz's conception of war governs "the regulation" of only "certain types of social relationship" that contain their "own particular logic" (i.e., Clausewitzian thought can explain only war between states).[55] Martin van Creveld, meanwhile, argued that in this new era "if any part of our intellectual baggage deserves to be thrown overboard, surely it is . . . the Clausewitzian definition of war."[56]

Such assertions by informed commentators denied any intelligible understanding of war. In effect, these commentators made a series of unfounded assumptions: first, they presumed rather than demonstrated that a distinction between "unconventional" and "conventional" war exists; second, they asserted rather than established that Clausewitzian "logic" applies only to warfare between state actors; and third, they implied rather than proved that rational political calculation in wars that do not involve state actors are radically different, if not nonexistent (reflecting unfathomable primordial drives, blind hatred, and naked bloodlust). Such reductionist thinking subsequently influenced contemporary U.S. counterinsurgency thinking. Thus, Montgomery McFate could contend: "Neither Al-Qaeda nor insurgents in Iraq are fighting a Clausewitzian war, where armed conflict is a rational extension of politics by other means. These adversaries neither think nor act like nation-states. Rather, their form of warfare, organizational structure, and motivations are determined by the society and culture from which they come."[57]

Here, we can observe the denigration of the intellectual conceptualization of war. By viewing insurgency as an entirely separate category of war, commentators focus on the form and organization of the nonstate actor at the expense of analyzing the actor's underlying motivations and political objectives. Because primitive social reflexes motivate these primitive insurgent actors, so the thinking goes, these objectives cannot possibly involve sophisticated political calculation. It is therefore assumed that these actors inhabit a radically different universe, one beyond rational intellectual appreciation.

However, what these assertions ultimately demonstrate is a profound ignorance of Clausewitzian thought. Clausewitz, a Kant-inspired philosopher of war, sought to reveal the philosophical essence of war rather than to treat it merely as an epiphenomenon of state activity. As Jan Honig maintains, Clausewitzian ideas are "easily adaptable to forms of warring social organizations that do not form states."[58] Clausewitz himself is explicit on this point, stating, "Wars will always vary with the nature of their motives of the situations that gave rise to them."[59] Wars are, in other words, always the product of the societies and cultures from which they emanate. It is the uniqueness of the time, place, and nature of the social actors engaged, whether state or nonstate, that affects how the course of any war unfolds. Reducing insurgencies to crude manifestations of primal instincts and presupposing that warfare is rational and instrumental only when it takes place between nation-states have implications for misguided policy making, which we elucidate further in the subsequent sections of this chapter. For now, it is sufficient to observe that asserting the existence of insurgency as an exceptional category of war denies that the practice of violence by nonstate actors is an expression of political purpose. The effect of this depreciation of the philosophy of war leads to a third analytical weakness: decontextualization.

The Decontextualization of War

Distinguishing a specific category of insurgent warfare on the basis of tactical level challenges in the context of intrastate conflict leads to a preoccupation with the physical manifestations of war rather than to an understanding of the play of passion, chance, and reason that endows each war with its unique character. The tendency to combine different wars into a single distinctive category of insurgency on the basis of tactical similarity risks superficial comparison and analysis.

Yet a predilection for subdividing the undividable nature of war into arbitrary categories has for decades been a notable feature in much academic writing on strategic affairs. The abundance of epithets (*revolutionary, conventional, unconventional, low-intensity, irregular, limited,* and *guerrilla*) illustrates the scholarly penchant for the ordering of supposedly different classes of war.

Yet, as Colin Gray argues, the preference for classifying war into typologies reflects a military and scholarly community that "typically overintellectualizes the challenges (problems/opportunities) that it perceives." Referring to the U.S. defense establishment in particular, he notes: "With a culture that privileges theory-building through disaggregation by categorical exclusivity, whole subject areas are conceptually deconstructed and reassembled for neater granular treatment." Creditable though the attempt to produce such categories may be, Gray observes that, "unfortunately, the actual and potential benefits of theoretical exclusivity are more than offset by the transaction cost in the loss of context."[60] The misguided effort to exceptionalize and categorize leads, as Gray suggests, to the decontextualization of war. Instances of war are as a consequence divorced from their contingent social and historical settings and lumped together merely by their tactical resemblance. A prominent feature of much commentary on insurgency and counterinsurgency evinces a penchant for collating otherwise unrelated cases of war under overgeneralized categories.[61]

But constructing categories of war upon the similarity of their tactical methods affords a poor basis for analysis. It is the equivalent of suggesting that the Gulf War in 1990–1991, World War II, the Vietnam War, the Six-Day War, the Korean War, and an assortment of other wars past and present are all in some way comparable because the combatants used rifles, grenades, and machine guns. It demonstrates the fallacy of classifying wars by their outward appearance. An analogous fallaciousness applies to the categorization of many wars as insurgency. Simply because one side employs the methods commonly associated with guerrilla war does not make an insurgency or mean that insurgency constitutes a clearly definable form of war.

The arbitrary subdivision of war into artificial categories can be illustrated if we consider the methods most associated with insurgencies—namely, guerrilla tactics. Any combatant can employ such tactics in any number of ways. Many of the aerial tactics employed by Fighter Command in the Battle of Britain in 1940 were classically guerrilla in character. German pilots observed that British fighters targeted Luftwaffe bombing formations but often flew away at the first sign of German fighter aircraft. Berlin-based American journalist William Shirer commented that these tactics led "many a Messerschmitt pilot to complain that the British Spitfire and Hurricane pilots were cowards, that they fled whenever they saw a German fighter." Shirer went on to note, however, that, given the steady losses inflicted on German bombers, "I suspect now the German pilots understand that the British were not being cowardly but merely smart."[62] The Royal Air Force adopted tactics that made sense in the operational context: playing to its strengths (fighting over home territory, using radar-guided fighter groups to inflict heavy losses on more vulnerable German bombers) while minimizing weaknesses (avoiding combat with often technically superior Luftwaffe fighters). In this manner, the Royal Air Force preserved its air defenses and foiled the German strategy to erode British fighter capabilities in large aerial battles.[63]

Analogously, the use of submarines to sink vulnerable merchant vessels in World War I and World War II is an example of guerrilla tactics at sea. Like the Battle of Britain, submarine warfare demonstrated all the characteristics associated with insurgent/guerrilla activity: the dispersal of forces, hit-and-run military engagements, the prevention of enemy concentration, and the avoidance of large-scale battle. When these tactics were first employed, they were regarded as novel, unconventional, and often cowardly. Yet few analysts have described Royal Air Force tactics in 1940 or commerce raiding by submarines as guerrilla, insurgent, or irregular actions. They are instead considered feasible, rational, and instrumental methods adapted to the circumstances and thus constituting tactical innovations aimed at achieving local superiority in combat actions. As such, these actions facilitated the combatants' wider strategic goals and were quickly assimilated into war-fighting practices. Yet when nonstate actors employ similar methods, these methods are classified not as tactics available to any kind of social actor to utilize if the actor thinks they serve its purposes. Even more incoherently, they are considered as separate kinds of war—insurgent wars, guerrilla wars, unconventional wars—entirely disconnected from mainstream understandings of war.

A prominent feature of much writing on counterinsurgency exhibits this preference for examining the surface manifestations of war while dismissing the need to comprehend the individual context of each instance of war. John Nagl and Brian Burton, for example, assert that a uniform set of "dynamics" inform all insurgencies. Accordingly, "insurgencies, like other forms of armed conflict, are better defined by their associated methodologies than by ideologies." They add: "While causes change regularly, the fundamentals of insurgent methodology remain relatively constant."[64] The preoccupation with the "fundamentals of insurgent methodologies" at the expense of understanding the unique social milieu from which all war arises leads to the fourth flaw induced by false categorization: an overly prescriptive approach to countering reputed cases of insurgency.

Overprescription in War

Like a medical practitioner who forms a diagnosis on the observation of a patient's symptoms, the COIN analyst examines tactical symptoms, diagnoses a case of insurgency, and prescribes the appropriate remedy in the form of a counterinsurgency program. The analyst subsequently prescribes a range of COIN remedies tested in other conflicts. However, unlike a physical disease, which responds to the same medicine everywhere, individual wars differ from one another, and so counterinsurgency remedies, applied to an ailing body politic, vary in efficacy. Although individual prescriptions might occasionally be effective, COIN risks becoming overprescriptive with misdiagnosis and ends up with damaging and costly policies. Wars are always based on a set of mutual interactions between contesting parties, each possessing their distinctive aims, capabilities and motives. Unlike disease, wars do not offer predictable symptoms. Therefore, treating the outward manifestations of "insurgency" never produces a holistic remedy.

Moreover, regarding insurgency as a set of symptoms of a distinctive kind of war facilitates inflexible policy responses. The counterinsurgent view assumes that when an adversary has adopted certain techniques in a particular social context (i.e., guerrilla methods in conditions of intrastate conflict), this adoption becomes a necessary and sufficient cause for a counterinsurgency campaign. In other words, both policy makers and military practitioners find COIN doctrine attractive because it proposes that general operational solutions can deal with complex political problems based on the application of a given set of techniques. President John F. Kennedy is said to have remarked to his advisers: "What are we doing about guerrilla warfare?"[65] Apocryphal or otherwise, the quote illustrates the potential for analytical and policy confusion and the bureaucratic predilection for devising countertactics to deal with the outward tactical manifestations of war. Here we can observe the fallacy of overprescription influencing the conduct of U.S. foreign policy in the early 1960s. The Kennedy and Johnson administrations equated nearly all outbreaks of "guerrilla warfare" as threats to Western interests, requiring counterinsurgency doctrine as the antidote.

The negative effects of rigidly adhering to the notion that tactical symptoms require the same set of countermeasures is most clearly demonstrated in two cases from this era: French military conduct during the Algerian War (1956–1962) and in Indochina, where the North Vietnamese insurrection in the South lured the United States into a military and political quagmire. The point is that, pace John F. Kennedy, one cannot do anything about "guerrilla warfare." Guerrilla warfare represents a set of tactics. Combating the tactics of the other side is only a small part of any response by a belligerent. The most important aspect of any war is to comprehend the underlying political dynamics that motivate a particular actor to take up arms. Only after addressing this first-order concern can tactical responses be considered. Putting tactics ahead of politics is an indication of overprescription in war.

More recent COIN analysis, such as that contained in the British Army's *Countering Insurgency* document, of course recognizes the importance of politics. Nevertheless, a close reading suggests that the relationship between the political dimension and combating insurgency remains insufficiently understood. For example, to illustrate that the army understands the key role of politics, *Countering Insurgency* approvingly cites the French theorist David Galula's claim that COIN is 80 percent political action and only 20 percent military action.[66] Yet Galula considered "political action" merely as the preference for nonviolent countermeasures. He did not consider politics involving an appreciation of the guiding motivations that lead actors to do what they do. His countermeasures were consequently highly prescriptive in content and approach. So in addition to stipulating technical-military measures, military manuals following Galula prescribe social and economic measures to drain the swamp in which insurgents apparently thrive. They thus promote "population-centric" projects such as building schools, hospitals, welfare services, and structures of governance as suitable prophylactics that will, along with more coercive remedies, cure the patient of the insurgent disease.

The medical analogy is not an exaggeration. *The US Army/Marine Corps Counterinsurgency Field Manual* explicitly exhibits the predisposition in COIN thinking to regard insurgencies as phenomena with definable characteristics amenable to established treatments. The manual maintains that "most insurgencies [like illnesses] follow a similar course of development. The tactics [treatments] used to successfully defeat them [to cure them] are likewise similar in most cases."[67] The problem is that implying that insurgency is a distinct form of war that is predictable in its course defies the Clausewitzian understanding that all wars move toward their own goals at varying speed. The precepts contained in COIN manuals consequently slip all too easily into rules for action. An overly prescriptive attitude to war therefore overdetermines the technical factors in war. Such an overdetermination obscures the questions as to why a political actor chooses to wage war and how that actor decides to conduct its campaign to secure its objectives.

The reasons any political entity goes to war and how it selects its methods to fight depend on a number of tangible and intangible factors related to the entity's physical and mental capacities, objectives, and perceptions of the nature of the obstacles to be overcome. These factors will also in part govern how an adversary responds to an initiation of hostilities. Because of the possible permutations involving this multiplicity of factors, the calculus for the belligerents is necessarily different in each and every case of war. Clausewitz's scheme of passion, chance, and reason precisely captures this infinite variation and the consequent inability to predict the character and direction of war. Rejecting Clausewitzian precepts—in other words, being overly prescriptive and searching for rules for action—has the further consequence of removing the *why* in war and focusing principally on the *how*: how to identify an insurgency and how to combat it. But because the how is always dependent on context, removing the *why* denies the proper role of strategy in war. This is the final and most damaging analytic flaw in COIN thought: the destrategization of warfare.

The Destrategization of War

Strategy is concerned with ways, ends, and means: the manner in which available resources are utilized to gain given objectives.[68] Strategy is not only about the crude application of the tangibles of power, the exercise of force being the most obvious. It also involves complex calculations about how far one party might be willing to invest its time, energy, and resources into trying to attain particular goals in conditions of political uncertainty. Uncertainty necessarily occurs because in striving to attain one's goals, one may well incur resistance from other political forces that wish to secure their own interests by denying those goals. If the collision of interests is sufficiently serious, a violent clash of arms—a war—might arise. War raises the stakes exponentially because the costs associated with particular outcomes increase the level of uncertainty.[69]

War, then, is a reciprocal activity involving interactions between opposing forces. In this context, the success of strategic decision making cannot be measured by an immutable standard, but in light of responses that actions produce or are expected to produce from an adversary at any one point in time.[70] Decisions about how far a belligerent is prepared to go to reach an objective are crucial if war is to be proportional to the goal sought. Proportionality in war keeps the activity within rational, instrumental bounds. What is proportional, moreover, depends on contingent judgment. Effective strategy is therefore about *good* political judgment, and good judgment is prudential and cannot be predetermined.

By contrast, a predetermined counterinsurgency response to a situation that is diagnosed as an insurgency removes all strategic judgment

from the equation. This identification of an autonomous sphere of conflict classified as insurgency and thus demanding prescribed counteractions obscures the importance that Clausewitz attached to the shaping of actions by the specific and protean context in which they occur.
From the perspective of policy making, such an approach worryingly
preempts discussion of more appropriate courses of action in the circumstances of a particular conflict,[71] something that chapter 2 explores
in more detail. With respect to the related and equally problematic notion of "irregular" warfare, Vacca and Davidson note that such labeling
"simultaneously weakens and limits theories of warfare, while leaving
strategists conceptually disarmed when confronted with strategic challenges that do not fit neatly in a[n] [insurgency-]specific model." They
further contend: "The use of the term 'irregular warfare' is not simply a
matter of harmless imprecision; it exerts a pernicious effect on the way
that policy makers plan for and conduct military operations."[72]

Such false categorization has a number of adverse strategic effects.
At the political level, a misleading obsession with invented modes of
warfare strips policy makers of the intellectual flexibility to conceive
an alternative course of action where there may be a pressing need
for one. Such inflexibility was apparent in the immediate aftermath
of the Cold War. Western defense establishments had habitually prepared for a "conventional war" between NATO and the Warsaw Pact
in central Europe, so in the early 1990s they had great difficulty comprehending how to meet contingencies that fell below the threshold of
"conventional" military operations. Military planners, as Paul Beaver
argues, could not cope with ideas of "asymmetric warfare" because
"traditional staff college and command school solutions just do not
work."[73] The outbreak of the ethnoreligious conflict in the Balkans,
following the disintegration of Yugoslavia in the early 1990s, demonstrated this rigidity. NATO and Western Europe more generally
froze into inaction because strategies that fell below the threshold of
the total destruction of the enemy fell outside the boundaries of accepted military thought and hindered the development of a flexible
policy of peace enforcement. Contingencies below threats to national
survival or major national interests had been destrategized. Because
nearly all instances of insurgency and low-intensity conflict fall below
this threshold, it became somewhat convenient to dismiss humanitar-

ian crimes as the product of barbaric, primeval drives that were beyond rational solution and best left to run their course (a feature of such thinking still affects policy making, witnessed in the prevalence of terms such as *hurting stalemate*).[74] The Balkanized outcome produced among both politicians and military practitioners alike a passive fatalism that could scarcely countenance anything stronger than humanitarian assistance.[75] Although these attitudes slowly changed, their impact on policy making almost certainly prolonged the brutal war in Bosnia[76] and very likely prevented preemptive action to stop the Rwandan genocide in 1994.[77]

Destrategization, based on erroneous categorization, also produces an equal and opposite defect. On the one hand, it leads to inaction, but on the other it predetermines actions and undermines proper strategic judgment. Identifying a conflict and consigning it to a predetermined category of war—an insurgency—to be met with a preconceived response—counterinsurgency—ignore the fact that war is reciprocal in nature and involves interactions by each combatant. In other words, the COIN model dismisses the importance of values: it ignores the circumstances and motivations that might lead an adversary to fight and dismisses the ways in which it decides to wage a particular campaign (utilizing guerrilla methods as one of its tools for instance). It also reduces the options that might be available to any political actor that chooses to respond to such a campaign. Such overdetermination, for example, embroiled the United States in South Vietnam and determined the military approach it adopted. Equally, the counterinsurgency mind dismissed any appreciation of the North Vietnamese motivation to wage war. It ignored the North Vietnamese patriotic commitment to achieve national unity and their consequent preparedness to make a higher sacrifice to achieve their goal than were the Americans. A more detached strategy that tried accurately to assess the nature of the enemy and the goals it sought, while recognizing the limits of American political commitment, might have offered the United States a more realistic set of options about how to prosecute its war in South Vietnam or, indeed, whether to prosecute it at all.

Treating instances of war as discrete manifestations of certain styles of conflict that come with prepackaged solutions closes down options and narrows the scope for decision making. Equally disturbing, the

idea that insurgencies must be met with a predetermined set of responses contains the potential to escalate war beyond what is feasible
and proportional in either military or political terms. As Vacca and
Davidson argue, by severing the conceptual link between war and
politics, "purely military" solutions that push toward "unrestrained
destruction" become all too prevalent. In such an atmosphere, they
say, "negotiated settlements become very difficult to reach, or even
propose."[78] This criticism is not merely hypothetical: these prescriptions affected American decisions to escalate the military campaign
in South Vietnam to no useful purpose and determined French policy
in the Algerian War, where the French armed forces convinced themselves they fought an irreconcilable enemy—a thesis that ultimately
resulted in the deaths of an estimated one million people.[79] A similarly
strategically challenged view of conflict has also caused incoherent
policy making in more recent conflicts. Thus, in Afghanistan policy
makers and diplomats endlessly lamented the lack of political direction in the NATO commitment to Afghanistan[80] and disagreed over
when or if to talk to the Taliban.[81]

The destrategized mind apparent in notions of insurgency and
counterinsurgency leads not just to unrestrained destruction but
also to a contradictory predilection for grievance settlement. Somewhat perversely, the categorization of types of war and their predetermined responses can promote inflexible policy response that can be
as politically damaging to Western interests as those policies that encourage military escalation. For example, as we explore in chapter 4,
much commentary on the threat posed by the "global insurgency" of
violent jihadism associated with al-Qaeda assumes that understand-
able socioeconomic and political grievance motivates their actions.[82]
Here COIN analysts somewhat contradictorily offer the antithesis to
an unrestrained military solution. Yet although negotiation and compromise might be valid in some cases, they are not by any means a
universal panacea or wise policy.[83] The practice of grievance reduction
requires an assessment of whether political compromises will pacify
an adversary or result in the abandonment of core interests.

As a result, we find in documents such as *The US Army/Marine
Corps Counterinsurgency Field Manual* pronouncements such as, "In
the end any successful COIN operation must address the legitimate

grievances insurgents use to generate popular support."[84] On the surface, grievance settlement may seem plausible and even politically prudent, but it holds the potential for adopting flawed policies of the kind Lawrence Freedman characterizes as "vague talk of hearts and minds." Good strategic judgment, as Freedman observes, requires an understanding of the causes for which an adversary fights, but even then, he cautions, "we must also recognize the limited quality of the political response available to us."[85] The response, in other words, does not necessarily require identifying grievances to redress, but trying to comprehend the dimensions of the conflict and the scope for achieving one's goals and keeping all action proportionate through available means, be they coercive or conciliatory.

Colin Gray coined the term *tacticization* to describe the problem generated by "unwise categorization," which erroneously tries to separate out different spheres of war. The preference for perceiving and reacting to war phenomena solely on the basis of apparent physical manifestations results in tacticization. The approach leads to the "neglect of strategy." Policy makers and military practitioners must understand that conceptually and historically "war and warfare are rarely option-pure by exclusive intellectual type."[86] From this categorical mistake, the errors of exceptionalization, deintellecutalization, decontextualization, overprescription, and destrategization follow. It is these errors that occasion bad policy and decision making. This chapter has therefore argued that the notion of insurgency and associated notions such as irregular warfare and unconventional war are faulty analytical abstractions. Their use does not enhance understanding of war phenomena but, on the contrary, undermines the attempt to appreciate its manifold complexity. Still less do these notions provide a stable basis upon which to apply a predetermined solution known as "counterinsurgency."

War is war, as Clausewitz understood. Each and every war is exceptional to its time and place and therefore cannot be reduced to general labels and false categories. As Clausewitz contended, "The first, supreme, the most far-reaching act of judgment that the statesman and commander have to make is to establish by that test [strategic judgment] the kind of war on which they are embarking; neither mistaking it for, nor trying to turn it into, something that is alien to its nature."[87] Forcing unrelated instances of war into the procrustean framework of insurgency and identifying the presumed solution of counterinsurgency violate this most basic strategic requirement. The curious obsession with identifying particular categories of war, based as it often is on superficial tactical manifestations, distorts the essence of war and, as chapter 2 shows, turns it into something that is alien to its nature.

2

Counterinsurgency and Strategy

Problems and Paradoxes

Interviewing General David Petraeus, the commander widely
seen as the architect of the revival of the theory and practice of
counterinsurgency in the U.S. armed forces, the journalist Rajiv
Chandrasekaran found that Petraeus "was defining COIN to include
every military tactic in his arsenal except the use of nuclear weapons."[1]
Chandrasekaran evidently had some reservations about Petraeus's
claims for COIN. His skepticism was warranted because shortly after
Barack Obama was elected to the U.S. presidency in 2008, he initiated
a high-level debate about whether a comprehensive COIN approach
to the U.S.-led NATO effort in Afghanistan should be adopted and in
particular whether troop numbers should "surge." Convinced of the
success of counterinsurgency and surge tactics in Iraq, Petraeus and
his top commanders assured the new administration of COIN's potential efficacy in Afghanistan.

Nevertheless, a group of civilian advisers and politicians in the administration led by Vice President Joe Biden questioned this line of
reasoning. They argued that shifting sectarian alliances and the Sunni
tribal awakening that rejected al-Qaeda's indiscriminate violence in
Iraq accounted for the reduction in violence in the country between
2006 and 2007, not COIN tactics.[2] Moreover, as Chandrasekaran observed, the Afghanistan challenge demanded something more than

separating the warring factions in a civil war. The challenge involved persuading the traditionally rebellious Pashtuns to "cast their lot with the Karzai government instead of [with] the insurgency." He continued: "The problem was that Karzai's administration was often more rapacious and corrupt than the Taliban. How could COIN work when the locals were turning to the insurgents to protect them from their supposed protectors?"[3] A memorandum from Biden to Obama following a conference on Afghanistan among the president's top aides and military staff in October 2009 crystalized the concerns within the administration. Biden argued:

> I do not see how anyone who took part in our discussions could emerge without profound questions about the viability of counterinsurgency. Our military will do its part: They will clear anything we ask them to clear. They will hold anything we ask them to hold. But no one can tell with conviction when, and even if, we can produce the flip sides of COIN that are required to build and transfer responsibility to the Afghans: an effective and sustainable civilian surge, a credible partner in Kabul, basic governance and services, and competent Afghan security forces.[4]

Biden's reservations were underlined two years later, in May 2011, when a Navy SEALS operation, sanctioned by President Obama, brought al-Qaeda's emir, Osama bin Laden, "to justice."[5] The al-Qaeda jihadist network in Afghanistan that originally nurtured the 9/11 conspiracy had been the ostensible justification for the U.S. invasion in late 2001 and the subsequent NATO coalition operation to stabilize the Karzai regime.[6] But with the elimination of bin Laden and the remnants of al-Qaeda's Afghan organization "in tatters," the rationale for a long-term counterinsurgency commitment was rendered increasingly elusive.[7] The fact that a precision intelligence and Special Forces operation had traced bin Laden to a compound in Abbottabad, Pakistan, further questioned what a long, costly COIN campaign in Afghanistan was actually meant to achieve.

In fact, raising this question reveals the constituting difficulty in defining just what counterinsurgency is as a concept and practice. Despite driving military operations in Afghanistan and before that in Iraq, exercising a dominant influence on the military thought and planning of the major Western powers, as well as fomenting a thriving intellectual industry in academia and think tanks,[8] COIN remains an ambiguous concept. The puzzle that this chapter addresses therefore is simple: What precisely is COIN? The chapter examines the assumptions and relevance of the thinking behind understandings of contemporary counterinsurgency as they have evolved among the major military actors in the West, notably the United States and United Kingdom. In particular, it poses a crucial question: Is COIN a military doctrine or a strategy? Advocates of counterinsurgency contradictorily imply that COIN is both. What this chapter demonstrates is that the effect of much COIN advocacy reduces the highly contingent nature of war, highlighted in the previous chapter, to a series of techniques. Whenever states confront conflicts defined as insurgencies, the argument goes, the application of these techniques is warranted. This assumption preempts difficult strategic judgments about how to ensure that proportional means are directed to achieve political ends in specific circumstances.

Is Counterinsurgency a Strategy?

The so-called Surge in Iraq in 2007 was the seminal event in modern counterinsurgency. The policy of doubling the number of troops and deploying them in population-centric roles rather than only in kinetic operations was widely accredited with reducing the violence and returning Iraq to a condition of security and stability.[9] As a consequence of this credit, COIN became the defining orthodoxy governing the Western state military response to purportedly low-intensity conflicts, small wars, and global asymmetric threats. Kimberley Kagan summed up the orthodoxy that emerged after 2007: "The Petraeus doctrine was innovative not so much in its emphasis on non-kinetic operations, as in recognizing the essential synergy between the kinetic tasks of providing security to the population and the non-kinetic tasks that had already been receiving the attention of American commanders and civilian leaders." Kagan added: "Petraeus emphasized that establishing security—with all of the risks, losses, and damage to the local population and their infrastructure attendant on combat—was not a distraction from the 'main effort' of the non-kinetic operations, but a key element that first made those operations possible and helped them succeed."[10]

Kagan represented General Petraeus's campaign as a "doctrine" of thought and action. Somewhat differently, other commentaries considered it a "counterinsurgency strategy." Both the media and larger discussions of U.S. and Coalition approaches in Iraq and Afghanistan used this phrase extensively. Thus, a U.S. Army War College workshop in 2007 was entitled "COIN of the Realm: US Counterinsurgency Strategy."[11] In a similar vein, in 2009 the *Guardian* reported that "the US military commander in Afghanistan, General Stanley McChrystal, has quietly launched a new counterinsurgency strategy aimed at bolstering popular support for the government in Kabul."[12] And as we have seen, in October 2009 the Obama presidency debated whether a surge should be applied to Afghanistan. The choices were presented in terms of either a "counterterrorism strategy" or a "counterinsurgency strategy."[13] Doctrine and strategy, conventionally understood, are very different things. So what is COIN: doctrine or strategy? Let us first consider whether COIN can be construed as a strategy rather than a doctrine.

In the introduction, we saw that COIN may be defined as an attempt to confound a challenge to established authority. It builds upon the notion that an insurgency (from the Latin term *insurgere*, "to swell or rise up") is a challenge to the legally constituted government. *Insurgency* is thus a somewhat nebulous term. For instance, it is not clear from such a capacious definition whether an insurgency has to be an armed challenge to authority. Can it be an unarmed challenge or constitute any form of dissent ranging from peaceful demonstrations to civil riots? Construing such action as insurgent in character, the definition stretches the concept to embrace any potential opposition, peaceful or violent. In theory, then, the terms *insurgency* and its antonym *counterinsurgency* are so all encompassing that any government, irrespective of its ideological and political composition, might be said to exist in a permanent condition of counterinsurgency to ensure its continuing authority. From such a stretched conceptual perspective, nonauthoritarian, democratic governments that minimize discontent that threatens their authority and legitimacy conduct counterinsurgency.[14]

Fortunately, *The US Army/Marine Corps Counterinsurgency Field Manual* and its British Army counterpart narrow the meaning of how counterinsurgency is understood in policy-making circles. These publications provide official statements of COIN theory and offer specific definitions. According to the *Counterinsurgency Field Manual*, an insurgency is "an organized movement aimed at the overthrow of a constituted government through the use of subversion and armed conflict." Counterinsurgency consequently is the "military, paramilitary, political, economic, psychological, and civic actions taken by a government to defeat an insurgency."[15] Such definitions offer some specificity to an otherwise elastic term. If, however, the less-euphemistic word *combatant* were inserted in place of the term *insurgency* and *war* in place of *counterinsurgency*, we would arrive at the following statement: "War involves military, paramilitary, political, economic, psychological, and civic actions taken by a government to defeat a combatant."

By this somewhat circuitous route, we arrive at a definition that applies, in fact, to *all* war, not simply to those conflicts that are termed insurgences. Yet the *Field Manual* calls for a uniform military response to all cases of what it has defined as an insurgency. The document informs us that "most insurgencies follow a similar course of development. The tactics used to successfully defeat them are likewise similar in most cases."[16] In other words, although the *Field Manual* ostensibly provides guidance for military conduct, it seems to maintain that counterinsurgency is a universal strategy—that is to say, a method that can be applied across time and space, regardless of contingent factors. The question follows: Does counterinsurgency as the set of principles set out in publications such as the *Counterinsurgency Field Manual* and the British army manual *Countering Insurgency* represent a coherent strategy?

As we defined *strategy* in the introduction to this volume, it denotes the attempt to attain goals with available means.[17] In a military context, this attempt entails the process by which armed force is translated into intended political effects.[18] Strategy is a practice guided by military planning that should not, at least in a functioning democracy of appropriate checks and balances, be determined by the military. This is because strategy requires answers to the following existential questions: What principles, values, and outcomes are being sought? How can the means available help attain desired outcomes? How will it be known when those outcomes have been achieved? How can those outcomes be achieved or maximized,[19] at what proportionate cost and without causing further problems later?[20] Ultimately, strategy in war can be distilled into two simple questions: For what is one fighting, and is that object likely to be worth the fight?

These questions are simple, but by their value-laden nature difficult to answer. Problematically, despite asserting COIN to be a strategy for combating insurgencies across time and space, neither current U.S. and British counterinsurgency manuals nor the commentary by COIN specialists addresses these strategic questions. Nowhere in these works on COIN do they expound why forces should be confronting insurgencies. Why, for instance, were Coalition forces fighting in Afghanistan, or why did they remain in Iraq? These works do not identify the political object of fighting or how to achieve strategic goals, however defined. They do not identify what success entails or offer any method for assessing proportionality. These questions are not raised or answered, it would seem, because they involve or require a political judgment. If, as we outlined in chapter 1, all wars are unique, all political judgments are contingent on the inimitable social setting of each and every instance of conflict. Any judgment about what and how to achieve outcomes through war should therefore rely on assessments of how armed forces can be used in circumstances that will never be repeated.

Contemporary COIN analysis is, however, silent about the political intent informing the recourse to armed force. Counterinsurgency, both as a concept and as an understanding outlined in COIN manuals, therefore *cannot* constitute a strategy. We explore the political lacuna at the heart of counterinsurgency further in subsequent chapters, but for now we confine our deconstruction of claims that COIN functions as a timeless prescription for insurgency by examining its equally difficult relationship with notions of doctrine.

Is Counterinsurgency a Doctrine?

If COIN is not a strategy, is it a doctrine? If we accept the idea that statements contained in military manuals compose tactical advice, then COIN nominally functions as military doctrine. So what is doc-

trine in this context? According to the U.S. military, doctrine constitutes the "fundamental principles by which the military forces or
elements thereof guide their actions in support of national objectives. . . . It is authoritative but requires judgment in application."[21]
Doctrine seeks to develop a set of agreed-upon methods by which
the armed forces will conduct their operations and establish a common language for doing so. In this manner, it seeks to render military
action and its effects predictable. In doing so, the notion of military
doctrine not only functions as a rationale for the existence of armed
forces and their respective budgets but possesses broader appeal,
particularly for political leaders uncomfortable with the prospect of
exercising "judgment in application" over the use of force but who
see in detailed doctrine a set of ready-made, off-the-shelf answers.
For such reasons, recent decades have seen the growing dominance
of doctrine in all spheres of military activity. Military doctrine now
encompasses all facets of operational activity—maritime doctrine,
air power doctrine, land warfare doctrine, and, new in the twenty-
first century, space and cyber doctrine.[22]

But what, it may be asked, does the term *doctrine* mean? Significantly, it derives from the tenets and structure of religious thought
laid out in a set of practices that the official priesthood inculcates as
the correct and orthodox path of belief. Thus, at its core, doctrine is
a system of faith, and faith ought by its nature to be unyielding. As a
consequence, someone who is rigid and inflexible in their orthodoxy
is described as dogmatic or even doctrinaire. Clearly, then, there is
a semantic tension between an understanding of a level of military
preparations conceived as doctrine and the practical and philosophical essence of war.

If, as discussed in the previous chapter, we accept Carl von Clausewitz's conception of war as "more than a true chameleon that slightly
adapts its characteristics to any given case,"[23] then all wars are exceptional in their origins, shape, and direction. Each is fashioned by its
time and place. What governs each instance of war and the way the
observer perceives it are always different, reflecting each case's contingent circumstances. At the same time, Clausewitz also maintained that
in its ultimate purpose war is the same: the pursuit of political ends
through violent means.[24] Yet each war's character is always unique,

formed by an ever-changing, unpredictable, and never reproducible mix of the variables of time, place, and the trinity of passion, chance, and reason.[25] Here lies a puzzle that confronts all strategic formulation: If each war is unique, how is it possible to plan for it? How can military planners and policy makers make stable assumptions about the likely course of the future wars they might have to fight?

The paradox is that all war is unique, yet all doctrine is—in theory—fixed. This paradox, it seems, can never be fully resolved. The course of any war cannot be predicted beyond the Clausewitzian formula of a known set of independent variables (passion, chance, and reason), which regulate all war. How those variables will interact in each instance is always unknown beforehand. Applying this understanding, we can see the tension between the claims made by counterinsurgency advocates and Clausewitzian theories of war.

COIN, according to its exponents, is a set of ideas and practices derived from the observation of historical cases, the lessons learned therein, and the identification of permanently operating factors in a specific area of war known as "insurgency." The core instrumental assumption of contemporary COIN doctrine is that, contra Clausewitz, there exist distinct "types" of war demarcated by their external, tactical manifestation. These types of war are repeated through history, so one can divine a robust set of prescriptions based on this typology. For those who believe in the validity of COIN, therefore, insurgencies are informed by a uniform set of "dynamics."[26] As a consequence, "insurgencies, like other forms of armed conflict, are better defined by their associated methodologies than by ideologies." Accordingly, "while causes change regularly, the fundamentals of insurgent methodology remain relatively constant."[27] For its advocates, then, counterinsurgency constitutes a military template that can be applied whenever a state recognizes that it confronts an insurgency. COIN thought thus assumes that there are enduring principles of action that underlie and inform the success of anti-insurgent campaigns. In particular, all insurgencies, it is maintained, are informed by similar practices. The timeless dynamics of insurgency, therefore, are the key to the timeless response of successful counterinsurgency. In this way, counterinsurgency is presented as a doctrine: an unyielding set of precepts that should guide thought and action throughout time.

Chapter 1 noted that such typologizing represents at best an over-simplification, illustrative as it is of an urge to classify the unclassifiable. Is "insurgency" a distinct and recurrent type of war? If so, how does insurgency differ from other forms of internal conflict such as civil war? And, indeed, how is insurgency differentiated from war per se? What are the factors that identify the type of conflict faced? Is there a standard matrix that can be discerned for all manifestations of internal war? Many years ago Bernard Fall, a notable commentator on counterinsurgency, criticized this penchant for classifying hostilities: "The [use of the] terms 'insurgency,' 'paramilitary operations,' 'guerrilla operations,' 'limited warfare,' 'sublimited warfare'" is, he noted, similar "to the position of the doctor faced with a strange disease. Whenever doctors are faced with a strange disease they give it a long name. It does not cure you, but at least it makes you feel good because you think they know what they are talking about."[28]

This lexical thicket underscores the incoherence at the heart of counterinsurgency thinking. Harry Eckstein, one of the most prominent scholars of "internal war," argued in the mid-1960s that "the term 'internal war' denotes any resort to violence within a political order to change its constitution, rulers, or policies. It is not a new concept. . . . Nor does it mean quite the same thing as certain more commonly used terms, such as revolution, civil war, revolt, rebellion, uprising, guerrilla warfare, mutiny, *jacquerie, coup d'etat*, terrorism, or insurrection. It stands for the genus of which the others are species."[29]

Eckstein's definition of internal war is strikingly similar to the definition of insurgency in *The US Army/Marine Corps Counterinsurgency Field Manual*. It is unclear whether the term *counterinsurgency* in the twenty-first century is intended to be synonymous with Eckstein's term *internal war* and, if so, whether one should conclude that the *Counterinsurgency Field Manual* and similar manuals offer cures to internal conflict of any variety. The implication in the *Field Manual*, with its assertions that all insurgencies follow a similar direction, is that COIN should be regarded as an all-encompassing doctrine, applicable in each case irrespective of context.

This claim, though, would be ambitious, particularly for a military manual. According to one commentator, "the probably accurate if pessimistic conclusion that the vast differences in the origins and nature of civil conflict make it difficult, perhaps even impossible, to achieve overarching solutions; [such solutions] are inevitably too general to be useful or too specific to apply to most or many cases."[30] In other words, if we follow Clausewitz's thinking, we must conclude that the uniqueness of such conflicts defies the development of a fixed, comprehensive doctrine.

Practitioner-Led Theory

The fact that counterinsurgency thought purports to be both strategy and doctrine reflects its origins and evolution in a policy-making community. COIN is not a product of the academy but emerges from the world of "practitioners," a designation many modern COIN theorists use to describe themselves. The traditional authorities in COIN thought who came to prominence after 1945—David Galula, Roger Trinquier, Robert Thompson, Richard Clutterbuck, Frank Kitson,[31] and others— were serving or retired French and British military or colonial officers. Likewise, the perceived forerunners of modern counterinsurgency theory and practice in the late nineteenth and early twentieth centuries similarly possessed military backgrounds,[32] such as the French empire builders Joseph Gallieni and Hubert Lyautey[33] and the British writers on colonial pacification Charles Callwell and Charles Gwynn.[34] With few exceptions, the more renowned contemporary COIN advocates tend to follow this pattern of being soldier-scholars, such as H. R. McMaster, John Nagl, Peter Mansoor, and David Kilcullen.[35]

The colonial origins of COIN also explain why many of its contemporary enthusiasts look to past conflicts in order to extract "lessons from history." As COIN thinking has evolved in contemporary American understandings, commentators have tended to rest their claim to COIN's efficacy and fundamental dynamics upon a dominant case: the British campaign in Malaya between 1948 and 1960 against a determined Communist revolt. The Malayan Emergency, in which British forces overcame the Communist rebellion via an interlocking program of military, economic, and social measures, constitutes the locus classicus of how a democratic state can win against a seemingly intractable insurgency through a policy of winning "hearts and minds."

COIN advocates have thus tended to apply lessons generalized from the Malayan Emergency to instances of insurgency after 9/11, as evidenced in the enthusiasm for population-centric approaches and the illocutionary "hearts and minds" rhetoric.[36]

In particular, a number of American soldier-scholar commentators drew on the British experience in Malaya to contrast it with the failure of U.S. efforts at countering the Communist insurgency in Vietnam.[37] John Nagl's 2002 book *Learning to Eat Soup with a Knife: Counterinsurgency Lessons from Malaya and Vietnam* exemplifies this approach. Learned though many of the COIN soldier-scholars undoubtedly were, they and like-minded commentators often treated the Malayan case not as a historian might, examining the causes of the insurgency and the plausible reasons for the failure of what Richard Clutterbuck termed "the long long war,"[38] but as a repository of methods and tactics that could be recycled and adapted to the analogously long wars in Afghanistan and Iraq. Abstracted from the counterinsurgency conducted by the British in the 1950s via Nagl's demonstration of the superiority of the British Army's adaptable small-wars organizational culture, COIN could be presented as socially and democratically palatable.[39] In this rendition, British success rested on the effective capturing of hearts and minds through programs such as the Briggs Plan to build safe new villages and relocate the squatter population from the edges of the jungle and plantations. Meanwhile, the tactic of securing "white areas" and then concentrating on the more troublesome "black areas" after 1955 resonates with the contemporary tactic of "clearing, holding, and building."[40] In Afghanistan, this practice took the operational form of Provincial Reconstruction Teams, comprising in part social anthropologists and aid workers who identified the levels of the frontier peoples' social needs and economic development.[41]

The use of the Malayan Emergency as the precursor COIN model, however, obscures the manner in which it cherry-picks the historical record. It ignores critical aspects of the campaign that were crucial to British success. First, it fails to recognize that the Emergency measures were conducted under conditions of colonial governorship. The United Kingdom might have been a democracy, but it conducted the "long long war" as a colonial power. Moreover, as Karl Hack argues in a revisionist account of Emergency historiography, the prelude to "hearts and minds" required forcefully "screwing down" the Communists and their supporters.[42] That is to say, coercive military power preceded the socioeconomic reforms that gave rise to the hearts-and-minds myth.[43] Notably, at the level of civil society and the British administered rule of law, the prelude required recourse to a highly repressive Internal Security Act (ISA). The postcolonial nations of Singapore and Malaysia have never repealed the ISA since 1965. Indeed, in these single-party-dominant states, the political elites maintain that the ISA constitutes the basis for social cohesion, internal resilience, and political stability. Nowhere, of course, do these new states advocate pluralism, accountability, and transparency.[44] Little acknowledgment is made in modern COIN advocacy of the utility of repressive legislation to curtail Communist Front activities or of the hard-power underpinnings of classic colonial era counterinsurgency success.[45] COIN devotees never advocate, for example, introducing a repressive internal-security regime, which would indeed be following the example of the British in Malaya.

A further feature of practitioner-led understandings of COIN is that they anachronistically distort the historical record in order to support less coercive uses of hard power.[46] This in turn supports a practitioner preference for grievance settlement as the default solution to winning hearts and minds. In the instrumentalist understanding of COIN, the rhetoric of hearts and minds in contemporary doctrine discloses an interesting syllogism:

- All insurgencies are a result of social contradictions.
- All social contradictions are a result of local grievances.
- All insurgencies are a product of local grievances.

From this syllogism, a number of false conclusions follow. Leading COIN advocates assume, for instance, that all socially produced grievances are in some manner legitimate and therefore deserve to be either remedied or appeased.[47] Thus, John Mackinlay asserts: "A dangerous insurgency . . . usually has legitimate grievances or cause [requiring a] change in direction in order to remove the pressure of the grievance."[48] Remedy the grievance, advocates contend, and the insurgency is substantively resolved. David Kilcullen notes that counterinsurgency ultimately requires a form of "armed social work." COIN, he argues, is "an attempt to redress basic social and political problems while being shot at. This makes civil affairs a central counterinsurgency activity, not an afterthought."[49] John Nagl and Brian Burton reinforce the emphasis on social grievance as the principal driver of insurgent actions:

> Political disenfranchisement, lack of economic opportunity, and social alienation at the personal level are more widespread within these [western Muslim] communities. For many of the young men who end up joining militant groups, the commitment to jihad is less important than the feeling of belonging and chance to avenge perceived indignities of the past. The militant "cause" may be couched in Islamist terms, but it is not simply bred into individual would-be jihadists with tabula rasa minds. They have pasts, grievances, and personal justifications for their actions that run deeper than the veneer of extremist religion.[50]

The grievance–resolution approach is not always wrong. Clearly, any sophisticated and humane policy response should address the social factors that may fuel a conflict. Yet although grievance settlement may constitute a set of practical responses on the ground, it should not function as a substitute for political judgment because, as we learned in chapter 1, the political circumstances of each war are always different, subject to the infinite variation of passion, chance, and reason. War is thus ever changing, and assertions that insurgencies are the product of grievance, political disenfranchisement, socioeconomic deprivation, or thymotic disregard, each of which requires redress in the form of armed social work, consequently do not hold as statements of timeless verity. Yet COIN thinkers regularly assert such monocausal explanations, which implicitly forms a political judgment. But political judgment in war is by its nature always contingent on war's unique social and geographical setting and not amenable to such reductionism. COIN advocates' assertions about the causes of conflict are therefore highly contestable, and the solutions they promote are not evidently applicable to each and every instance of so-called insurgency. They are not timeless principles of understanding.

The fact that such claims aspire to universal truths about the causality of insurgency, however, leads COIN theorists into a curious and paradoxical relationship with the concept of politics.

COIN's Antipolitical Relationship with Politics

COIN thus enunciates policies that have profound political implications. Yet contemporary American and British COIN manuals primarily offer only tactical and operational advice. The reader struggles to find any discussion of overt political goals or ideals for which a counterinsurgency campaign might be fought. Although COIN thinkers claim to understand the causes of insurgency (social, political, and economic grievances), these documents as well as much commentary on the subject eschew articulating any higher purpose for the wars fought. Political considerations involve complex calculations about the outcomes sought, and the sometimes coercive means to achieve them may entail actions that require a degree of dissimulation. At the same time, the deliberations that lead a democratic polity to pursue war or peace require presentation in a persuasive manner.[51] Above all, the political aim requires the state—or other social actor—engaged in war to articulate the values it upholds and wishes to secure. In this context, COIN manuals share a curious family resemblance to a recipe book by a fashionable TV chef inducting the amateur enthusiast in the arcane skills of cordon bleu cookery. But, unlike these technical cookbooks, counterinsurgency manuals can never guarantee the perfect COIN mix because they deny the critical ingredient in all war—political judgment, the prerequisite for all successful strategy.

Paradoxically, therefore, while offering somewhat simplistic political evaluations about the causes of war, COIN advocates nevertheless characterize themselves as disinterested connoisseurs of combat, neutral observers beyond the compromises of quotidian politics. COIN thinkers seek to assume the impartial role of an engineer who offers technical solutions to fix problems. The COIN image repertoire epitomizes an apolitical style of policy making that is bureaucratic or, more precisely, technocratic.[52] It abjures anything that compromises this rationalist character. As Michael Oakeshott explains, such "rationality in conduct" is the product of "a determinate instrument, and asserts that the 'rational' way of going about things is to go about them under the sole guidance of the instrument."[53]

The technocratic instrument in the case of contemporary warfare is COIN doctrine, and, like all such antipolitical rationalism, COIN doctrine seeks to break up human behavior "into a series of problems to be solved, purposes to be achieved and a series of individual actions performed in pursuit of these ends."[54] This perspective informs the seemingly objective consideration of every project. As Oakeshott shows, however, the rationalist's craving for this sort of "mistake proof certainty" and the "instrumental mind it reflects may be regarded in some respects as the relic of a belief in magic."[55]

Two distinguishing features of the counterinsurgency discourse clearly illustrate both this instrumentalist approach and its antipolitical consequences. First, the antipolitical character of the COIN "instrument" is evident in the attempt to deny the Clausewitzian conception of war—namely, that war always has a political object. A London-based COIN consultative group that met in 2007 to discuss the development of British Army counterinsurgency doctrine concluded its attempt to reframe doctrine with the injunction: "Be wary of Clausewitz . . . some of his theories complicate rather than inform an effort to explain the complexity of the current version of insurgency."[56] But the group never explained why it considered Clausewitz's thought problematic. Montgomery McFate, the anthropologist who assisted the U.S. military in formulating its field manual, similarly maintained: "Neither Al-Qaeda nor insurgents in Iraq are fighting a Clausewitzian war, where armed conflict is a rational extension of politics by other means."[57]

Why is Clausewitz treated so disparagingly? On one level, such indifference or even opposition almost always reflects numerous commentators' misunderstanding of Clausewitz's view of war, assuming that the Prussian general was concerned only with third-generation or nation-state warfare.[58] Concealed within this nescience, though, is a more compelling reason for COIN analysts to reject Clausewitz: Clausewitz emphasizes the centrality of politics in war. Politics—that is, the values and goals of the state's higher decision-making echelons—and the contingent political circumstances that govern such decision making render war uncertain and ensure that war manifests itself in different guises on each and every occasion. The chameleon-like nature of war negates the view that there exists a precise, universal, and rational template to guide conduct in warfare, regardless of any superficial tactical similarities (such as those that manifest themselves in insurgencies). Clausewitz's conception of war therefore rejects the view that terms such as *counterinsurgency* possess meaning or applicability beyond any single instance of war.

Strategy, Doctrine, and Counterinsurgency

As chapter 1 argued, what governs any instance of war is always different in some degree, reflecting each case's contingent circumstances. For Clausewitz, the unique character of war is the result of the "paradoxical trinity" arising from the interplay of "primordial violence, hatred and enmity . . . the play of chance and probability with which the creative spirit is free to roam: and of its element of subordination, as an instrument of policy, which makes it subject to reason alone."[59] In Clausewitz's estimation, the foremost influence on war is politics. When he describes war as a continuation of politics by other means,[60] he means not only that politics gives rise to war, but that it also exerts a primary influence over the manner in which war is conducted. As a consequence, warfare can never be, as COIN theorists contend, a set of technical/operational practices but rather is always an activity that must be shaped in accordance with the overriding political purposes for which it is fought.

The complex contingency of war creates difficulty for strategy—that is, the process by which armed force is translated into political ends. The process of translating military means to serve political ends is subject to the competing demands of military necessity (often perceived as the demand to win quickly), with the requirements of policy possibly demanding more moderate or subtle forms of action and communication to attain desired ends. These imperatives are not obviously compatible. Strategy therefore acts, in Colin Gray's words, as the "bridge" between tactical actions on the ground—the violent actions of combat—and the higher purpose to which those acts are di-

rected.[61] Strategy must therefore be capable of providing timely direction for military activity in the midst of war. For although peacetime
militaries spend a great deal of time planning for war, these plans are
often overtaken by events once hostilities commence. Military professionals have long recognized this problem. As Chief of the Prussian
General Staff Helmut von Moltke remarked, "No plan survives first
contact with the enemy."[62] At the same time, strategy must also remain
sensitive to the broader political context within which war is conducted if it is to produce military outcomes that are not disproportionately
costly in relation to the value attached to victory. The imperative to do
something quickly, in other words, should not override the need to do
something that is commensurate with the political context.[63]

In order to reduce the uncertain landscape arising from the contingency of war, policy and military professionals have sought to address the problems associated with the need to plan and rapidly revise
plans by developing doctrine as a source of guidance for action. This
doctrine may be informal, ad hoc, and based on past experience, or it
may be, as it is increasingly in modern bureaucratic polities, codified
in military manuals. The evolution of counterinsurgency theory in the
first decade of the twenty-first century evidently attempted to provide
some kind of strategic bridge between past experience, present campaigns (in Iraq and Afghanistan), and probable wars of the future in
which the major Western powers might find themselves engaged. This
was the purpose guiding the publication of both *The US Army/Marine
Corps Counterinsurgency Field Manual* in 2007 and the British Army's
Countering Insurgency manual in 2009.[64]

In theory, military doctrine is utilitarian. It provides a set of di-
rectional propositions for action distilled from the "lessons" of the
past and applied to inform decision making in the current era. In
this way, doctrine is intended to replace the requirement of deriving
plans and courses of action from first principles. As Geoffrey Till has
stated, doctrine is "something designed to provide military people
with a vocabulary of ideas and a common sense of purpose about how
they should conduct themselves before, during and after the action."
Accordingly, "if strategy is about the art of cookery, doctrine is concerned with today's menus." In the absence of doctrine, Till observes,
"commanders would have either to rely on luck and blind instinct or

to convene a seminar to decide what to do when the enemy appears on the horizon."[65]

If doctrine is to possess validity as a guide to strategic decision making, its "vocabulary of ideas" and "common sense of purpose" must nevertheless be subordinated to political considerations. The successful application of appropriate military doctrine, in other words, requires prudence, the practice of judgment in light of prevailing circumstances. As another British Army document explains, doctrine is about "how to think; not what to think."[66] This is an important distinction because without the prudential application of judgment, doctrine has a tendency to degenerate into dogma—that is, a rigid assertion of rules of questionable relevance to any given instance of war and functioning as the harbinger of poor policy making.

A brief examination of current official U.S. and British doctrinal publications on insurgency reveals the problems experienced in reconciling the tensions between the differing imperatives of politics, strategy, and doctrine. The British COIN manual *Countering Insurgency* superficially appears more attuned to the centrality of politics than does the U.S. *Counterinsurgency Field Manual.* The British document acknowledges, albeit cursorily, the primacy of political purpose in counterinsurgency. Yet it misconstrues the notion of political purpose, presenting it solely in terms of nonmilitary operations supporting social developments to drain sympathy away from the insurgents. The manual does not conceive politics in terms of the state's pursuit of objectives based on a prudential calculation of costs, interests, and values. Thus, tactical advice is accentuated over the core political calculations of the relationship of means to ends, proportionality, and the definition of success.[67] The manual's hostility toward Clausewitzian postulates becomes further apparent in its enthusiastic quotation of somewhat vacuous statements by David Miliband, the British foreign secretary at the time the manual was published. Miliband asserted in July 2009 that "people like quoting Clausewitz that warfare is the continuation of politics by other means. But in Afghanistan we need politics to become the continuation of warfare by other means."[68] Miliband apparently was suggesting that nonmilitary operations can be considered acts of war within the context of counterinsurgency. Such comments might be deconstructed to mean that building schools and hospitals and inculcating democratic values might help undermine the Taliban insurgency in Afghanistan. At the same time, however, they also obscure Clausewitz's appreciation of the relationship between warfare and political ends, which firmly subordinates the former to the latter.

Clausewitz prioritized the political in an attempt to ensure that the resort to war would produce better outcomes than those that preceded war. In the context of Afghanistan, this political outcome should not entail a limitless commitment of troops and material to a weak state that, absent al-Qaeda, possesses little strategic interest. Here COIN's focus on winning hearts and minds through nonkinetic operations (social programs, the building of schools and hospitals, etc.) confronts the principle of proportionality. More than a decade after 9/11, this focus resulted in a mission stalled in the Pashtun tribal hinterlands, where the Taliban enemy received covert support from Pakistan.[69] Yet the United States regards Pakistan, locked between the rising powers of China and India on the one side and a reinvigorated Russia on the other, as a crucial pillar upholding the stability of South Asia.[70] The negative impact of waging a long counterinsurgency campaign in Afghanistan has been disproportionate because the outcomes are of little real political value. Indeed, the counterinsurgency campaign against the Taliban has drained financial and material resources, damaged Western credibility, and succeeded only in destabilizing Pakistan.

Similar limitations permeate the U.S. *Counterinsurgency Field Manual*. As noted earlier, the manual confidently asserts that most "insurgencies follow a similar course of development" and that the "tactics used to successfully defeat them are likewise similar in most cases." The manual thus conceives itself to be comprehensive in its potential application across time and space. In other words, the *Field Manual* ostensibly provides rules for action, which all too frequently become dogmatic. In doing so, it too ignores the importance that Clausewitz attached to the shaping of actions with regard to the wider political context in which a social actor seeks to use the military instrument to achieve its goals.[71] Contemporary COIN analysts reinforce this view, holding that "while causes change regularly, the fundamentals of insurgent strategy remain relatively constant. . . . So too do the fundamentals of counterinsurgency."[72] COIN's emphasis on the tactical means a combatant employs rather than on the comprehension of the broader political reasons that motivate an adversary to fight ultimately preempts effective strategic judgment.

COIN Discourse

We understand that armed forces doctrine has an important role to play in facilitating military decisions under time constraints by providing some ready-to-hand generalizations as a guide to action. Doctrine cannot, however, be a substitute for the application of judgment in relation to strategic matters. Effective strategic decision making must be made with reference to war's political dimension.[73] It is the political dimension that confers on war its chameleon-like characteristics. Yet COIN doctrine habitually descends into dogma and thereby impedes the formulation of strategy. Doctrine as dogma is attractive quite often because it is bureaucratically more acceptable to rely on checklist solutions than to venture into the shifting, prudential, and contingent domain of politics.[74] The exercise of judgment, after all, is difficult and can provoke deep misgivings, especially when a great deal may rest on the outcome of decisions made. It is far easier, therefore, to apply a known formula that can be followed under all circumstances. The Western embrace of counterinsurgency after 2007 can be readily explained, perhaps, by the desire to believe that a technical formula drawn from the "lessons of history" can replace the complex strategic decisions associated with prosecuting difficult wars in far off places.

But if COIN is not a strategy, based as it is on a selective use of history and a confused theoretical foundation, how can we explain its prominence in strategic discourse? After all, insurgency is assumed to constitute the likely challenge that the major Western powers will confront in the future and is almost synonymous with war in current thinking.[75] From what we have seen of COIN's promotion into contemporary discursive appeal, we can discern that COIN is, in fact, not just one thing, not just a doctrine or a strategic pretense, but a discursive conflation of a number of not necessarily clearly related things.

COIN AS A NARRATIVE

We can see, first, that COIN is a narrative. It is a story about triumph
over adversity. To illustrate by means of a cultural metaphor, it is particularly suited to the genre of the Western movie. It also fits with the
foundational American myth of a manifest destiny to overcome both
nature and hostile natives to achieve the teleological goal of liberal
democratic enlightenment. In this context, Petraeus's advisers framed
a view of the Surge in Iraq after 2007 in terms of innovative thinking and a new commander breaking up a sclerotic establishment.[76]
Thus, COIN advocates present the Surge like a Hollywood script: the
old commanders, General George Casey and others, fail to speak to
the natives, and things are going from bad to worse on the frontier.
Fortunately, a new sheriff, Marshall Petraeus, strides into town with
a new purpose and clear ideas. He cleans out the local saloon (a.k.a.
Multinational Forces Iraq) and with his trusty advisers treats with the
tribal leaders and smokes the pipe of peace (the "Sunni Awakening").
A new bond is forged, the border is settled, and the outlaws (al-Qaeda
in Iraq) are put to flight.[77]

The triumph-over-adversity narrative, along with its associated
historical and cultural references, is easily detectable in American
public discourse. After 2007, the story of the Surge was retailed to
a popular audience seemingly eager to believe in a tale of ultimate
success after so much carnage and pessimism.[78] "There are lessons
to be learned from the dazzling success of the surge strategy in Iraq,"
proclaimed media commentator Michael Barone in late 2007: "Lesson one is that just about no mission is impossible for the United
States military. A year ago it was widely thought, not just by the new
Democratic leaders in Congress but also in many parts of the Pentagon, that containing the violence in Iraq was impossible. Now we
have seen it done." Discerning a historical pattern, Barone suggested:
"We have seen this before in American history. George Washington's
forces seemed on the brink of defeat many times in the agonizing
years before Yorktown. Abraham Lincoln's generals seemed so unsuccessful in the Civil War that in August 1864 it was widely believed
he would be defeated for re-election. But finally Lincoln found the
right generals. Sherman took Atlanta and marched to the sea; Grant

pressed forward in Virginia." Extending the historical parallel, Barone noted: "George W. Bush, like Lincoln, took his time finding the right generals. But it's clear now that the forward-moving surge strategy devised by Gens. David Petraeus and Raymond Odierno has succeeded where the stand-aside strategy employed by their predecessors failed."[79] In more measured but no less emphatic terms, scholar and National Security Council adviser Peter Feaver similarly asserted: "Over the past sixteen months, the United States has altered its trajectory in Iraq. We are no longer headed toward a catastrophic defeat and may be on the path to a remarkable victory."[80]

As such statements illustrate, the narrative tradition is not confined to recent conflicts, nor—it should be observed—is it something peculiar only to U.S. national stories. In fact, COIN's most celebrated historical cases reflect comparable portrayals. The traditional narrative of Malaya holds that General Gerald Templer's inspirational leadership saved the operation from his predecessor's mistakes (when in fact his predecessor, conveniently assassinated, had established the groundwork for later success).[81] Analogously, in Vietnam, according to popular accounts such as Lewis Sorley's 1999 book *A Better War*,[82] General Creighton Abrams arrived almost in time to save the disastrous situation created by a decade's worth of political mismanagement and General William Westmoreland's failure to implement an effective counterinsurgency plan.[83]

Following the setbacks after the years of supposed failure by the Coalition in Iraq, the public's reception of the triumph narrative fed the idea that the Surge led by Petraeus fitted the notion of "a better war." Although much derided by later critics such as Gian Gentile for its oversimplifications,[84] the notion of "a better war" undoubtedly arrests the American collective unconscious. It is the plot of John Ford's films *Rio Grande* (1950) and *The Horse Soldiers* (1959) as well as later John Wayne war vehicles such as *The Green Berets* (1968),[85] crafted for the needs of a new U.S. command and for mass commercial consumption. Somewhat differently in the UK context, it plays instead into the continued British quest for colonial adventure. In the latter case, the image repertoire drawing upon the practice and legend of T. E. Lawrence, classically evoked in David Lean's cinematic masterpiece *Lawrence of Arabia* (1962), informs the romance of British COIN. Quixotic advisers hang out with the natives, learn their ways, and ride with the camels to create a new tribal dawning.[86] It is no surprise, perhaps, that the front-cover photograph on the British Army manual *Countering Insurgency* features a rugged British officer conversing with a group of tribal elders in a local village somewhere, presumably in the Afghan hinterland. The COIN narrative, in other words, not only attempts to provide guidance for military conduct but also communicates a myth for popular consumption. It reassures public opinion that difficult wars can be prosecuted successfully provided the right leaders follow the right tactics: the tactics of counterinsurgency.

COIN AS SUBTEXT—MODERN ARMIES MUST BE FLEXIBLE

Grand narratives are of course important, especially in mass-media-driven, modern democratic polities. They provide the myths that generate popular support for preferred courses of action. COIN discourse in this respect can also be understood as providing a subtext—that is to say, it contains an underlying theme or message belied by its immediate surface manifestation or its apparent technical sophistication. COIN analysts, we would argue, may privilege doctrine and technique at the expense of strategic understanding. They may, in our view, be excessively simplistic. Yet we equally maintain they are not disingenuous. They want to promote an unequivocal message that speaks to extant foreign-policy and security concerns. Unlike, for instance, the radically pacifist normativism and critical security theory that prevails in departments of international relations on Western university campuses,[87] the motivation of most COIN advocates is that they wish to ensure that modern armed forces are mentally equipped to prevail in the kinds of wars that the West currently fights and might wage in the future.[88] Informing all COIN thought, then, is often a simple message: modern Western armies must be flexible.

This message—the need for flexibility—comes across clearly in *The US Army/Marine Corps Counterinsurgency Field Manual* and in John Nagl's study of colonial and postcolonial insurgencies, *Learning to East Soup with a Knife*. Nagl's study marks a seminal moment in the theoretical evolution of contemporary counterinsurgency. Although

he subsequently somewhat overidentified with the prescriptive for-
mulae of COIN doctrine, he initially showed some sensitivity to the
view that U.S. military theorizing had often misrepresented Clausewitz's ideas. Nagl noticed that "soldiers—and most statesmen—are
uncomfortable with ambiguity, with Clausewitzian 'it depends' answers."[89] In fact, Nagl's early work did not assert that colonial-era
conflicts and the way they were fought afforded a model counterinsurgency, extrapolated from the Malayan jungle onto a global canvas.
Instead, Nagl argued that British success in Malaya reflected the British Army's facility for patient, adaptive learning and that this quality is something to be admired and emulated. It was the example of
organizational flexibility, not the instances of "on-the-ground" counterinsurgency experience that really served as the crucial "lesson" of
Malaya, according to Nagl.[90]

COIN AS A STATEMENT OF THE OBVIOUS

Understanding the subtext embodied in much COIN discourse
leads to the revelation of the key point about contemporary COIN
doctrine: it offers an attractive repackaging of statements of the
militarily obvious. It is self-evident that any military organization
should be supple, learn from mistakes, and jettison old ways of doing things as the unique circumstances of war demand. Indeed,
Colin Gray notes somewhat caustically that the contemporary fascination with military precepts about the asymmetry of conflict involve little more than "the rediscovery of the stunningly obvious."[91]
We can demonstrate this pursuit of the obvious from *The US Army/
Marine Corps Counterinsurgency Field Manual*, which advocates the
following tactical practice:

- Develop COIN doctrine and practices locally.
- Establish local training centers during COIN operations.
- Regularly challenge assumptions, both formally and informally.
- Learn about the broader world outside the military.
- Promote suggestions from the field.
- Foster open communication between officers and subordinates.
- Establish rapid avenues of disseminating lessons learned.

- Coordinate closely with governmental and nongovernmental partners at all command levels.
- Be open to soliciting and evaluating advice from local people in the conflict zone.[92]

Such advice applies to all war. In the sense that this advice outlines nostrums of positive practice, it offers rules of conduct that any professional armed forces would adopt, regardless of context.[93] This advice suggests that people should be encouraged to talk to each other, share information, and be receptive to the new and unusual. There appears in COIN thinking a commitment to "talking diversity" and for armed forces to be operationally flexible and learn what does and does not work in a particular context. Regardless of the virtue of such obvious counsel, it ultimately fails to formulate effective strategy that functions as the bridge between military conduct and the political effects sought through war.

COIN AS POLITICAL SPIN

It is no coincidence that COIN doctrine rose to prominence at the same time as the Surge, a politically controversial decision by the Bush administration to double-down troops in Iraq in early 2007. The new *Field Manual*, first issued in December 2006, was seen as the new commander in Iraq David Petraeus's playbook. It is significant that he played a key role in the writing team that authored the document. The subsequent decline in violence in Iraq seemed to validate not only the Bush administration but COIN doctrine itself.

Significantly, this manual was drafted and presented very differently from the way prior manuals of military doctrine were. The drafting process was widely advertised as "inclusive," involving groups traditionally suspicious of military action and opposed to the operation in Iraq. The drafting team even included the director of Harvard's Carr Center for Human Rights Policy.[94] The doctrine, moreover, satisfied a remarkably broad constituency with its emphasis on "protecting the population."[95] It appealed not only to neoconservative advocates of muscular American interventionism for democracy promotion (by force if necessary) but also to liberal internationalists and even human rights organizations. Subsequent evaluations of the Surge have questioned whether the fall in violence in Iraq did indeed correlate with Petraeus's arrival and the implementation of a fully-fledged counterinsurgency campaign, but to its architects the connection was beside the point.[96] The construction of the doctrine served the Machiavellian purpose of providing ethical cover to sell the continuation of a controversial war to an increasingly skeptical public.

Overall, the constituent components detected in the counterinsurgency narrative leads to the conclusion that COIN is an insoluble paradox. Doctrines, as we suggested at the start of this chapter, by their nature lend themselves to inflexible assertions of principle. COIN doctrine supports unfalsifiable statements of the obvious that hold that military organizations should stay flexible. Although armies should always adapt, COIN doctrine maintains contradictorily that all insurgencies are similar and can be countered by a standard COIN methodology. In essence, COIN doctrine, as it has evolved among the major powers of the West, purports to uphold the need to be flexible but yields to the underlying momentum of doctrine—namely, dogmatism.

As the first chapter showed, the contention that insurgencies and counterinsurgency can be defined by a uniform set of dynamics assumes that manifestly disparate conflicts compose a distinct category of war on the basis of tactical similarity. It further assumes that all insurgencies share predetermined commonalities. Counterinsurgency thinking is a paradox because it tries to apply rigid doctrine to circumstances that defy rigidification. Further, as this chapter has argued, it cannot resolve this paradox because it is not a strategy.

Ultimately, as we have demonstrated, insurgency and counterinsurgency are not separate, exclusive categories of conflict. What COIN should more modestly claim requires returning to Clausewitz and appreciating that each war is unique and that military establishments must be prepared to encounter war at any level based on the political effects and goals sought. Yet, we would argue, one does not need COIN doctrine to appreciate this point because, in the end, there is only one meaningful category of war, and that is war itself.

3

Counterinsurgency and the Ideology of Modernization

The classic vision of effective counterinsurgency practice—as David Petraeus, the U.S. Army commander of the 101st Airborne Division in the Mosul region of Iraq between 2003 and 2004, emphasized—required rebuilding the local infrastructure and economy as the essential accompaniment to long-term stability.[1] According to John Nagl, writing the foreword to the University of Chicago edition of *The US Army/Marine Corps Counterinsurgency Field Manual*, Petraeus inspired "his command with a question: 'What have you done for the people of Iraq today?'" Nagl continued: Petraeus "worked to build Iraqi security forces able to provide security to the people of the region and quickly earned the soubriquet *Malik Daoud* (King David) from the people of Mosul."[2]

Such praise suggests that in addition to the narrative, subtext, spin, and paradox involved in modern counterinsurgency, COIN also entails an ideology, or what Eric Voegelin terms a "political religion."[3] Former diplomat Sherard Cowper-Coles intimates this aspect of COIN when he observes, "Like its first cousin, stabilisation, counterinsurgency, or COIN, has acquired some of the characteristics of a cult." COIN's "disciples speak of its properties with evangelical fervour. There are different routes for gaining admission to its mysteries, but most involve field experience in a conflict zone, recently in

Iraq or Afghanistan, and a period of post-graduate study of uneven rigour. Qualifying involves at least as much faith as works." Summing up the political faith that permeates COIN, Cowper-Coles contends that "associated with the cult is a vast literature of pseudo-academic tracts. Many refer back to historical experience of counter-insurgency campaigns in Southeast Asia, Ireland and Algeria, to name only a few. For serious historians or political scientists, the revelations offered by the new apostles are seldom new, or far removed from common sense. The COIN cult's main contemporary source of revelation is the U.S. Army Field Manual No. 3-24, the *Counterinsurgency Field Manual*, the fruit of General Petraeus's tour at Fort Leavenworth in 2005–6."[4]

Other commentators also suspect that COIN represents an ideologically closed system of thought rather than a coherent strategic concept. Gian Gentile, for instance, criticizes the "cult of counterinsurgency" because it "lulls people into thinking that war is about soft power, that American soldiers sent overseas to tame a civil war or stop an insurgency will do so in a less harmful way."[5]

If COIN is a cult or political religion, the question is, Of what kind? Cowper-Coles and Gentile, in part, view counterinsurgency as a personality cult; in the case of Iraq, it was focused on Petraeus at the height of his career. The personality cult feeds into a familiar military hagiography that requires "savior generals." Such cults simplify historical narratives, projecting a distorted myth of war. This perspective presents wars initially going awry as a result of unimaginative military leadership but providentially saved from the jaws of defeat by the appointment of a flexible, innovative, and inspirational commander. The mainstream accounts published in the wake of the Iraq Surge follow this pattern, such as Thomas Ricks's *The Gamble* and, indeed, Victor Davis Hanson's *The Savior Generals*.[6]

However, there is more to COIN's cult status than an excessive reverence for the "great man" theory of history. Rajiv Chandrasekaran suggests that ideological and structural forces reinforced the ascendancy of counterinsurgency thought after 2006. Like Cowper-Coles, Chandrasekaran notes that following the Surge into Baghdad in 2007, "America's military leaders embraced COIN with the fervour of the converted." He perceives that "it became their defining ideology, just as free-market economics and Jeffersonian democracy were to the neo-conservatives who had led the United States into Baghdad."[7] COIN, then, has an ideological dimension imbued with a distinctively American liberal philosophical and political self-understanding. The promotion of Jeffersonian notions of democratic enlightenment, as Chandrasekaran implies, characterizes this system of thought. Indeed, it is plausible to infer that a cult of democratic modernization—an ideology of development—that dates back to the early decades of the Cold War forms the problematic milieu to U.S. understandings of COIN.

"Success in counterinsurgency (COIN) operations," the *Counterinsurgency Field Manual* declares, "requires establishing legitimate government supported by the people and able to address the fundamental causes that insurgents use to gain support." Fundamental to defeating an insurgency, it asserts, is to "render [insurgents] irrelevant" through the rule of law and the provision of essential services and security for the bulk of the population.[8] The premise informing such assertions, as David Kilcullen explains, is that insurgencies arise largely as a result of "bad government policies or security forces that alienate the population."[9] As a consequence of this view, the *Field Manual* again avers that the "primary aim of any COIN operation" is to foster "legitimate government."[10] These and similar asseverations permeate formal documents such as the *Field Manual* and consistently figure in the advocacy of academic and military COIN supporters. Ultimately, they consciously invoke restatements of modernization theory.

As the term implies, modernization constitutes a process by which societies move from tradition to modernity, from status to contract, and from rural to industrial and urban socioeconomic forms of organization. Modernization further assumes this process of change to be necessary and progressive. Whereas nineteenth- and early-twentieth-century political and social theorists as various as Georg Hegel, Karl Marx, John Stuart Mill, Émile Durkheim, and Max Weber drew attention to this stadial pattern of modern historical development, a distinctively American social science methodology arose in the 1950s to explain how industrial nations in Western Europe and North America evolved into complex societies through changes in technology, productivity, education, and communications.

The development of modernization theory in the United States also considered how these processes might apply to the developing, non-

Western world. More precisely, modernization as a social system and how it might apply to the developing world in the Cold War defined the research activity of the U.S. government–supported Committee on Comparative Politics (CCP) of the Social Science Research Council and the Center for International Studies (CIS) at the Massachusetts Institute of Technology from the early Cold War years through to the 1970s. Building on the work of Talcott Parsons and Edward Shils conducted at Harvard University's Department of Social Relations in the 1930s and 1940s, modernization theory dominated the U.S. social sciences during the Cold War. Its attraction to government lay in its confident assumption of the inexorable course of development and its willingness to define plans for entire societies to move along a universal path from tradition to modernity. From the late 1950s, the CIS and CCP offered policy programs that showed how elites in developing states might facilitate what the CIS termed the "modernity syndrome." From this perspective, as Daniel Lerner, quoting Andre Siegfried, explained in *The Passing of Traditional Society* (1958), " 'the United States is presiding over a general reorganization of the ways of living throughout the world.' "[11] Nils Gilman argues that modernization theory in the 1960s became the U.S. "foreign policy equivalent to social modernization at home."[12] It assumed that a rationalist, technocratic state could solve all social and economic ills. Academic scholar-bureaucrats who came to occupy key advisory or administrative roles in the Kennedy and Johnson administrations, such as Robert McNamara and W. W. Rostow, reinforced the assumption that modernization had to be guided by elites. In this view that came to influence both the conduct of U.S. counterinsurgency thinking during the Cold War and the rebirth of neoclassical COIN after 2003, Western-trained "mandarins of the future" could impose the modernization syndrome upon the masses by coercion if necessary. How, then, did modernization theory evolve into modern counterinsurgency's default ideological drive?

The Cold War Modernization Agenda

The answers given to three methodological questions came to dominate the U.S. government–sponsored modernization research program and by extension the social and economic goals of its COIN program. First, what policies and processes determined what W. W. Rostow, the doyen of the CIS, identified as industrial "take off" in late-developing economies? Second, what was the relationship between economic and political development? And third, to what extent did culture or contingent historical experience impede or promote development? This approach subsequently fashioned alternative answers to a fourth question: Did modernization necessitate democratization?

Tracing the evolution of modernization theory, Samuel Huntington contended in the early 1970s that prior to the 1950s "political change tended to be ignored because comparative politics tended to be ignored." A renewed postwar American interest in "the comparison of modern and traditional political systems" consequently engendered a "renaissance in the study of comparative politics."[13] However, in order to map the various paths, routes, and stages that facilitated the transition from tradition to modernity, the emerging disciplines of comparative politics, political sociology, and historical sociology had to identify the characteristic features or "systems" that distinguish traditional from modern society. This concern with system, syndrome, and structure reflected a growing interest in "a more scientific practice of political inquiry."[14] Leonard Binder, reflecting on the natural history of liberal development theory, contends that it consisted in the aspiration that the dominant "pragmatic pluralist system" in American political science "could be the basis of a universal political science."[15]

To this developing process of scientific redescription, Talcott Parsons and Edward Shils contributed the factors that governed the pattern variables or values within which political actors structured their social action.[16] In the mature Parsonian scheme, the social system consists of "interdependent elements that cohere into a self-regulating whole."[17] As a consequence, the functions of adaptation, goal attainment, integration, and latent pattern maintenance sustain the social system. In this context, pattern maintenance, otherwise known as "values," engender a hierarchy of "cybernetic" controls that support the "homeostatic" propensity of social systems.

According to modernization theory, modern societies, unlike primitive or less-developed ones, had evolved highly differentiated social systems that enable concrete subsystems to develop. The success of the modern condition consists in the integration of sub-system complexity through an institutionalized normative culture. The secret of modernity, then, is the movement from ascription to functional differentiation, mobility, and specialization. Central to the success of this transformation is the manner in which the normative order adjusts to new realities without abandoning basic understandings upon which the system depends.

The problems that modernity generated, therefore, were not primarily cultural, but inclusionary and institutional. In particular, modernization posed the question of how the culture of a modernizing elite can be integrated with that of the mass society. Inclusion and the effective transmission of modernizing values require institutionalization. Modernization consequently sought to establish inclusionary values that transcend local or traditional attachments of religion, kin or ethnicity, while at the same time adapting those understandings to the process of development. Parsons saw democratic citizenship, industrialization, and education as inclusionary processes central to creating new institutional forms, legal structures, market mechanisms, and bureaucracies that bring isolated and dependent populations into normatively regulated social participation. Parsons somewhat optimistically considered these institutions to have such "great adaptive capacity as to suggest that they will ultimately dominate the social life of all modern societies."[18] From a cybernetic perspective, Karl Deutsch subsequently emphasized the fact that political systems are networks of decision and control "dependent on processes of communication" resembling aspects of man-made communication equipment because they depend on the processing of information.[19]

The problem of political development, according to Deutsch, thus consists in "the integration of sets of autonomous units with their own strategic value; and the success or failure of political integration could also be evaluated in terms of the presence or absence of a second-order strategy of value, or a 'common spirit' that could be identified in the different value patterns and steering systems of the smaller autonomous units."[20] Attention to the processing of information and the transmission of values ineluctably leads to considerations of national character, culture, and nation building, which all political elites, in particular modernizing ones, have to address. In functional terms, the stability of the system requires not only an inclusionary group of shared values but a shared language. In other words, modernization needs a people constituted as a nationality that can be cybernetically ordered. From this functionalist viewpoint, shared ethnicity or history is tangential to order. All the political system requires is a people who possess "a wide complementarity of social communication." Communication makes a people cohere. In the structural functional view, the modernization process accordingly involved greater inclusiveness achieved through the institutionalization of norms in an evolving network of communicatory practice. Ultimately, this liberal theory argued that "modernization, and hence democracy[,] would result in the short or long run so long as change was introduced into any part of the social system."[21]

Even so, these lucubrations upon the social system shed little direct light on the *process* of modernization. What did modern conditions actually entail, and how were they distinguished from tradition and the practices that linked or inhibited the transition from one to the other? These questions became an area of growing scholarly attention in the course of the 1960s coincident with the growing U.S. entanglement in Vietnam and the growth of classical counterinsurgency thinking. By 1971, the CCP contended, a modern polity called for, among other things, a differentiated and functionally specific system of government; a prevalence of rational and secular procedures; efficacious administrative decisions; popular identification with the state's history, territory, and national identity; the allocation of roles by achievement rather than by ascription; and an impersonal and secular legal system.[22] Bridging what Huntington termed the "Great Dichotomy between modern and traditional societies" required the "Grand Process of Modernization."[23] This process involved a bewildering variety of procedures and processes as well as elite guidance imposed by force if necessary.[24] From a structuralist perspective, it required the shift from uniformity to differentiation and from ascription to achievement. For Marion Levy, modernization was a "universal social solvent" that involved a shift in the ratios of inanimate to animate power.[25] For Dankwart Rustow, more prosaically, it included "industrialization, rationalization, secularization and bureaucratization,"[26] and for David Apter it required commercialization and, in its noneconomic dimension, embodied "an attitude of inquiry and questioning about how men make" moral, social, and personal choices.[27] Summarizing the practices involved, Huntington contended that modernization was revolutionary, inducing "total change in the patterns of human life"; complex; systemic; global; lengthy; phased, in terms of the stages of the process; homogenizing toward interdependence among societies so constituted; irreversible and ultimately progressive.[28]

Increasing attention to this process revealed a number of difficulties in earlier structural models. Later developmental theorists argued that the cybernetic model failed adequately to capture what Samuel Huntington termed the "change to change."[29] In *The Passing of Traditional Society*, Daniel Lerner had proposed in the late 1950s the sequence of urbanization, literacy, extension of mass media, wider economic participation, and political participation as the natural order of political modernization.[30] By the 1960s, however, it had become evident to CCP members that all political systems are in some senses transitional, combining elements of modernity and tradition. Following Gabriel Almond and James Coleman's collected volume *The Politics of Developing Areas*,[31] the Social Science Research Council on comparative politics gave increasing attention to the dynamics of the development process.

The identification of sequences and crises further facilitated the differentiation of political development as a concept for policy purposes. By the early 1970s, Lucian Pye and James Coleman identified a "development syndrome" that promoted increasing equality, capacity, and differentiation within the political system. Nevertheless, somewhat problematically, it was never entirely clear whether the syndrome represented a description of processes transforming a system in transition or a teleological destination for the system.[32]

Given the different dimensions of the development syndrome, it became incumbent upon the CCP to identify the sequential character of development and the crises that might afflict a system. This problem became increasingly acute, for, as Huntington observed, "political decay and political instability were more rampant in Asia, Africa and Latin America in 1965 than they were fifteen years earlier."[33] It was argued that, given that political development ultimately understands "the prerequisite political environment essential for economic and industrial development,"[34] the failure to traverse the Great Dichotomy constitutes a problem that resides in the "crisis and sequences in political development," as another CCP work intimated.[35] For Dankwart Rustow, a sequence of national identity, state authority, and equal participation represented the least-traumatic modernization sequence.[36] By 1971, the CCP had arrived at five potential sequential crises that the modernizing state has to negotiate: identity or nation building, state legitimacy, penetration of the wider society by a state bureaucracy, political participation, and the effective distribution of resources as a consequence of the development process.

The evidence of the friability of new states created in the wake of decolonization after 1945 elicited additional concern with the character of political stability, the preconditions for economic development and their relationship to the political variety, and the role of culture in the development process. This concern, too, had implications for the practice of what was later to be described as "neoclassical COIN" after 2003. In his 1968 study *Asian Drama: An Inquiry Into the Poverty of Nations*, Gunnar Myrdal located the obstacles to economic development in the "inefficiency, rigidity and inequality of the established institutions and attitudes."[37] The internal weakness handicapping developing South and Southeast Asian states demonstrated the need to consolidate the state. These states were "soft" in that they lacked the penetration to implement policy. For Myrdal, "national character" and a variety of "Asian values" that emphasized consensus and agreement as well as religious inertia and ignored legal procedure, together with lack of access to world markets, had inhibited Asia's economic "takeoff."

From a related perspective, Rostow also considered national stability and legal procedures necessary political preconditions to economic growth. Elaborating on the politics that shape the "stages of economic growth," as his 1958 book put it, Rostow maintained that it was the British economic takeoff from the 1780s and the subsequent diffusion of this model that broke a preindustrial "cyclical pattern of expansion and decline." A sense of national identity forged by external threat and institutions engendering a sense of national consensus "formed part of the back-drop for the take-off in the 1780s."[38] Subsequent takeoffs reflected a purposeful modernizing elite's response to actual or threatened foreign intrusion. Significantly, Rostow maintained that "the troubled and contentious nature of the transition from a traditional society to one capable of sustained industrialization did not lend itself easily to stable democratic rule."[39]

The 1970s thus witnessed a shift in developmental thought toward establishing the legitimating preconditions for economic development and the crises that could lead not to political stability but to political decay as latecomers embarked upon an increasingly fraught transition to modernity. For Samuel Huntington, modernization theory neglected the fact that "as social forces became more variegated, political institutions had to become more complex and authoritative." Worryingly, according to Huntington's view, in the newly industrializing economies "the development of the state lagged behind the evolution of society."[40] As the comparative method evolved, it became apparent that a frequently overlooked distinction existed between "political modernization defined as movement from a traditional to a modern polity and political modernization defined as the political aspects and political effects of social, economic and cultural modernization."[41] The gap between the two could be vast. "Modernization in practice," Huntington contended, "always involves change in, and usually the disintegration of, a traditional political system, but it does not necessarily involve significant movement toward a modern political system." Instead, it might involve an "erosion of democracy" and the promotion of autocratic military regimes and one-party states.[42]

Furthermore, whereas those states that had achieved modernity tended to be wealthy, liberal democratic, and stable, those seeking to achieve modernity frequently encountered political disorder and political decay. Hence, although modernity meant stability, modernization often meant the opposite. As Huntington suggested, it was "not the absence of modernity but the efforts to achieve it which produce political disorder."[43] This disorder, it now seemed, reflected the failure to develop stable political institutions to deal with the economic, social, and psychological demands generated by rapid development, the frustration of rising expectations, and the growing economic disparities between rich and poor, town and country. In most modernizing countries, therefore, the lack of "mobility opportunities," the absence of mechanisms for political participation, and "the low level of political institutionalization" threatened to produce "a correlation between social frustration and political instability."[44] Significantly, Huntington further contended that the extent to which a society undergoes "complete political decomposition during the modernization process" reflects the character of its traditional political institutions.[45]

Despite these difficulties, however, it appeared by the late 1980s that a number of non-Western societies, notably in Pacific Asia, had made the transition across the big ditch that separated tradition from modernity. Modernization theory further held, therefore, that effective economic modernization creates an irresistible pressure for liberal democratic political change. Authoritarian rule may offer the initial stability necessary for economic growth, but as fully developed modernity approaches, it becomes increasingly redundant and reluctantly withers away. Depending on one's theoretical preference, the overt or covert hand promoting this change is an articulate, urban, and self-confident middle class. In the argot of development studies, the presence of this new socioeconomic phenomenon intimates both liberalization and democratization. As Seymour Martin Lipset, an early proponent of the modernization thesis stated, "the more well-to-do a nation, the greater the chances it will sustain democracy."[46]

Modernization theory has been the subject of much debate since the 1960s. It suffered from its association with Kennedy-era foreign policy and the application of modernizing COIN ideas "as rationales and strategies for foreign development aid and military action."[47] Meanwhile, from an academic perspective, the criticism that modernization theory presented a too mechanistic account of political and economic development caused it to fade but never disappear from the comparative study of politics. Indeed, its animating concerns came to inform a particularly American conception of the international environment, one that Walter A. McDougall has described as "global meliorism." It assumes that the world can advance through the application of human effort and, as the CCP contended in the 1960s, that America has a "responsibility to nurture democracy and economic growth around the world. It is all about Doing and Relating . . . and [is] designed to give America the chance to shape the outside world's future."[48] The vision accepts that, modernization difficulties notwithstanding, the course of human development will ultimately lead to an interconnected and integrated world characterized by the values of liberal institutionalism.[49]

At the end of the Cold War, a revived and revised version of modernization theory and America's mission to promote it experienced a notable renaissance. The fall of communism in Eastern Europe, Francis Fukuyama optimistically believed, witnessed the triumph of liberal democracy over its ideological rivals, communism and fascism, resulting in a polyarchic end of history.[50] In its most anodyne form, this Jeffersonian version of manifest destiny held out an essentially benevolent view of human development where modernization would lead to a convergence of shared political and economic norms, resulting in a liberal democratic universalism. At its core was the "assumption that America can, should, and must reach out to help other nations share the American dream."[51] After 9/11 and more particularly the invasion of Iraq in 2003, though, critics of U.S. hyperpower detected a more aggressive project to advance the end of history by force if necessary. Driven by a globalizing neoconservative ideology, the Bush presidency advanced the U.S. Empire of Freedom and sought to impose democracy and open markets by both hard and soft means.[52]

It was out of these ideological and political paradigms that modern counterinsurgency evolved. The rediscovery of COIN after 2001, in other words, possesses elective affinities with the U.S. modernization agenda following that agenda's revival in the 1990s under the influence of the "end of history" and democratic convergence thesis. Informing U.S. counterinsurgency thinking was a modernization mission to transform traditional societies into modern, market friendly, pluralist arrangements. This project, as with classic Cold War iterations of the theory, required a program of nation building through both military and civilian measures to convert broken or failing autocracies into stable states and fledgling democracies.

As we have noted, writers as various as Cowper-Coles and Chandrasekaran, among others, show how inapplicable American developmental approaches have been to failing states such as Afghanistan and Iraq. This chapter, by contrast, explores a broader question: Why was the rediscovery of COIN connected with an ideological program that dated from the Cold War and the policy misadventures that flowed from it? COIN's revival in the post–Cold War era evinced a continuing U.S. political elite preoccupation with promoting modernization and the purportedly universal enlightenment values upon which it is premised. However, its reappearance in Baghdad and Helmand also conjured up darker Cold War avatars, in particular the sometimes brutal application of rigid, apolitical, and doctrinaire techniques to facilitate the ineluctable goal of modernity.

The modernizing project even informed the conduct of counterinsurgency in theater. It found quotidian exemplification in the attempt to combine military tactics with civic actions. The *Counterinsurgency Field Manual* made this clear: "Long term success in COIN depends on the people taking charge of their own affairs and consenting to the government's rule." Fundamentally, therefore, it is the role of the "counterinsurgents to enable a country or regime to provide the security and rule of law that allow the establishment of social services and growth of economic activity."[53] Sarah Sewall spelled out what this dictum entailed in practical terms in her introduction to the *Field Manual*: "COIN relies upon nonkinetic activities like providing electricity, jobs, and a functioning judicial system." This means "preparing ground forces to assume the roles of mayor, trash collector, and public works employer."[54] Likewise, Kilcullen, in his tract "Twenty-Eight Articles: The Fundamentals of Company-Level Counterinsurgency," emphasizes that "counterinsurgency is armed social work; an attempt to redress basic social and political systems while being shot at. This makes civil affairs a central counterinsurgency activity, not an afterthought."[55]

Such emphasis on civic action and de-emphasis on hard, kinetic operations sit somewhat uneasily with customary notions of military power. For the U.S. Army especially—an institution steeped in traditions of force concentration and the ability to bring combat power and technology into symphonic conjunction, demonstrated consistently in practice from World War II to the Gulf War of 1990—the notion of participating in a "Wilsonianism with boots on" mission should have possessed little appeal.[56] For this reason, COIN's rise to prominence in Western military thought and its complex, sometimes subtle relationship with modernization theory deserve further investigation. What we observe, in the first instance, are industrially advanced bureaucracies performing progressively through an interrogation of their own past assumptions and practices.

The Complex Renaissance of COIN

Prior to the Iraq War of 2003 and its immediate aftermath, military studies treated counterinsurgency somewhat disdainfully and as a secondary activity. As the first chapter showed, often disparaging labels such as *unconventional war* and *irregular war* permeated military and strategic discourse. These terms implied that insurgencies were abnormal and of lesser importance than actions requiring high-tempo force-on-force concentration. This prejudice persisted despite the fact that insurgencies and "low-intensity small wars" began to constitute the norm of war—the convention—after 1945 in terms of their incidence.[57]

In 2007, Lieutenant General Sir John Kiszley of the British Army summarized the reasons traditional military thought evinced an ingrained antipathy toward insurgencies. Kiszley maintained that counterinsurgency comprises "features with which the pure warrior ethos is uneasy: complexity, ambiguity, and uncertainty; an inherent resistance to short-term solutions; problems that the military alone cannot solve, requiring cooperation with other highly diverse agencies and individuals to achieve a comprehensive approach; the need for interaction with indigenous people whose culture it does not understand; and a requirement to talk to at least some of its opponents, which it can view as treating with the enemy." He continued:

> Such a military sees its task hedged about with unfair constraints; over-tight rules of engagement, negating the use of its trump card— firepower; perceived overemphasis on force protection and its disciplinary consequences; the need to accommodate the media. Moreover, in the eyes of the warrior, counterinsurgency calls for some decidedly un-warrior like qualities, such as emotional intelligence, empathy, subtlety, sophistication, nuance and political adroitness. Armies that find difficulty with these unwelcome features tend to view counterinsurgency as an aberration, look forward to the opportunity of returning to "proper soldiering," and see subsequent training as an opportunity to regain their warfighting skills rather than to learn the lessons of counterinsurgency.[58]

In the United States, the armed forces, scarred by memories of the Vietnam War, demonstrated this reluctance to address anything that smacked of insurgency. For the latter part of the twentieth century, decisions about military action were ruled by the "Powell–Weinberger Doctrine," which emphasized the precision application of military power for clearly defined and time-limited purposes. Getting embroiled in dirty wars that lacked popular support, firm objectives, and a clear exit strategy were to be avoided, for this route had led to the disaster of Vietnam and other foreign-policy misadventures, such as the troubled intervention in the Lebanese Civil War, which witnessed the loss of hundreds of U.S. personnel in 1983.[59] Mistaken interventions abroad and the apparent lessons for the United States that it evidently held for the future reinforced the assumption that counterinsurgency constituted a form of warfare from which no good could come. "After the Vietnam War," according to General Jack Keane, "we purged ourselves of everything that had to do with irregular warfare or insurgency, because it had to do with how we lost that war."[60] Even so, as David Ucko argues, the U.S. military's post-Vietnam "aversion to counterinsurgency and stability operations" in fact "confused the undesirability of these missions with an actual ability to avoid them."[61] The aftermath of the 9/11 attacks by al-Qaeda-sponsored jihadists dictated a policy of preemptive intervention to forestall emergent threats to U.S. security and thus served to buttress the point that avoidance was not a realistic policy proposition.

The most graphic expression of the commitment to preventive war was, of course, demonstrated first in the invasion of Afghanistan in late 2001 and then by the ousting of the Saddam regime in Iraq in 2003. It was the U.S.-led Coalition's subsequent failure to stabilize Iraq in the aftermath of the 2003 invasion that prompted a radical reevaluation of traditional military priorities.[62] The breakdown of civil society, the descent into lawlessness, and the tenacity and brutality of organized resistance to both the occupying forces and the fledgling Iraqi government presented the United States and its allies with a desperate problem.[63] From the military perspective, according to John Nagl, then a lieutenant colonel in the U.S. Army, the difficulty in dealing with the evolving chaos stemmed from a failure to identify "a common understanding of the problems inherent in any counterinsurgency campaign." This in turn reflected the army's institutional culture and orientation, which discouraged the study of such conflicts. As a consequence of this orientation, the military establishment ignored both the lessons of such wars and the "ways to achieve success in contemporary counterinsurgency campaigns." Nagl insisted in 2007: "It is not unfair to say that in 2003 most Army officers knew more about the U.S. Civil War than they did about counterinsurgency."[64]

The U.S. Department of Defense's eventual recognition in 2004 that a deep-rooted insurgency prevailed in Iraq constituted the prelude to an impressive period of learning and adaptation within the American military establishment.[65] Ucko notes that "an uncommon level of humility and lack of chauvinism" informed this learning process.[66] In the course of 2004–2005, the U.S. armed services and Coalition partners such as the United Kingdom undertook a critical examination of military conduct in Iraq.[67] This process of critical reevaluation culminated in 2007 in the publication of the joint U.S. Army/Marine Corps manual on counterinsurgency, the *Counterinsurgency Field Manual*, one of the most comprehensive operational documents published on COIN operations. More importantly, the new thinking reflected ongoing changes in operational practice taking place on the ground in Iraq, along with more general shifts in military policy in Iraq that culminated in the so-called Surge. As a result, discernible improvements in the security situation were evident after 2007. Iraq was stabilized, and an impending catastrophe averted.

In contemplating the renaissance of counterinsurgency thinking within U.S. military institutions, it is possible to identify two distinctive schools of thought. Writers such as Frank Hoffman called one of these schools "neo-classical counter-insurgency."[68] The term *neoclassical* refers to the rediscovery of an underlying set of verities about COIN that drew on canonical case studies and key thinkers once overlooked or forgotten but whose relevance now appeared irresistible. This school conceived the challenge presented by insurgencies as one that operated within a Maoist framework, seeking to win the allegiance of the population to the rebel cause. From this perspective, the practice of counterinsurgency demanded an appreciation of the social and political conditions that pertained in a given territorial space and a strategy that tailored this knowledge to military and socioeconomic policies in order to contest the insurgents' claim to popular support. It is this school of COIN that most closely drew on the principles that underlay modernization theory for its inspiration and practice.

By contrast, a second, though related, school of thought reflected an ambitious attempt to draw connections between the specifics of local insurgencies and broader currents at work in the international system after 9/11. It viewed deterritorialized Islamist jihadism as a "global insurgency." It further perceived such insurgency as "post-Maoist," unbounded by space, where the local and global interact to produce a transnationally networked resistance movement. This second school presented an altogether more radical appreciation of insurgency. The evolution of this global insurgency school is explored more fully in chapter 4.

Taken together, however, these schools might be described as "neo-counterinsurgency," or "neo-COIN" for short. Although the neo-classical and global counterinsurgency schools involved elements of overlap and frequently asserted similar programs, they are nonetheless worth examining individually. The analytical separation permits us to reveal the complexity and differing perceptions at work within neo-COIN thought and how their complex interplay leaves us with a confused understanding of the phenomenon. The remainder of this chapter therefore addresses the impact of modernization theory on the neoclassical school of counterinsurgency.

The Rise of Neo-COIN

Systems of thought rarely evolve in a vacuum or as an immediate response to a crisis. They have origins that are often deep rooted and highly contingent. The rise of neo-COIN thought did not begin with the failure to stabilize Iraq. Indeed, its genesis preceded the invasion of Iraq by at least a decade. The premonitory snuffling of neo-COIN appeared in the 1990s, which in itself throws an interesting light onto the evolution of the counterinsurgency debate after the turn of the millennium.

In other words, if the immediate cause of a popular revival in COIN was the evident failure of the Coalition's occupation of Iraq, those reviving this interest drew upon evidence derived from a number of post–Cold War events. The two seminal sources of modern counterinsurgency thinking derived first from the attempt to understand why the Northern Ireland conflict ended in the manner it did and second, somewhat relatedly, from the wider study of the number of asymmetric challenges to the post–Cold War international order.

The settlement of the seemingly intractable insurgency in Northern Ireland inspired a number of scholarly and journalistic studies from the mid-1990s on.[69] Almost certainly the most significant figure in influencing later neoclassical COIN thought after 2003 was American anthropologist Montgomery McFate.[70] McFate had lived and studied in Northern Ireland's Republican community in the early 1990s while conducting fieldwork for her doctoral thesis. Early on she recognized the importance of acquiring "cultural knowledge" as a means of "enhancing military prowess."[71] In a series of papers written for U.S. military periodicals and published in the years following the invasion of Iraq, McFate reiterated the need for the nuanced appreciation of the social milieu from which insurgencies arose. In the Iraqi context, this meant understanding the nature of Sunni tribal networks.[72] She argued that U.S. "military operations and national security have consistently suffered due to lack of knowledge of foreign cultures," and so she urged the development of specialist centers in the Department of Defense to "produce, collect, and centralize cultural knowledge, which will have utility for policy development and military operations."[73] The *Counterinsurgency Field Manual* readily repeated these strictures, noting that "cultural knowledge is essential to waging a successful counterinsurgency" and stressing that "American ideas of what is 'normal' or 'rational' are not universal."[74]

The second source affecting the post-2003 focus on counterinsurgency developed in the late 1990s.[75] It focused on the nature of asymmetric conflict as it appeared to evolve in the decade following the first Gulf War of 1990–1991. Military and strategic thinking after the Gulf War concentrated on the Revolution in Military Affairs and Fourth Generation Warfare, the technology of precision-guided weapons, and integrated all-arms combat. Some analysts, however, questioned this revolution. They questioned in particular whether major battlefield operations represented the most likely form of confrontation for Western states in the future. Skeptical commentators, such as Rupert Smith, observed that those wishing to test the resolve of the major powers would be unlikely and arguably extremely foolish to confront Western and especially U.S. military and technological superiority through face-to-face combat. Instead, an enemy would attempt to mount assaults below the level of conventional combat operations, avoiding open confrontation with these materially superior opponents.

These analysts contended that the wars of dissolution that befell the former Federal Republic of Yugoslavia and the former Soviet Union, along with the increasing number of civil wars and violent nonstate actors in failed and failing states, notably in Africa and Central Asia, which sometimes compelled Western forces to intervene in humanitarian and peacekeeping or peace enforcement roles, meant that accepted understandings of military power required radical rethinking.[76] Specifically, they perceived a need for a more flexible military capable of adapting quickly to multiple and diverse roles in "out of area" operations, and this capability implied, among other things, the necessity of contemplating tasks that were perceived to fall into the category of counterinsurgency.[77]

The key texts on asymmetric warfare, out-of-area operations, and the changing nature of military power were published from 2001–2002 on, although almost all their research data derived from pre-9/11 source material. If Montgomery McFate's work epitomized the renewed interest in insurgency/counterinsurgency deriving from the latter stages of the Northern Ireland conflict, then John Nagl's 2002 book *Learning to Eat Soup with a Knife: Counterinsurgency Lessons from Malaya and Vietnam* exemplified this second trend in the evolution of neoclassical COIN. Nagl's principal concern was how military institutions innovate and adapt or sometimes fail to adapt to military challenges. Contrasting what he saw as the very different organizational cultures of the British and American armies, Nagl observed that the British preference for patient and adaptive learning, small-unit forces, and decentralized command as well as willingness to embrace civil–military cooperation could explain the relative success they enjoyed in the Malayan Emergency compared with the American army's rigid adherence to "big-unit" concepts in Vietnam that invariably emphasized firepower to resolve what were essentially deeply entrenched political problems.[78]

From these two distinct strands of thought arose a growing admiration for the British approach to COIN, which in historical terms accentuated ideas of proportionality and long-term commitment.[79] Nagl argued that the British Army's institutional culture forged over centuries of colonial war "reflected varied experiences outside conventional conflicts on the European continent" and explained its capacity to adapt to new challenges. "The leadership of the British army," he stated, "shared a common belief that the essence of the organization included colonial policing and administration." Thus, when "conventional tactics and strategy failed in Malaya, the British Army had few problems creating an internal consensus that change was needed and that political rather than purely military solutions were well within the purview of the British Army." Nagl concluded that "an innovative and varied past created a culture amenable to the changes in organizational process required to defeat a complex opponent in a new kind of war."[80]

By contrast, McFate's respect for British methods derived primarily from the British Army's ability to acquire deep cultural knowledge of its adversary. In her attempt to persuade the American armed forces to take anthropological approaches seriously, McFate related "an epiphany" she experienced while living in Belfast. "The common view of the Troubles as a battle between Catholics and Protestants, or Loyalists and Republicans, or even terrorists and the government was not how the warring sides saw it."[81] Irish Republicans legitimized their campaign of violence out of a belief that they formed part of a continuous resistance movement against eight hundred years of British military occupation. Yet, rather than deny this perspective, the British Army understood the Irish Republican myth that inspired Irish Republican Army (IRA) actions. "They may think that these people are terrorists and despise them, but they understand what's motivating it," McFate reflected. "They [the British] could not have built an effective strategy in Northern Ireland as they did without having a very full understanding of their enemy, which by the way, it took them 30 years to get."[82]

The rise of neoclassical counterinsurgency thus had its origins in the United States and had developed its thinking well before 9/11. Grappling with the troubled occupation of Iraq after 2003, elements in the U.S. military establishment, as a matter of course, turned to those who had established their credentials in the field prior to the invasion. It was natural, too, that those associated with the neoclassical school would advocate the American embrace of COIN. Indeed, they were soon at the forefront of deliberations on improving Coalition strategy in the face of what, by 2005, seemed an increasingly intractable insurgency. It was no surprise, therefore, that John Nagl, a serving officer in the armored divisions of the U.S. Army with firsthand experience both of the original invasion of Iraq during Operation Desert Storm and later with occupation forces in Khalidiyah Province, played a seminal role in shaping the debate over U.S. counterinsurgency doctrine,[83] eventually writing a foreword to the *Counterinsurgency Field Manual*.[84] Analogously, Montgomery McFate actively promoted the view that "cultural and social knowledge of the adversary" should be on the American counterinsurgency agenda. As she argued, "In a counterinsurgency situation such as the United States currently faces in Iraq, 'winning' through overwhelming force is often inapplicable as a concept. . . . Winning on the battlefield is irrelevant against an insurgent adversary because the struggle for power and legitimacy among competing factions has no purely military solution."[85]

For some commentators, the fact that McFate and others had to restate established maxims of counterinsurgency reflected the inertia in Western armed forces thinking.[86] The neglect of insurgent warfare meant that even the British Army, with its "repeated engagement in counterinsurgency, has historically found it difficult to internalize the lessons drawn from these campaigns necessitating quick adaptation on the ground with each new engagement [rather than being able to draw upon a strong institutional memory and systematic operational doctrine]."[87] The problem was even more acute for the U.S. military, deeply imbricated in an institutional culture that predisposed it toward thinking almost exclusively in terms of application of combat power above all else.

The institutionalized neglect of counterinsurgency therefore demanded the reiteration of the basic principles of counterinsurgency. In the context of the failure of the Coalition's policies in Iraq, necessity was the mother of reinvention. The neoclassical school of thought in effect reinvented the study of counterinsurgency as a core rather than a peripheral focus of military practice. It is "neoclassical" in the sense that it reinvigorated traditional counterinsurgency principles. The influence and authority of this neoclassical school was first evident in military and scholarly research that rediscovered the major counterinsurgency campaigns of the later twentieth century. Much of the research in this area highlighted the largely successful British campaigns in Malaya (1948–1960) and Northern Ireland (1969–1998), but it also looked at the failed but no less instructive French tactics in Algeria (1954–1962).[88] American military commentators in particular drew inspiration from the overarching strategies adopted by the British in their campaigns, while admiring aspects of French doctrine and operational technique. The republication of key texts from the 1960s, ranging from David Galula's reflections on the Algerian War in *Counterinsurgency Warfare*, originally published in 1964, to John McCuen's seminal 1966 publication *The Art of Counter-Revolutionary Warfare*, exemplified this growing interest in colonial-era insurgencies.[89]

Interestingly, those with an established track record in this area predating the 1990s were often skeptical of this renewed interest in matters counterinsurgent.[90] Colin Gray observed: "In the history of strategic ideas, the contemporary American fascination with asymmetry comprises the rediscovery of the stunningly obvious."[91] A restatement of the obvious, nevertheless, seemingly constituted a necessary prerequisite to raising awareness in the U.S. armed forces. More importantly, this renaissance in counterinsurgency produced a series of thoughtful articles about how to develop U.S. counterinsurgency practice in Iraq.[92] According to Sarah Sewall, these works established the terms for a critical analysis aimed at "breaking the conventional paradigm." "For decades," she maintained, "the US Army in particular had discounted the need to prepare for counterinsurgency—a messy, hydra headed conflict that can, by its very nature, only be won incrementally." "American culture and US military doctrine," Sewall averred, "prefer a technological solution and the overwhelmingly decisive blow. Americans have a penchant for black-and-white clarity and have historically shown little patience for complexity and extended commitment."[93] Commentaries such as Sewall's soon established a COIN narrative. It held that progressive military commanders such as Generals David Petraeus and Peter Chiarelli, who had experienced the "messy" realities on the ground in Iraq, "recognized a responsibility to prepare troops to meet the wars that call them, not the wars they might prefer to fight."[94]

Yet the preparation of American troops to confront insurgent conflicts accounted only in part for the revival of COIN. The U.S. armed forces' unprecedented willingness to open themselves to criticism provided space for both soldiers and scholars to reflect upon the conduct of U.S. military operations in Iraq and what needed to be done to prevail in the long run. This openness to criticism represents one of the most remarkable aspects of the COIN revival. Thus, writing in the U.S. Army journal *Military Review* in 2005, John Lynn of the University of Illinois vigorously condemned orthodox military approaches in Iraq:

> The most short-sighted statements I hear are: "They only understand force." Or, "If only we could take the gloves off, we could win." The truth is that everyone understands force, and everyone can be battered or intimidated by violence, but such use of violence generates the three "Rs": resentment, resistance, and revenge. People who argue that the enemy only understands force imply that force wins respect. In reality, force usually only instills fear. We are not trying to recreate Saddam's regime of fear, so we must use more than force.[95]

"The wisest analysis of the counterinsurgency," Lynn continued, "came from an unidentified colonel on CNN who state[d] that we cannot really win the hearts and minds of the Iraqis but we can provide security and establish trust. In security lies the support of the majority and the environment in which a new and better state may emerge."[96] As Lynn suggested, providing a critical framework that questioned conventional wisdom was one thing, but it was the experiences of military commanders on the ground in Iraq, combined with the new reflective mood, that decisively reoriented military thinking. Critical reflection, moreover, quickly assumed a distinctively modernizing cachet. Officers returning from tours of duty in Iraq offered practical insight into dealing with insurgent forces and the local communities that afforded them succour.[97] Lieutenant Colonel Chris Gibson, for example, writing of his experience in Nineveh Province, maintained that COIN forces needed to "be able to convince the people that they can provide security." "Without that," he contended, "locals will not associate themselves with—or even be seen in the presence of—security forces. . . . Once security is established, however, locals can see that COIN forces offer a better vision for the future than insurgent forces do."[98] Building on these affirmations, other serving officers offered practical evidence to support McFate's call for cultural knowledge and the need to attain practical awareness of the particularities of the local surroundings. In this context, the experience of Captain Travis Patriquin (who was later killed in action in Tikrit in December 2006) was particularly notable. Patriquin developed a practical understanding of how to work among and obtain the cooperation of the traditionally pro-Baathist Turkomen population of Tal Afar.[99]

Although the neoclassical school of thought began by reclaiming the insights of previous counterinsurgency campaigns, the experience of the Iraq insurgency also meant that this renewed interest quickly led to the reorientation of much mainstream military thought in the United States.[100] The publication of the *Counterinsurgency Field Manual* apotheosized this influence.[101] The regeneration of COIN thinking also moved from general restatements of principle to the promulgation of theoretical and practical insights that raised the standard of in-theater operational analysis. Reflecting on the experience of stabilization efforts in Iraq and applying it to the traditional principles of counterinsurgency, both soldier and civilian analysts developed technical, doctrinal, and operational understandings in such areas as equipping COIN forces; understanding tribal networks; denying sanctuary; developing negotiation strategies; and implementing population control.[102] The experience also facilitated the examination of what constituted the center of gravity in such operations and its implications for existing conventional forces.[103]

Technique as a Substitute for Political Understanding

The first page of the *Counterinsurgency Field Manual* evinces both the renaissance of and the expansive claims for neoclassical thinking: "This publication's purpose is to help prepare Army and Marine Corps leaders to conduct COIN operations anywhere in the world. It provides a foundation for study for deployment and the basis for operations in theater. Perhaps more importantly, it provides techniques for generating and incorporating lessons learned during those operations—an essential requirement for success against today's adaptive foes. Using these techniques and processes can keep U.S. forces more agile and adaptive than their irregular enemies."[104]

Curiously, however, the "techniques and processes" identified do not appear to be especially novel or adaptive. To the extent, moreover, that they incorporate the "lessons learned," these techniques were not drawn from particularly successful historical examples of COIN campaigns. Colin Jackson compares the conduct of French forces in Indochina and Algeria in the 1950s and 1960s with American experiences in Iraq and Afghanistan and finds a "familiar theory of influence" playing itself out: a belief that the "provision of humanitarian relief and public goods" will win "over [the] 'hearts and minds' of the liberated population."[105] This belief assumed the form of remarkably similar operational tactics, wherein "small groups of military advisers and civilian bureaucrats [are] inserted to restore the formal institutions of the state, distribute public services, and rebuild the authority of the government through benevolent administration."[106] Examining the performance of Provincial Reconstruction Teams in Afghanistan, Jackson argues that these teams—like the other examples he studied—did little to boost the central government's authority and win over the people. He found that local communities cooperated with the teams simply to capture the benefits of Western aid. The teams had no impact on altering traditional tribal allegiances and undermined rather than reinforced the role and authority of the central government in Kabul.

Why did the Americans embark on a course of action that had ultimately been unsuccessful for the French fifty years earlier? Jackson contends that the similarity arose from common theories of victory and influence in civil war that were reflected in contemporary counterinsurgency ideas such as "clear, hold, and build" and adhered to a standard paradigm: separate the insurgents from the people, then reintroduce good governance and public services. Effective administration and the provision of material incentives, so the theory goes, will dampen resistance, loosen ties with the insurgents, and shift allegiances to the state. Such thinking assumes material inequality accounts for resistance movements and that the source of political authority consists in a functioning state bureaucracy delivering efficient administration and distribution of welfare. The paradigm possesses an enduring appeal for Western theorists, Jackson suggests, because of its apparent logical consistency and the progressive modernizing outlook that assumes good works improve the lot of the citizens.[107] The problem, however, is that this outlook is a "technocratic conceit." Counterinsurgency experts from established states assume that resistance results from a failed social contract. According to Jackson, these theorists, following thinkers such as Steven Pinker,[108] "regard the outbreak of resistance as a reflection of the failure of governance and the absence of material prosperity. Based on this understanding, they believe that a combination of population security, improved local and national governance, and economic development will induce collaboration and restore a durable political order." Crucially, Jackson observes that in this understanding, "politics . . . is an essentially technocratic problem of imposing formal institutions, introducing competent and virtuous administration, and delivering public services and prosperity."[109]

Thus, far from developing "cultural knowledge" in order to understand different ideas of rationality, Western-style counterinsurgency thinking imposes an ideology of modernization upon societies that may, for deep-rooted cultural reasons, resist them. This assessment applies particularly to a custom-based tribal society such as Afghanistan, where a sense of national identity or belief in central state authority is lacking or nonexistent. The ideology convinces its adherents that counterinsurgents act out of progressive motives, seeing themselves, in Kilcullen's words, as in "competition with the insurgent for the right and ability to win the hearts, minds and acquiescence of the population," where the "most beneficial actions are often local politics, and beat-cop behaviors."[110] Benign though this approach sounds, it stems from a paternalistic, if not mechanistic, attitude that reduces the population to passive recipients. "COIN is fought among the populace," the *Counterinsurgency Field Manual* pontificates. "Counterinsurgents take upon themselves responsibility for the people's well-being in all its manifestations." This responsibility includes, inter alia, the provision of security, policing, economic and health needs, public utilities, and cultural and welfare services.[111]

Even while asserting cultural sensitivity and humanitarianism, a Eurocentric and secularist ideology informs Western COIN. Its underlying modernization agenda, far from empowering the local populace, reduces it to dependence. Sarah Sewall, somewhat paternalistically, holds that COIN's belief in the civil reconstruction of a conflicted society "is not a responsibility that can be left to a beleaguered host nation." For Sewall, an "unwillingness to govern other nations" is not something admirable, but a shortcoming in national policy.[112] As a consequence of the military's reluctance to embrace "foreign policy as social work" during the 1990s, she maintains, the "US failed to develop critical nation-building capabilities that could have proved crucial in Iraq."[113] Nation building is the concrete expression of a developmental dogma. COIN, therefore, rediscovers and reasserts Cold War U.S. assumptions about the virtue of nation building. Thus, Sewall contends, "counterinsurgents must harness the ordinary administrative functions to the fight, providing personnel, resources, and expertise," and assume the "enormous demands that governance and nation-building place not simply upon military forces but also on civilian agencies."[114] Sewall, however, like other COIN analysts, suffers from an acute case of historical amnesia. Nation-building COIN led the United States in particular into its most disastrous foreign-policy encounters. South Vietnam, in particular, was perceived as a "beleaguered host nation" demanding modernization.

The Politics of COIN Rationalism

The default assumption that nation building is the answer to the complex social conditions in which insurgencies invariably arise demonstrates most graphically the fallacies inherent in modern Western notions of counterinsurgency. It returns us to the "managerial rationalism," that chapter 2 identified as central to contemporary COIN. As Jackson argues, a technocratic approach to instrumentalizing bureaucracy and governance negates and simplifies the complex politics of insurgency. COIN theory and doctrine address the problem of how to implement a program of civic development. They ignore and exclude first-order questions of why an insurgency happens or why an intervening power should choose to become involved and with what ends in mind. COIN's reductionist view of policy options, moreover, overlooks the fact that some individuals will hold multiple loyalties simultaneously and that although some members of a population may be able to alter their loyalties, others never can.

Avoiding the *why* questions arises from a managerial rationalism that assumes that the instrumental mind bled of all prior assumptions can efficiently address problems. The flaw in instrumental rationalism and the mechanistic assumptions at work in modernization theory occur because these two ways of thinking give the answer in advance of the question. As Michael Oakeshott observed of this disposition, "To call an activity rational on account of its end having been determined in advance and in respect of its achieving that end to the exclusion of all others" is erroneous "because there is in fact no way of determining an end for activity in advance of the activity itself."[115] The truth is that to understand the *how* you must first understand the *why*.

Concentrating on the second-order instrumentalist *how* without serious consideration of the first-order *why* further invites a rationalist preoccupation with highly technical, jargon-heavy, and abstruse discussions of tactical minutiae. From David Galula's classic discussion of counterinsurgency technique in the Algerian War in *Counterinsurgency Warfare* to more recent neoclassical accounts, managerial rationalism permeates the COIN literature. COIN instrumentalism requires a managerial vocabulary complete with flow diagrams that rhetorically reinforces its claim to expertise. The COIN argot—with its population-centric approaches, discussions about centers of gravity and hearts and minds, and accounts of how to win the confidence of tribal hinterlands—forms a technical vocabulary available only to an elite who speak this exclusive language.

As noted in chapter 2, Oakeshott considered rationalism the basis of modern ideological faith. In 1964, Jacques Ellul similarly identified "the technique of a more or less spiritual nature that we call magic," which is "basically a 'scholasticism of efficiency.' "[116] COIN's propensity for ex cathedra statements that assert as fact what is in fact supposition or opinion reflects this character. The *Counterinsurgency Field Manual*'s mechanical assumption that the host population is an inert mass illustrates this predilection. "In almost every case," the manual declares, "counterinsurgents face a populace containing an active minority supporting the government and an equally small militant faction opposing it." If the government is "accepted as legitimate by most of that uncommitted middle, which also includes passive supporters of both sides,"[117] then success against an insurgent campaign is guaranteed. Nowhere is this ruling assumption tested or falsified; it is merely asserted as truth. The simplistic division of the "population" into three groups according to their presumed view of the insurgency (insurgent supporters, neutral or passive, and pro-government)[118] implies a deterministic, causal link between counterinsurgent actions along "lines of operation" and change in public opinion. These rationalist assumptions inform both contemporary COIN manuals and the writings of prominent theorists. *The US Army/Marine Corps Counterinsurgency Field Manual*, with its list of eighty-four different "tables, figures and vignettes,"[119] exemplifies this scientistic technology of practice.

COIN tactics may, of course, have some utility at the operational level and may indeed be relevant in specific theaters of conflict. However, once COIN's modernizing rationalism is exposed, it becomes possible to challenge the idea that this localized tactical knowledge has wider strategic application. Creating universal principles from local techniques and abstracting them into a universally applicable instrument do not constitute a stable basis for prediction. Instead, at best, such rationalism recites bland injunctions, and, at worst, the erroneous application of the instrument to a situation in which it does not apply has potentially disastrous consequences.

In its fullest application after 2007, COIN's modernizing project involved, among other things, military governance, law and order, infrastructure, building the Afghan National Security Forces, and development. Ironically, employing the lessons of Malaya to capture "hearts and minds" led, by a curious process of mission creep, to the same type of the nation building and economic and social reconstruction program associated with the disastrous intervention in South Vietnam.[120] It is precisely toward more drawn-out involvements along Vietnam lines that much current counterinsurgency thinking inexorably leads. The lure of modernization ideology and its predisposition toward nation building appeals to an American mindset predisposed to global meliorism and manifest destiny. Gian Gentile, for example, points to General Tommy Franks's remarks to the House Armed Services Committee in February 2002 that defeating al-Qaeda required a commitment to pursue a "permanent solution . . . based on strengthening Afghanistan's capacity." For Gentile, the reference to restoring the capacity of the Afghan state's resources and institutions revealed that the "United States has been in the nation-building business from the start."[121]

In the 1960s, the prevailing paradigm in American political science held that the transition from tradition to modernity in the developing world demanded U.S. intervention in Southeast Asia to forestall the threat of communism. Walt Rostow observed in his classic modernizing study *Politics and the Stages of Growth* that opposing communism would grant "to the rest of Asia a decade to find its feet and begin to fashion a framework of progress and cooperation which might balance in the long run the power and influence of . . . China."[122] In this understanding, political stability and security constituted the necessary preconditions for investment in developing states, and "finding the terms on which private capital flows can make a rational contribution to development" would lead to economic takeoff and political as well as economic development.[123]

In 1961, President John F. Kennedy sent Rostow, one of his key national-security advisers, to South Vietnam to assess conditions and propose recommendations. Rostow suggested sending more advisers and equipment and recommended a fundamental "transition from advice to partnership" with South Vietnam.[124] A nation-building and modernizing agenda thus superseded any limited advisory commitment. By 1962, it was the "clearly stated objective of the Kennedy administration," according to Robert McNamara, "to train the South Vietnamese to defend themselves."[125] In the same year, a RAND Corporation Symposium on counterinsurgency agreed on, among other things, the need to "identify and redress the political, economic, military and other issues fueling the insurgency" and to "gain control over and protect the population which the counterinsurgent must see as the prime center of gravity."[126]

COIN methodology and its ideological commitment to modernization consign its adherents to historical amnesia and doom them to repeat foreign-policy mistakes. Advanced as a standard model for guidance, COIN's instrumental rationalism leads to flawed judgments and commitments. It reduces insurgencies to their "methodologies"— that is, their tactics. Accordingly, all the respondent requires to solve the problem are countertactics. COIN theory negates political judgment because it can never identify the interests that need securing with these tactics, and as a matter of instrumental rationalism there is no clear criterion to judge political success. Technique is not a substitute for strategy.

By 1965, analysts such as Hans Morgenthau were already questioning the expanding American commitment to South Vietnam. Morgenthau presciently observed that the American approach treated the complexity of the war as a "self-sufficient, technical enterprise, to be won as quickly, as cheaply, as thoroughly as possible and divorced from the foreign policy that preceded and is to follow it." He continued: "Thus our military theoreticians and practitioners conceive of counterinsurgency as though it were just another branch of warfare, to be taught in special schools and applied with technical proficiency wherever the occasion arises."[127]

COIN's reductionist rhetoric is heard in modern-day injunctions such as "clear, hold, and build."[128] But this slogan never actually explains what requires clearing, holding, or building. More to the point, if it is recognized that NATO forces need to clear the enemy from an Afghan province and then hold it at great cost, such a formula never offers a means of rhetorically framing why this is being done, to achieve what end, and for how long. COIN analysis cannot establish, given its constituting instrumentalism, when NATO in Afghanistan— or any other theater for that matter—will have sufficiently cleared, held, and built and thus achieved its strategic goal.

Only politics can determine what success entails. But this is now a problem. For as we have seen, the modernizing, technical discourse sounds plausible and compassionate: it promises a universal panacea for insurgencies regardless of context. The politics of war is discounted in favor of the application of the rationalist technique of an instrument to guide conduct. Such rational instrumentalism appeals to both liberal-minded policy makers and military practitioners alike because it offers the seductive blandishment of predetermined remedies to otherwise complex political problems. Whether in Vietnam or in Iraq or Afghanistan, the cheap, self-sufficient, technical enterprise described by Morgenthau so many years ago subtly appeals to those inculcated in the ideology of modernization.

This chapter has shown that the instrumentalist, reductionist, technocratic character of modern COIN thinking reveals an apparent contradiction at its center, arising from a Western commitment to developmental goals. COIN assumes that the population is the "center of gravity."[129] Counterinsurgent forces must win the population's loyalty, which is the key to defeating insurgents, and this imperative must drive all operations. As the *Counterinsurgency Field Manual* makes clear, "At its core, COIN is a struggle for the population's support. The protection, welfare, and support of the people are vital to success."[130] From this axiom all other requirements flow, most notably the felt need to develop a deep understanding of the local cultural, linguistic, and sociological context, which in Alex Marshall's words represents a "powerful military-anthropological tradition, one which remains an active part of most European counterinsurgency doctrine even today."[131]

But COIN theory also asserts the irrelevance of specifics. All insurgencies, it is claimed, possess similar dynamics and the solution to each is the same throughout time and space. The U.S. counterinsurgency "strategy" for Afghanistan, leaked to the press in late 2009, made this clear. As Ambassador Robert Blackwill declared, "I notice that in the entire treatise, more than 23,000 words, the . . . Pashtun, who are after all the primary objects of that strategy, [are] mentioned exactly once. Unless all references to them are redacted and extensive, those folks are Banquo's ghost at the feast."[132]

Thus, a set of tactical responses, contained in a rational instrument such as a field manual, aspires to the status of a universal understanding. It promotes itself as a closed system of thought, complete with its own distinctive language, available only to the cognoscenti. It is, in other words, a cult.[133] Furthermore, when doctrine is accepted as faith in the corridors of power, it affords a vehicle for professional preferment that silences debate about alternative ways of analyzing a security problem.[134]

COIN's mutation from tactical guidance into a faith is, however, a symptom of a wider ideology. The ubiquitous promulgation of its doctrinal faith offering value-neutral technical solutions to complex problems inexorably assumes the character of a modernizing ideology. This is somewhat paradoxical given COIN doctrine's aversion to politics. Rhetorically presented as apolitical technique, COIN ultimately promotes contestable positions as incontrovertible truths, somewhat conveniently unsupported by evidence or empirical tests.

4

The Paradoxes of Counter-insurgency and Globalization

The U.S. *Counterinsurgency Field Manual* consistently refers to American forces supporting the "Host Nation." In fact, the phrase is so commonplace in the manual that it acquires an acronym: HN.[1] The implication is clear: counterinsurgency is practiced on others elsewhere. "The primary objective of any COIN operation," the manual declares, "is to foster development of effective governance by a legitimate government." Legitimate government, "in the Western liberal tradition," the manual helpfully explains, "derives its just powers from the people and responds to their desires while looking out for their welfare is accepted as legitimate." The manual clearly separates the counterinsurgents from their hosts. Thus, we find that "both counterinsurgents and the HN government ensure that their deeds match their words." Analogously, both "counterinsurgents and the HN government . . . carefully consider the impact on the many audiences involved in the conflict and on the sidelines."[2] Patently, the counterinsurgent and the host are rarely, if ever, one and the same.

In other words, the *Counterinsurgency Field Manual* for the most part unambiguously situates itself within the neoclassical tradition that assumes Western nations intervene in distant conflicts in a quasi-imperial role. Yet the post-9/11 epoch revealed that threats to the security of the state did not necessarily originate in far-off places. The events of 9/11 announced the arrival of transnational, deterritorialized jihadism, which could asymmetrically strike stable and legitimate, or at least presumed stable and legitimate, Western nations. The threat had gone global.

A number of commentators recognized that the globalized threat of violently apocalyptic Islamism posed new challenges that called for responses different from those offered by neoclassical techniques. The notion of a "global war on terror" somewhat crudely captured this new perspective. As a result, alongside the neoclassical school, an alternative view of neo-COIN arose that emphasized the linkages between the apparent growth of asymmetric challenges to Western power after 2001 and broad trends at work in the international system that multiplied the threat. The global war on terror thus required a new focus and different priorities. This line of thinking eventually developed into a distinctive "global counterinsurgency" school. This chapter examines the evolution of this school of thought and its problematic COIN advocacy.

The global counterinsurgency thesis offered a more critically aware appreciation of contemporary security problems. A careful evaluation, however, shows that the thesis has more in common with the thought and practice of the neoclassical school than might at first sight be supposed. Indeed, the projection of counterinsurgency onto a global canvass, we argue, advances an even more ambivalent conception of insurgency, especially in its transnational jihadist version, and of the strategies required to combat it.

From Here to Modernity

To appreciate the emergence of the global counterinsurgency school, it is necessary first to grasp what globalization entails from a security perspective and its relationship to the modernization thesis that the previous chapter identified. Western policy makers, as we have seen, considered modernization crucial to an effective counterinsurgency program. As Anthony Giddens explains, the notion of globalization may be understood as the "intensification of worldwide social relations which link distant localities in such a way that local happenings are shaped by events occurring many miles away and vice versa."[3] Globalization is, in this respect, associated with a rapid quickening in the speed and volume of international communications, electronic or physical. The increase in the pace of transnational connectivity compresses time and space.[4] It also facilitates the formation of networks of associations that possess the potential to alter and remake patterns of social relations. Because globalization entails a "process by which events, decisions and activities in one part of the world can come to have significant consequences for individuals and communities in quite distant parts of the world,"[5] it has profound social, economic, and political implications.

Globalization since the end of the Cold War, moreover, is often seen as an outgrowth and validation of the modernization process. From this perspective, the creation of an integrated international order is something desirable. Globalization, according to Thomas Larsonn, announces "a world shrinkage, of distances getting shorter, things moving closer. It pertains to the increasing ease with which somebody on one side of the world can interact, to mutual benefit, with somebody on the other side of the world."[6] From a positive perspective, globalization presages a harmonious global convergence and a neoliberal order based on the rule of the free market, democracy, and universal humanitarian values. Francis Fukuyama's post–Cold War declaration of "the end of history" and Thomas Freidman's identification of a flat world in *The Lexus and the Olive Tree* are two of the more influential endorsements of this process.[7]

In the debates on globalization at the end of the twentieth century and the beginning of the twenty-first, those of a more historically minded disposition questioned this meliorism. They considered globalization a fluid process with no necessary endpoint. Jan Nederveen Pieterse saw globalization as a product of modernity and transformational in its impact but considered its effects uneven and contradictory.[8] The world is increasingly interconnected but by no means integrated, and the outcomes might be negative. The new dispensation raised "economic, social and ecological questions." The resulting anxiety and uncertainty exacerbated problems ranging from "pollution, human rights, drugs and terrorism."[9]

To its more vociferous critics, the globalization and modernity nexus appeared a vehicle for Western imperialism or, more accurately, the Americanization of discourse, culture, and values across the political, economic, and social spheres. Such homogenization might evoke resistance rather than be welcomed.[10] The rise of the antiglobalization movement—a paradoxical term in itself—in the course of the 1990s exemplified this opposition.[11] After 1990 antiglobalization was first associated with what Bernard-Henri Lévy termed a new Zombie, left, anticapitalist, anticonsumerist, and environmentalist movement,[12] which inspired anarchistic violent protests at G8 summits and elsewhere. However, it was the rise of international jihadi violence that constituted the gravest and most violent reaction to the globalization process.

Some assessments presented the rise of al-Qaeda as a hybrid form of resistance—a transnational insurgency—by the weak and oppressed of the "global South" against the exploitation of a hegemonic and homogenizing "West."[13] More accurately, violent jihadist activity was a by-product of the slow-motion collision between modernity in its more recent globalized form and an Islamic social character. This collision has been fateful but little understood and less researched.

Modernization, extending from the European Enlightenment to the late twentieth century, advanced a vision of science, education, and technology that would tame the passions of traditional society.[14] The civilizing effects of modernity would result in a democratizing, modular, but above all secular order. Overcoming religious customs as the basis for ordering society was the inexorable outcome once the forces of modernization had been unleashed. Yet more acute observers realized that the secular assumptions governing Western thinking about modernization could not explain social and political developments in the contemporary Muslim world. Thus, Ernest Gellner observed that Islam's engagement with modernity had led Islam to grow stronger and purer since its nineteenth-century encounter with the West.[15] He noted that Islamic societies had avoided secularization even as they assimilated many other nonreligious modes of modern technological, scientific, and social conduct. Gellner contended that modernization—"the deadly angel who spells death to economic inefficiency"—was as a consequence "not always at the service of liberty."[16]

We can therefore provisionally suggest the lineaments of a plausible sociology based on Gellner's neglected insights. From at least the early nineteenth century, what was considered the predicament of Islam (its evident political and economic weakness and the psychic pain this engendered) required reopening the gates of *ijtihad*, or interpretation of what the Prophet's message might entail for the challenge modernity presented. The challenge elicited a range of responses, from the privatization of religion to create an Arab equivalent of the modern European nation-state (the Atatürk/Pan-Arab/Baathist response) through a moderate program of moral reform to a radical transformation that would strip Islam of any cultural accretions it had acquired over time. It is the latter response, taken in a notably ideological or political direction in the course of the twentieth century, that concerns us here.

From the elusive Jamal Afghani in the mid–nineteenth century to Islamic modernizers such as Rashid Rida in Egypt, Abu al-Mawdudi's Jemmat-i-Islami (Islamic Party) in South Asia, and the Muahmadiyah movement in Southeast Asia in the early twentieth century, we find everywhere a movement to reform the folk Islam of the countryside with the High Islamic culture of the city—a movement from mimetic to analogic reasoning premised upon the sacred text. Such neo-orthodoxy became associated with greater piety as well as with upward mobility. Its special provenance in the context of modernity was the diasporic community or the growing urban and anxious middle class.

In this reformist context, authority moved from clan elder to mullah, mosque, and madrassa, while standards were transmitted via the printed page and later the Internet site rather than through oral tradition leavened by local customary practice. In Islamic terms, this movement was advancement. Indeed, it was modernization. In the postmodern, postcolonial, globalized world, identification with scripturalist high culture became the hallmark of urban sophistication. This evolution, which required a specific form of self-disclosure and self-enactment but did not necessarily entail violence to achieve it, nevertheless bulged with paradox. It exemplified a network-based social order without a real society that was atomized without individualism.[17]

From this neo-orthodox perspective, the path of Westernization was one of *jahaliya*—a debased state of ignorance—and so this perspective looked to scriptural certitudes to codify an Islamic response to a decadent and increasingly secularized modernity.[18] Although the return to authenticity was initially a call for spiritual rejuvenation, the purification of Islamic thought and practice inevitably acquired political overtones that transformed it into an ideological system (*nizam*) that demanded individual and societal fidelity to holy law, a movement now commonly termed "Islamism."[19] For Islamism's most important ideologist, Sayyid Qutb, the revival of Islamic purity involved the Manichean division of humanity into the sphere of Islam (*darul Islam*) and the "house of war" or the sphere of "not Islam" (*darul harb*) that existed in a condition of ignorance (*jahaliya*). In Qutb's view, it was the complete "submission to God alone in its beliefs, in its observance and its legal regulations" that constituted "the only civilised society." The Islamist, therefore, seeks a condition where "sovereignty belongs to God alone, expressed in obedience to the Divine Law," for "only then is every person in that society free from servitude to others, and only then does he taste true freedom."[20]

This Manichean worldview inevitably invited an activism that legitimized the use of violence to bring about the will of Allah.[21] Qutb, for example, considered it the duty of all Muslims to struggle against *jahaliya* in order to replace infidel arrangements with Quranically approved alternatives.[22] Over time, the ideology fashioned a confrontation that relied increasingly upon a deterritorialized transnational *umma* (community of believers) to lead the assault against what one of al-Qaeda's most prominent theorists, Ayman al-Zawahiri, called "domineering western enslavement."[23] In its most apocalyptic form, Islamism's all-embracing ideological system encouraged a will to action—a holy war (jihad)—that affirmed the right to "slaughter" unbelievers "like lambs."[24] An Islamist training manual declared in the 1990s: "Islamic governments have never and will never be established through peaceful solutions and cooperative councils. They are established as they always have been . . . by pen and gun . . . by word and bullet . . . by tongue and teeth."[25]

The evolving militancy associated with the program of Islamism in its clash with secularized modernity reflected the political repression that groups such as the Muslim Brotherhood had encountered in Egypt and Syria from the 1960s onward. After Qutb's arrest and subsequent execution by the Egyptian regime in 1966, his spiritual followers, such as Muhammud Abd al-Salam Faraj, and militant organizations such as al-Jihad (Holy War) rendered explicit the neglected duty of waging jihad against the infidel in order to establish the Islamic realm by direct action.[26] The economic failures of the corporatist nation-state model in the Middle East as well as the region's growing corruption, defeat by Israel in 1967 and later 1973, and inability to solve the problem of Palestine only reinforced the call for a purified utopian Islamic revival. It was in the aftermath of the assassination of President Anwar Sadat in Egypt in 1981 and the suppression of the Muslim Brotherhood in Syria that Islamists such as Ayman al-Zawahiri and the Palestinian Abdullah Azzam sought to internationalize their struggle. According to Zawahiri, they sought to launch a new force "outside the international order."[27] To set in motion this new force, Zawahiri's group broke with the increasingly pragmatic Muslim Brotherhood and joined with the Arab Mujahideen in Afghanistan and Pakistan, sponsored by Osama bin Laden after 1988 in order to establish the lineaments of what we now call al-Qaeda.

The Evolution of Global Counterinsurgency

The most obvious geopolitical consequence of the evolution of the Islamist *internationale* was that its objective of violently provoking the forces of Western modernity made itself felt beyond the Middle East. The transnational promulgation of the Islamist message reached Africa, South Asia, North Africa, Southeast Asia, and, after 2001, North America and Europe. A totalizing Islamist style, confident and clear in its goals, both local and global, demanded a response that necessarily went beyond the conventional approaches of classical understandings of counterinsurgency. Even before COIN entrenched itself in military establishments following the troubled interventions in Afghanistan and Iraq beginning in 2001, John Mackinlay had identified al-Qaeda as a qualitatively new kind of threat. Mackinlay, writing just after 9/11, proclaimed that classical counterinsurgency could not frame an adequate response because it failed to take into account the "linkage between the Qaeda [sic] network's tactics in the field" and its " 'long-term aspiration' of a restored Caliphate." He maintained: "For

Western audiences, this political objective might appear unrealistic, but viewed from al Qaeda's perspective and the constituency to which it appeals, the 'acute sense of the symbolic' embodied in its actions overrides any 'apparent strategic weakness.'" Indeed, he concluded, "Al-Qaeda's preference for huge statements, for bold acts of extreme violence in place of a long-term incremental strategy, appeals to the expectations of a society which is also conditioned by the same global imagery as the west. Whether negatively or positively, the 11 September attacks gripped our attention and changed our lives in a way that justifies [Osama bin Laden's] military concept from an insurgent's point of view."[28]

Mackinlay identified in al-Qaeda the features of a global insurgency, which required a response that went beyond anything that the renaissance in classical counterinsurgency proposed.[29] Global counterinsurgency as a concept that took shape after 9/11 thus offered a distinctively original interpretation of the global war on terror, which provided a more complex analysis of the phenomenon that accepted Zawahiri's claim that al-Qaeda embodied a new force in the international order.

Nevertheless, proponents of the global counterinsurgency thesis could not be initially separated from those who promoted the neoclassical approach that set the terms of debate in North America and Europe after 2003 as the challenging occupations of Iraq and later Afghanistan preoccupied Washington and its closest allies. Exponents of neoclassicism and global COIN shared a common desire to rehabilitate counterinsurgency thinking and advance its status within defense circles.[30] In this context, David Kilcullen represents a crossover analyst who accepted many features of neoclassical thinking as exemplified in *The US Army/Marine Corps Counterinsurgency Field Manual*. Kilcullen empathized with the neoclassical commitment to deep, anthropological understanding of local conflicts,[31] and his professional soldiering background enabled him to write "Twenty-Eight Articles: Fundamentals of Company-Level Counterinsurgency," a treatise admired by neoclassicists for its distillation of practical counterinsurgency methods for armed service personnel. However, Kilcullen also recognized that counterinsurgents did not function in terms of Cold War verities and required an appreciation of the globalized condition in which they were compelled to operate. "One of the biggest differences between the counterinsurgencies our fathers fought and those we face today is the omnipresence of globalized media," he wrote, adding: "Beware the 'scripted enemy,' who plays to a global audience and appeals to the court of global public opinion."[32] His awareness of the global environment that affected the conduct of counterinsurgency subsequently broadened into more explicit misgivings about the neoclassical school. He argued the "re-discovery of classical, 'proven' counter-insurgency methods" had been "misplaced." "Today's insurgencies," he declared in another article, "differ significantly at the level of policy, strategy, operation art and tactical technique—from those of earlier eras." In fact, the classical paradigm and the "prescriptive application of 'received wisdom' derived from the classics . . . cast a long shadow." Yet in the era of globalization "the 'classic' version of counter-insurgency is less relevant to current conflicts."[33]

Kilcullen became a consultant on counterinsurgency thinking with the U.S. State Department after 2005 and then an adviser to General David Petraeus in 2007. His influence can be discerned in a number of key passages in the *Counterinsurgency Field Manual* that recognize the global COIN case. These remarks reveal difficulties with the prevailing neoclassical understanding that informed the rest of the document. "Today's operational environment," the manual stated, "also includes a new kind of insurgency, one that seeks to impose revolutionary change worldwide. Al Qaeda is a well-known example of such an insurgency." Noting the capacity of al-Qaeda-linked groups to exploit "communications and technology" to harness local causes to the broader goal of recreating a new, purified, Islamic caliphate, the manual continued: "Defeating such enemies requires a global, strategic response—one that addresses the array of linked resources and conflicts that sustain these movements while tactically addressing the local grievances that feed them."[34]

Although the manual conceded the theoretical case for a new appreciation of counterinsurgency, the notion of global COIN was not elaborated and was elsewhere given short shrift. Sarah Sewall cynically remarked in introducing the volume: "Increasingly, analysts argue that the Al Qaeda–inspired Salafist terrorism network functions as a modern-day global insurgency. . . . Some have warned that classical

counterinsurgency theory is insufficient for tackling the modern terrorist threat. The most prescient critics are ahead of themselves, since
not even the U.S. military has yet internalized the new field manual."[35]
Sewall insinuated that although global COIN theorists might have an
intellectual point, it was irrelevant to the current crisis. For the U.S.
military, the imperative was to stabilize the host nation—in this instance, Iraq. In fact, Sewall contended that although a distinction of
sorts might be drawn between efforts to tackle interventions such as
those in Iraq and those to defeat al-Qaeda, nevertheless, "the overall
strategic problem is uncannily parallel: sustaining the statist norm in
the face of radical and violent revolutionaries."[36] The notion of global
counterinsurgency, in other words, was irrelevant.

Others did not share Sewall's skepticism. Indeed, the distinction between global and classical COIN thinkers constituted a fault
line that increasingly divided analysts. Former U.S. Marines officer
Frank Hoffman, despite belonging to the team that wrote the U.S.
military's counterinsurgency doctrine, expressed misgivings about
neoclassicism's influence over the manual. Echoing Kilcullen, he
claimed that the neoclassical position focused, "myopically, on the
glorious heyday of revolutionary warfare in the 1950s and 1960s."[37]
The *Field Manual* failed, therefore, to deal with the reality that the
wars in Iraq and Afghanistan formed part of a broader global insurgency, evidenced by the involvement of foreign and local Sunni
fighters in Iraq's civil war who were progressively associated with
the Islamic State in Iraq and Greater Syria and who were more commonly called "al-Qaeda in Iraq."[38]

More specifically, critics considered both the manual and much
contemporary writing on counterinsurgency overdetermined by
what David Betz called a "Maoist-style People's Revolutionary Warfare, which is not the sort of insurgency now being faced."[39] The
Maoist paradigm held that insurgency occurred within a defined
territorial space. For Frank Hoffman, "the classicists ignore the
uniqueness of Maoist or colonial wars of national liberation, and
over-generalize the principles that have been drawn from them. Today's insurgent is not the Maoist of yesterday."[40] Maoist theories of
revolutionary war certainly exerted a formative influence over much
neoclassical writing. Sustaining a modern parallel with the war in

Iraq, Montgomery McFate, for example, quoted Mao's aphorism that the " 'people are water, the Red Army are fish; without water, the fish will die.' "[41] Similarly, the *Counterinsurgency Field Manual* acknowledged Mao's thinking about protracted people's war and was predicated upon the Maoist assumption that counterinsurgency is about the domination of a given geographic setting.[42]

The global COIN school maintained that excessive reverence for Maoist theories of guerrilla warfare ultimately led neoclassicism into a strategic, Iraq-centric (and later Afghan) dead end. Hoffman argued that classical precepts were either "blatant flashes of the obvious"[43] or else simplistically one-dimensional. His criticism and the criticisms coming from the global counterinsurgency tendency more broadly could certainly validate their claims. Indeed, much COIN writing in the early 2000s presented clichés as insights. Hence, a monograph of the neoclassical persuasion published in 2007 somewhat adventurously criticized the British campaign in Malaya on the grounds that the "promise to withdraw once the situation was stabilized" intimated the campaign's failure. This was because "the British had to surrender their role as occupier to defeat the insurgents."[44] Such a view naively equated success with the retention of territory rather than with the attainment of political objectives, which not only repeated a view first articulated by the radical journalist Robert Taber in *War of the Flea* in 1970[45] but implied that any concession, no matter how minimal, represented a victory for the insurgent.[46] Such reductionism ultimately leads, as the global COIN critics observed, to a rudimentary Maoist/counter-Maoist dialectic that assumes that holding onto physical territory, no matter the cost, is the supreme goal of any combatant.

The outdated approach evident in neoclassical counterinsurgency texts represented a legitimate concern. These texts implied that any withdrawal of forces from an occupied territory constituted a defeat. They also risked repeating French approach to COIN during the Algerian War (1954–1962) and similarly disastrous consequences. Given the excessive reverence for French COIN thinkers such as David Galula exhibited in much neoclassical writing,[47] the global counterinsurgency advocates were right to signal their disquiet. Somewhat worryingly, the French military had presented its conflict with the Front de Libération Nationale as a war to save Western civilization. Such a misrepresentation resulted in great brutality and loss of life on all sides and witnessed during the campaign the creation of a clandestine bureaucracy that institutionalized policies of torture and atrocity.[48] This approach did not have much to recommend itself to Coalition forces in Iraq and Afghanistan, particularly in the wake of the political damage caused by revelations of prisoner abuse in the notorious Abu Ghraib (Baghdad Central Prison) detention facility.[49]

Thus, the questions global COIN theorists raised about the requirement for military awareness of changing operating environments, the impact of greater media intrusiveness, the need for strategic messaging, and the broader threat inherent in transnational jihadist activism were by no means inconsequential. In fact, much writing in the neoclassical idiom represented an attempt both to understand and to rectify the failures arising from the Iraq occupation and to that extent often exhibited only minimal awareness of the wider implications of threats to the international system. Most important for this idiom was that the renaissance of classical counterinsurgency thinking possessed direct utility for the U.S. armed forces, facilitating an appreciation of, for example, small-unit operations, effective collation of intelligence, and cultural understanding of and engagement with local communities in order to contain the threat posed by a concerted rebellion.

However, in an age of transnational threats that emanated from deterritorialized jihadist groups, the wider applicability of neoclassical maxims beyond the theaters of Iraq and Afghanistan were open to question. Global COIN theorists were therefore right to doubt the underlying assumption of neoclassical thought that insurgencies happen "somewhere else," requiring support to the "host nation." This perspective meant that insurgencies represented external threats that resided beyond the realm of the modern liberal democratic state: over there, but not here. It reflected neoclassicism's overdependence on a view of COIN practices that derived from the twentieth-century experience of colonial struggles wherein imperial powers sought to suppress violent opposition to their rule.

Yet as the twenty-first-century experience demonstrated, treating counterinsurgency as a foreign affair was untenable when threats, plots, and physical attacks emanated not only from the Middle East and from South and Southeast Asia, but also from the modern urban landscapes of Europe, North America, and Australia. The theorists of global COIN were thus correct to see the modern insurgent phenomenon as an existential reality that had the capacity to be not somewhere else, but everywhere.

The Limitations of the Global Counterinsurgency Critique

One important difference distinguishes the neoclassical counterinsurgency school from the global counterinsurgency school of thought. Unlike the neoclassical version, the global COIN school never achieved codification in an official manual. As a body of thought, neoclassical COIN possessed a unity and consistency that could be evaluated and critiqued. The global counterinsurgency school never achieved such coherence. Instead, a variety of thinkers expressed its distinctive ideas in disparate papers and publications, rendering both its analysis and practical program elusive. Ultimately, the global COIN school rested on a paradox. It proposed a more sophisticated treatment of the threats posed by violent transnational Islamism in its confrontation with modernity, yet its solutions amounted to little more than equivocal reformulations of modernization, democratization, and developmental theories that groups such as al-Qaeda had already sworn to resist. In other words, global COIN realized that the jihadist was in collision with modernity but could propose nothing beyond modernization to solve the problem.

Although the global counterinsurgency school invited analysts to question their understanding of the sociology of contemporary Islam, it failed to answer the challenge that the contemporary Islamist posed to Western secular, pluralist modernity—namely, how to integrate diaspora communities into secular, postnational, market states.[50] As a consequence, the global COIN thesis ignored the manner in which an ascetic, militant brand of Islam had since the 1970s promoted its appeal to migrant communities in Europe and North America, as manifested in the indiscriminate bombing and shooting attacks from Madrid and London to Fort Hood after 2001 that demonstrated that the counterinsurgent and the "host nation" could be one and the same thing. The constituting weakness of global COIN was that although it accurately described the problem, it offered no real answer. It shared, in this respect, the shortcomings of the neoclassical school, particularly in its negation of ideological motivation, its confused relationship with strategy and notions of terrorism, and its elevation of technique above political understanding.

Despite its more perceptive characterization of the threat posed by a transnational Islamist insurgency, global COIN analysis and policy prescriptions were vague. What, we might wonder, did a "global counterinsurgency" campaign entail in practice? Its proponents appeared unable to define such a program with any precision. As a result, global counterinsurgency seemed long on assertion but short on specificity. David Kilcullen offered perhaps the most plausible outline of what a global COIN plan entailed. His concept of "disaggregation" sought to "interdict the Al Qaeda core leadership's ability to influence regional and local players—by cutting off their communications, discrediting their ideological authority, and global operations to keep them off balance. At the regional level, disaggregation would isolate theater-level actors from global sponsors, local populations and local insurgent groups they might seek to exploit in support of the *jihad*."[51]

The global counterinsurgency agenda, according to Kilcullen, would among other things encompass "attacking the 'intricate web of dependency,' which "allow[s] the *jihad* to function effectively"; "interdicting links between theaters of operation within the global insurgency"; "denying the ability of regional and global actors to link and exploit local actors"; "interdicting flows of information, personnel, finance and technology (including WMD [weapons of mass destruction] technology) between and within *jihad* theaters"; as well as "denying sanctuary areas (including failed and failing states, and states that support terrorism) within theaters."[52] These suggestions have aspirational validity, but how to operationalize them in practice across the globe remained worryingly unclear. Global COIN's attempted policy solutions made up little more than a transnational wish list.

The concept of a global counterinsurgency superficially improved on nebulous terms such as *war on terrorism*. Its adherents recognized the danger posed by the uncompromising and transnational character of jihadist movements such as al-Qaeda. Global COIN appeared to acknowledge the totalizing mission inherent in al-Qaeda's Islamist ideology, and this acknowledgment represented a crucial difference from the neoclassical view.[53] In his critical appraisal of *The US Army/ Marine Corps Counterinsurgency Field Manual*, Hoffman noted that it was "relatively mute on the subject" of religious motivation in jihadist activism. The document, he argued, "offers few indications that the classical approach to terrorist or insurgent activities are altered at all by religions based groups."[54] The manual acknowledged, for example, that "ideas are a motivating factor in insurgent activities" but only as an artifice to gain recruits and garner local support and not as a motivational force to achieve radical strategic ends. "Stories are often the basis of strategies and actions," it announced, and "insurgent organizations like Al Qaeda use narratives very effectively in developing legitimating ideologies."[55]

Relegating ideological motivation to the status of a narrative reflected the permeation of modernization throughout the manual. The manual privileged local, material factors rather than the credal appeal of a political religion, thus reinforcing the secular, liberal assumption that "religion is a secondary factor next to political grievances and nationalism—that [the] religious language of terrorists is instrumental and culturally idiomatic rather than causative."[56] Such assumptions, as Hoffman noted, were ethnocentric, adducing that the target population in the host nation shared an American value system that desired to construct societies that "are consistent with representative democracy". "But," Hoffman contended, "if the population's values system is not consistent with these basic elements of the U.S. approach, or if they reject [American values] in favor of something founded in the thirteenth or fourteenth century, we may need a drastically revised counter-insurgency strategy."[57]

Given this critique of neoclassical COIN's ethnocentric bias, one might suppose the global counterinsurgency thesis to be more sensitive to the ideological forces at work in movements such as al-Qaeda. Surprisingly, though, when it came to exposing the drivers of jihadism, global counterinsurgency theorists also dismissed the politically religious motivation for Islamist activism. Curiously, instead of trying to understand al-Qaeda's ideology, global COIN theorists focused on peripheral organizational characteristics, social networks, psychological profiling, and patterns of recruitment to understand the new global threat. In this context, the "global insurgency" thesis suffered from the definitional ambiguity that haunted the much criticized notion of a war on terrorism. Like the amorphous notion of a war on terrorism, a global counterinsurgency denoted an unspecific threat that obfuscated rather than clarified the object of the war—namely, a militant, political religion: Islamism.

Indeed, the key proponent of global COIN, David Kilcullen, specifically discounted Islamist ideology as the motivation to jihad. Instead, he considered the "sociological characteristics of immigrant populations" responsible for Islamist-inspired violence. These characteristics, he asserted, better explained "contemporary threats rather than Islamic theology." Islamic thought, he declared, "has little functional relationship with violence."[58] For an article in the *New Yorker*, he even claimed that "after 9/11, when a lot of people were saying, 'The problem is Islam,' I was thinking, It's something deeper than that. It's about human social networks and the way they operate." In justifying his analysis, Kilcullen argued that his postgraduate research into the Indonesian Darul Islam movement led him to conclude, "It's not about theology." He maintained, rather confusingly, that "there are elements in human psychological and social makeup that drive what is happening. The Islamic bit is secondary. This is human behavior in an Islamic setting. It is not 'Islamic behaviour.'" He added: "People don't get pushed into rebellion by their ideology. They get pulled in by their social networks," remarking, somewhat tangentially, that fifteen of the 9/11 Saudi hijackers "had trouble with their fathers."[59]

What is one to make of this curious sense of denial about the role of political religion in both the neoclassical and the occasionally more perceptive global COIN position? Obviously, the process of radicalization is complex, and any individual's willingness to transit from ideological conviction to violence in support of the cause cannot be attributed solely to religion or ideology. Nevertheless, it is somewhat perverse to dismiss it or relegate it to a second-order concern. Numerous violent al-Qaeda-linked assaults from 9/11 on were, whatever else, *Islamist acts* in a Western setting. The view that religion is at best a secondary motivation defies the evidence. All the jihadist groups that have undertaken high-profile attacks dating from 9/11 and stretching from Bali to Madrid, London, and Mumbai have acted in the name of a militant understanding of Islam. Such a pattern of worldwide attacks exhibiting a profound devotion to a politically religious cause intimates, if nothing else, a politically religious dimension to jihadism.[60] To reduce jihadism to individual pathology, as Kilcullen and others do, merely explains away political religion as a social fact. Curiously, this reduction assumes that when a highly motivated jihadist claims to undertake an operation to advance a cause, he does not mean it, as if Kilcullen and the others know the jihadist mind better than the jihadist himself.

To deny the relevance of political religion to jihadist insurgency is ultimately akin to maintaining that the armed campaigns waged by Che Guevara, the Red Brigades, and the Baader-Meinhof gang had nothing to do with Marxist–Leninist and Maoist thought. Various factors may "push people into rebellion," but it is ideology that justifies the violent act and gives it meaning. Paradoxically, Hoffman's criticism of neoclassical COIN—namely, that it misunderstands a worldview that wishes to re-create an Islamic caliphate—applies with equal force to global counterinsurgency thinking. The lasting irony, then, is that global COIN supporters, although recognizing the transnational danger posed by jihadism, in their own turn discounted the ideology of Islamism that made the threat global.

Resolving the Paradox

Why, we might wonder, are counterinsurgency theorists of both global and neoclassical persuasions reluctant to confront the politically religious dimension of modern insurgency? COIN discourse and the counterinsurgent mind help answer this question. As we have observed elsewhere, counterinsurgency thinking in the West possesses a somewhat problematic relationship with strategy and politics, evident in the dismissal or downplaying of Carl von Clausewitz.[61] This denial of Clausewitz facilitated the avoidance of politics and the recourse to technique in its place.

Chapter 2 noted the June 2007 meeting of a group of influential academics and soldiers to consider a draft of the British Army's doctrine for the manual *Countering Insurgency*, which sought to marginalize Clausewitz's thinking. The group evaluated modern counterinsurgency thought not in Clausewitzian terms but in light of the "characteristics which might distinguish what might be described as the post Maoist era." The group recognized that "insurgency has become a globalized technique[;] the response is now international and multi-disciplined; the strategic centre of gravity lies beyond the territorial boundaries of the operational space; success is determined more in the virtual dimension than by events on the ground in the operational space; [and] in the 1950–60's the vital ground comprised a single nation's population[, but] now there are multiple populations involved."[62]

Such statements reveal a curious desire to dismiss a theorist whose writings remain seminal to any understanding of insurgency in the modern era. In the late 1950s, Raymond Aron, one of the more significant interpreters of Clausewitzian thought, with some perspicacity speculated that "revolutionary" or guerrilla war "would figure just as prominently as the theory of nuclear weapons in the treatise of a twentieth century Clausewitz."[63] Clausewitz intimated this very point, contending that "wars will always vary with the nature of their motives and of the situations which gave rise to them."[64] War is *always* determined by the "society and culture," and it is strange indeed that COIN analysts such as McFate, who urged the United States to understand its adversary's culture, should deny that al-Qaeda might possess a "rational" worldview, albeit one framed by an Islamist ideological prism and its distinctive understanding of global politics.

For Clausewitz, the interaction of tangible and intangible factors govern the course of war, influencing its direction and duration. War always "moves on its own goals with varying speed."[65] The Napoleonic era of warfare between nation-states shaped Clausewitz's thinking, but his concern was not interstate war exclusively.[66] He presented an ontology of war, something more than an epiphenomenon of state activity. As Jan Honig observed some two decades ago, Clausewitzian ideas are thus "easily adaptable to forms of warring social organizations that do not form states."[67] In this regard, McFate's assumption that rational warfare occurs only among nation-states seriously misrepresents the Clausewitzian argument. David Kilcullen commits a similar categorical mistake when he argues that "Al Qaeda–linked insurgencies" do not necessarily "seek to *do* or achieve any practical objective, but rather to be a *mujahid*, earning God's favour (and hope of ultimate victory through his intervention) through the act itself."[68] It is curious that anthropologists of both a neoclassical and global COIN provenance ostensibly dedicated to understanding the customs and traditions of particular social groups reach the conclusion that nonstate actors, such as al-Qaeda, are incomprehensible and function without meaningful objectives because they are not states and are motivated by a religiously inspired value system.

The reluctance of both neoclassical and global COIN to find religious motives in jihadist action, global COIN's emphasis on "post-Maoism," and their shared disdain for Clausewitz reveal a profound discomfort on the part of all contemporary counterinsurgency analysts to address the political dimension of war. It is the *politics* of modern jihadist resistance that all the varieties of contemporary counterinsurgency theory avoids, for politics involves complexity, particularity, ambiguity, controversy, and the need to challenge or defend specific value systems. As Honig discerned, what many commentators find disconcerting about insurgent conflicts "is the seemingly irrational motivations of parties which originate in the murky depths of history."[69] Accordingly, Clausewitz, who emphasized the politics of war above all else, returns us to the central problem identified in earlier chapters—namely, that modern COIN thinkers believe that any exploration of the underlying value systems shaping the societal and cultural complexity from which war arises somehow undermines their objective approach to the phenomenon.

This aversion to the politics of war is itself ironically an ideological position. COIN theorists can dismiss the significance of Clausewitz's thinking on war only by assuming that insurgent movements act irrationally and function outside any form of political discourse because their motives are deemed unfathomable. Thus, a depoliticized and rationalized analytical framework is constructed that disengages from any attempt to address the "murky depths" of history, politics, and religion from which the global threat sprang. This process of exclusion and disengagement has enabled the modern counterinsurgency agenda to address the phenomenon in the rationalist terms with which it is most comfortable—namely, that of managerial technique.

Global COIN, like classical and neoclassical renderings of counterinsurgency, emphasizes technique over politics. Although professing to understand the cause and spread of deterritorialized jihadism, a global countertechnique ultimately temporizes with the claims of Islamist ideology. Ignoring the politics of Islamism, contemporary global COIN thinking avoids what might be politically necessary to defeat Islamism's appeal within the modern West. Focusing on apolitical operational concepts, statements of aspiration, abstruse debates on the insurgent centers of gravity, the policy minutiae of countering radicalization, and what Lawrence Freedman has described as "vague talk of hearts and minds"[70] amounts to a policy of evasion.

Global COIN was particularly guilty of such equivocation. Whereas the neoclassical school focused on the tactics necessary to counter armed challenges in "host nations" such as Iraq and Afghanistan, global counterinsurgency advanced global techniques that were either vaguely aspirational or strategically ambivalent. For all their criticism of neoclassical thought, when global COIN advocates defined their approach, it amounted to little more than the application of colonial, Malaya Emergency–style counterinsurgency methods practiced on an international stage. Accordingly, Kilcullen considered the global insurgency a "better model" than the more operationally well-defined "counterterrorism" paradigm because "the key to defeating global jihad" did not "lie in traditional counter terrorism (police work, intelligence, special operations or security measures) at all." Instead, he contended somewhat nebulously, global insurgency must be "regarded as representative of deeper issues or grievances within society. We seek to defeat insurgents through 'winning the hearts and minds' of the population, a process that involves compromise and negotiation."[71]

Similarly, Mackinlay considered that a "dangerous insurgency" "usually has legitimate grievances or cause," which require a successful counterstrategy to be "politically strong enough to change direction in order to remove the pressure of the grievance, and at the same time hopefully remove a substantial element of popular support from the insurgent."[72] Kilcullen reinforced this view, asserting the need to "counter the grievances on which insurgencies feed, denying their energy to their recruiting and propaganda subsystems, and ultimately marginalizing them." Drawing directly from the Malayan experience,

he noted approvingly that the British "countered the Communist appeal to nationalism by setting a clear date for independence and com-
mencing transition to self-government."[73]

Global COIN as Appeasement

Paradoxically, global counterinsurgency thinking, rather than expressing a global outlook, accentuates local grievance settlement as its
practical solution to global insurgency. It shares this perspective with
the neoclassical approach, which asserts that a "focus on supporting
the local population and the [host nation] government" through social and economic programs is the most effective means of addressing
the "root causes of conflict."[74]

Global COIN's projection of the Malayan Emergency way of grievance settlement onto a global canvas has had, however, serious political consequences, which have been overlooked in the technical literature devoted to it. This is particularly the case when it applied itself
to "the unbearable sense of grievance" that energizes support for the
jihadist struggle.[75] In fact, this depoliticized, technical approach to insurgency and the reluctance to confront Islamism's ideological worldview led to policy prescriptions that were either dangerously naive
or radically utopian. Grievance removal necessarily raised political
questions such as, What level of conciliation would placate disaffected
Muslim opinion? Are the ends of militant Islamism amenable to real-
world solutions? Moreover, if they are, does the price paid for peace
in the short term unduly compromise Western states' national interests? These questions have been widely debated beyond the realm of
counterinsurgency,[76] but rarely by global COIN thinkers themselves,
whose answers, in those rare instances when they did offer them, were
notable only for the lengths they were prepared to go to appease the
global Islamist threat. Thus, for example, Mackinlay opined that the
"global developments" that engendered al-Qaeda-inspired violence
"cannot be arrested by a democratic, free market society; they are
the consequences of that society," which might have been true in one
sense but not especially helpful in identifying practical measures to
tackle the danger posed.[77] Kilcullen similarly chose to feel the Islamist

pain, perceiving that "for Muslims in much of the world, there is no middle way: only a stark choice between *jihad* and acceptance of permanent second-class citizenship in a world order dominated by the West and apparently infused with anti-Islamic values. For many self-respecting Muslims, the choice of *jihad* rather than surrender is both logical and honorable."[78]

These and similar statements from global COIN advocates evince an interesting family resemblance to understandings expressed by the fashionable but radically pacifist and critical school of international relations theory. This fashionable branch of study denounces globalization as the problem, yet it asserts cosmopolitan Western liberal solutions of global justice and emancipatory norms as the solution. Hence, critical international theory perceives *globalization* as a synonym for a capitalist world order, hence a "late-modern sociological term for the 'civilizing process'" and thus oppressive of the non-Western "other." As a consequence, "terrorism—as a form of barbarism," in the form of al-Qaeda, can be "seen as a challenge to international order and the civilizing process of globalization."[79]

In a similarly critical spirit, global COIN theorists such as Mackinlay and Kilcullen argued that the prevailing Western economic and political order represses Muslims everywhere. Such a diagnosis closely resembles the analysis of critical international relations scholars who considered al-Qaeda-style violence either a "construction" of or a reaction to Western "elite power." From this perspective, the "westernised world system" imposes a global economic "apartheid" that reduces Muslims to second-class citizens via the markets that create a burgeoning economic divide between the rich "West" and the exploited poor of the "majority world."[80] This viewpoint sees insurgency and terrorism as weapons of the weak[81] used against the hegemonic West and inexorably arising from the "global capitalist system."[82] In this context, "Al Qaeda is not a state nor [*sic*] a great power" but a "transnational network and more importantly an idea around which resistance is organised globally and locally."[83] From this standpoint, the solution demands the radical transformation of the international order into "a system of sustainable security" "based . . . on justice and emancipation."[84] The details of this radically transformed order, like the techniques of global COIN, remain opaque but at a minimum require the abandonment of market economics and the radical revision of Western foreign policy. Such transformationalism finds echoes in the global COIN perspective advanced by Mackinlay, who argued that "disarming the hatred of the disaffected Islamic communities means a new US policy on Israel and in the long term, for the US to . . . learn to talk to insurgents."[85]

Global COIN analysis ultimately, if somewhat equivocally, supports a radical transformation of the global order. Like critical theory and classical COIN, it rejects political religion as the driver of Islamist action while at the same time claiming to know the technical causes that inspire Muslim disaffection—namely, Western sociocultural and economic oppression. This of course is not to deny that governments should in some circumstances negotiate with those insurgents able to compromise. Such negotiation may be prudent in a specific theater, whether talking to Sunni tribal leaders in Iraq or elements of the Taliban in Afghanistan. But it is an entirely different case to extend "grievance settling" per se to the international arena because it invokes the logic of appeasement without examining whether global jihadism is capable of being appeased.

Lawrence Freedman's skepticism about "vague talk of hearts and minds" reflected his belief that for Westerners, as potential victims of jihadist violence, it was important to understand the political causes of that violence. Moreover, he argued, "even when we do [understand those causes], we must also recognize the limited quality of the political response available to us." For Freedman, this learning process does not mean "finding grievances" to placate. Rather, it requires comprehending the nature of the forces that wish to establish an illiberal, theocratic world order, considering why this problem has arisen, and appreciating the limited scope for agreement, conciliation, and amelioration.[86] It represents a far more credible understanding not only of jihadist adversaries but also of the values and interests that Western societies need to defend.

Neo-Maoism, Not Post-Maoism

If contemporary jihadism constitutes a globalized insurgency, then what might convincing a global counterinsurgent response involve?

Ultimately, it would have to address the ideologies that motivate protagonists, not the practice of local grievance settlement, as the key battle against the global insurgency. And where does this crucial struggle occur? It occurs, in fact, within the borders of the modern state, not in some abstract global sphere. In this regard, neoclassical COIN thinking possesses insights that elude the global COIN perspective. Here it is worth reiterating Sarah Sewall's introduction to the *Counterinsurgency Field Manual*, "There are important differences in the analogy between counterinsurgency and an effort to defeat Al Qaeda and its allies, but the overall strategic problem is uncannily parallel: sustaining the statist norm in the face of radical and violent revolutionaries."[87]

Although global COIN insists on the "post-Maoist" nature of insurgency, the reality of any counterstrategy, global or otherwise, is that it is always prosecuted within the spatial confines of the state. In fact, Kilcullen's global COIN conception of "disaggregation," with its emphasis on "de-linking local issues from the global insurgent system," acknowledges this point.[88] Rather than transcending the Maoist of idea insurgency, addressing the threat at the local level returns us, by a somewhat circuitous route, to the Maoist paradigm of "sustaining the statist norm." However, global COIN theory's failure to countenance the ideological motivation to jihadist activism obscures what is happening at the domestic political level in Western cosmopolitan cities. Interestingly, its diagnosis of the threat invariably conflicts with the thinking and experience of intelligence and law enforcement officials, who often possess a greater insight into the specific factors that motivate local actors.

Thus, Jonathan Evans, the director general of the British Security Service, MI5, in a speech in Manchester in November 2007 diametrically opposed Kilcullen's contention that political religion is a second-order concern, possessing little "functional relationship with violence." Evans maintained that

> the main national security threat that we face today is from al Qaida and its associated groups. But before we look at the violent manifestations of that threat in the UK, we need to remember where this threat comes from. The violence directed against us is the product of a much wider extremist ideology, whose basic tenets are inimical

to the tolerance and liberty which form the basis of our democracy. So although the most visible manifestations of this problem are the attacks and attempted attacks we have suffered in recent years, the root of the problem is ideological. Why? Because the ideology underlying al Qaida and other violent groups is extreme. It does not accept the legitimacy of other viewpoints. It is intolerant, and it believes in a form of government which is explicitly anti-democratic. And the more that this ideology spreads in our communities, the harder it will be to maintain the kind of society that the vast majority of us wish to live in.[89]

Such statements reveal the constituting weakness in the global COIN thesis. The term *global insurgency* itself, rather than clarifying the nature of the current security condition, ignores it. In reality, the phrase *"global" insurgency* obscures something more prosaic—namely, a *domestic* insurgency arising from the political forces promoting Islamism both at home and abroad. It is, moreover, the ideology that the insurgency promulgates that renders its threat transnational and requires governments operating multinational coalitions to deal with jihadism both through external interventions (such as the removal of the Taliban regime in Afghanistan in late 2001) and through domestic, police-level interventions.

In this way, the global threat presents a challenge to the modern democratic state as much as it does to "host nations" that Western interventionism attempts to stabilize. In the case of a number of European states such as the United Kingdom, which has possessed acute problems in integrating second-generation Muslims into its multicultural society, this challenge requires reasserting political sovereignty, securing state borders, and elaborating an inclusive national identity as part of a shared public morality and counterideology.

The notion of defeating the ideology that inspires jihadist militancy, then, does not detract from the Maoist concept of insurgency but actually supports it. Indeed, it accentuates the political and ideological struggle within a given territorial space. The sovereign state ought to provide security for its citizens and through its territorially limited authority contribute to the defeat of Islamism globally. Yet the global COIN school obfuscates this dimension of what Steven Pinker terms the "Leviathan state."[90] Its reluctance to confront the political dimension of the struggle means that it ignores the contest over values at home. The internal dimension of the conflict is problematic, controversial, and value laden, which is why global COIN theorists ignore it. Moreover, when they address this dimension, they focus not on the illiberal ideology of jihadism but on second-order issues such as social networks, prisons, urban deprivation, and family breakdown as sources of jihadist recruitment. Even here, global COIN's casuistry is evident as its agenda deliberately overlooks the schools, mosques, colleges, and universities that provide the ideological energy for jihadist recruitment.[91]

The main puzzle identified in this chapter is that global counterinsurgency thinking, despite recognizing the complexity of the post–Cold War world, avoids the politics of the current conflict and its implications for an effective counterstrategy. Yet it is the contest about values at the state level that renders the conflict political in nature. The need to consider state security, however, poses difficult questions relating to civil liberty, surveillance, public morality, sovereignty, and the problem of multicultural identity for analysts and public agencies functioning within a secular and liberal democratic paradigm. Rather than confront this dilemma, global COIN evades it. This evasion contrasts with law enforcement agencies' growing awareness of the threat jihadism poses to policing a liberal democracy. For instance, in 2007 Deputy Assistant Commissioner Peter Clarke, head of Counter-Terrorism Command at the London Metropolitan Police, admitted that counterterrorist policing (that is, internal counterinsurgency) has become more "political" because it has had to preempt plots and target resources against an identifiable section of the population.[92] This is awkward terrain, but it requires traversing to construct coherent public policy.

In this context, a state-oriented "Maoist" paradigm for insurgency demonstrates the enduring relevance of classical COIN thinking to the dilemma of policing the modern cosmopolitan condition. It also raises difficult questions about the application of counterinsurgency principles in both the democratic state as well as any state of concern requiring external intervention. The central Maoist revolutionary warfare objective remains the control of the people: the battle for hearts and minds. We should finally ask, therefore, the question that global COIN theorists prefer to avoid: What are the implications for internal security of a Maoist strategy operating globally and locally? In fact, the notion of a transnational insurgency poses other questions: Who are the people? And whose hearts and whose minds need to be won? Global counterinsurgency thinking offers a recipe of grievance settling and assumes that Muslim communities in Western states and on the Arab street must be the focus of "hearts and minds" operations.

Certainly, a comprehensive counterinsurgency strategy must attend to those communities to interdict plots and deter those who might be attracted to the path of violence. However, a properly conceived political strategy that effectively confronts the existential threat presented by a globalized insurgency requires more. In an age of polymorphous violence inspired by clashing ideological and religious visions, "hearts and minds" operations must also address the growing insecurity of majority populations in multicultural states. The silent majority also requires security and public order before it can consider second-order redistributive concerns.[93] Sustaining popular support for protracted struggles abroad, such as the Western commitment to fighting the Taliban insurgency in Afghanistan, while countering the internal jihadist threat at home minimally requires this political assurance from a coherent counterstrategy.[94]

The notion of a global insurgency recognizes that the contemporary security challenge is a complex transnational one, which manifests itself simultaneously at both the state and the international levels. Even if global COIN's theorists negate the role of ideology, a realistic understanding that the threat is global would see that the totalizing political religion driving jihad conceives "over there" as "here." As a consequence, countering this postmodern style of revolutionary warfare requires a political strategy that transcends conventional, classical counterinsurgency precepts. A properly conceived global counterinsurgency effort would entail a global "hearts and minds" campaign, but one very different from that offered in the global COIN theorists' grievance-settling playbook. Maintaining security and facilitating development in places as diverse as Iraq and Afghanistan, as classical and neoclassical insurgency thought contends, would remain essential ingredients in a properly conceived "global" counterinsurgency program. At the same time, that program would also entail the quite separate task of neutralizing the ideology that inspires diasporic Islamic communities to violent jihadism in open Western democracies while ensuring the necessary social cohesion to sustain a protracted campaign.

This point returns us to a key Clausewitzian insight—namely, that in considering any kind of response in war, the first principle is to understand what the fundamental struggle is about, "neither mistaking it for, nor trying to turn it into something alien to its nature."[95] This means recognizing that the contemporary conflict is ideological and permeates both the global system and the domestic politics of both Western and non-Western societies. Ultimately, it is a struggle between an illiberal and totalizing political religion, Islamism, and a secular, cosmopolitan, liberal democracy. Resolution of this struggle requires not only recalibrating Muslim hearts and minds but also crafting a coherent political response. The global insurgency, then, among other things, takes place within modern democracies and involves the whole population and its shared public morality, not just a particular minority and its cultural concerns. Democratic governments must persuade the majority of the validity of the struggle. This cannot be achieved by conceding important points of principle in foreign policy or compromising political values at home to appease vocal but intolerant minorities under the aegis of grievance settlement.

The evolution of neoclassical and global counterinsurgency evidently represents a remarkable rediscovery of both archetypal conflicts and the revolutionary style of warfare that define the contemporary polymorphous condition. Its precepts continue to affect conflicts such as those in Iraq and Afghanistan. Global counterinsurgency techniques that identify the transnational connections between local conflicts and the external factors that sustain them have enhanced the understanding of the modern international system. Nevertheless, we should not exaggerate global COIN's influence, take its theories at face value, or accept that we have entered a new era of post-Maoist insurgency that marginalizes state responses.

The state, on the contrary, remains central, particularly in the domestic political arena, where transnational threats manifest themselves and have to be combated. Global counterinsurgency thinking, despite its insights, fails Clausewitz's first principle. It evades the political issues at the state level in order to defeat the threat of deterritorialized jihadism at the transnational level. In this respect, the global insurgency thesis fails to recognize that contemporary transnational threats manifest themselves not "somewhere else" but have profound implications for the hearts and minds of liberal and pluralist societies in a globalized world.

5

The Illusion of Tradition

Myths and Paradoxes of British Counterinsurgency

Introducing *The US Counterinsurgency Field Manual* in 2007, Sarah Sewall contended that "the new U.S. doctrine, embraces a traditional—some would argue atavistic—British method of fighting insurgency. It is based on principles learned during Britain's early period of imperial policing and relearned during responses to twentieth century independence struggles in Malaya and Kenya."[1] This respect for the British way of conducting COIN seemingly coincided with the British Army's own high opinion of its capabilities. According to the 1995 *Army Field Manual*, volume 5, "The British Army has for over 100 years been involved with insurgency of one type or another and from this experience has evolved a doctrine for countering insurgency."[2] The official statement accepted as fact that a tradition of counterinsurgency existed in British military conduct. The British manual proceeded to list the verities of this "doctrine": the maintenance of political primacy; the development of effective government structures; the utilization of intelligence; the separating of insurgents from any popular base of support; the neutralization of the insurgency; and the creation of a long-term plan.[3] Later iterations of the *Army Field Manual* in 2001 and 2007 reaffirmed these precepts. Meanwhile, the army's handbook *Countering Insurgency*, issued in 2009,[4] explicitly referenced and endorsed a British "tradition" of counterinsurgency.

Recent American and British writing on the subject take this tradition for granted. Thus, British counterinsurgency experience constitutes the historical reference point from which most contemporary COIN theory takes its cue. Whether complimentary or critical, recent commentary assumes that Britain possesses or at least once possessed a venerable COIN tradition.

Yet, in spite of the endorsements of eminent commentators and statements in modern military manuals, should the British Army's self-proclaimed tradition of counterinsurgency be taken as an accurate appreciation of its experience? The argument in this chapter questions whether such a tradition ever existed. In fact, the idea that the British state in general or the British Army in particular had "evolved a doctrine for countering insurgency" functions as a myth. The invocation of a one-hundred-year-old tradition frames a discourse constructed by commentators and subsequently endorsed by the British Army through the regularization of statements that reaffirm the myth, even while sometimes criticizing aspects of it. A careful dissection of the British "experience" of combating soi-disant instances of insurgency evinces that there is no discrete tradition in the sense of a common pattern of understanding or action. To the extent that the British Army asserts the features of a tradition of counterinsurgency, it is largely a post–Cold War construct that was reified in the mid-2000s following Western Coalition interventions in Afghanistan and Iraq. Prior to these developments, the British Army itself (as opposed to academic commentators upon its practice) had never identified a particular "British way" of counterinsurgency.

For the purpose of this chapter, we understand myth to be a representation of something that fictionalizes, explains, and mobilizes a coherent structure of meaning.[5] A fictionalization of the British historical experience frames the current debate about a distinctive British approach counterinsurgency. If, as we contend, there is no actual pattern of activity that can be distilled into a British approach, then, a fortiori, the invocation of an explicit *tradition* of counterinsurgency cannot constitute the basis of any perceived British success in military encounters over the past century.

Conversely, the purported decline of a tradition that is in fact a myth cannot account for any recent British military shortcomings in so-called small wars. A persistent mistake made by military commentators and lately by the British Army itself, which the chapter further demonstrates, is to treat "small wars" as a notion reducible to an operational art rather than as an instrument of politics. This treatment reflects a common theme of this volume—namely, the absence of politics from discussions of COIN. The British experience of insurgency over the past century and a half comprises examples of war that no matter how "small" are always acts of policy—British national policy—that cannot be reduced to a technical debate about methods, operations, and tactics. The tradition of a British way in counterinsurgency is a myth because political commitment rather than military technique determines success or failure in military encounters.

Experience Does Not Amount to a Tradition

The 1995 *Army Field Manual* stated: "It is curious to record, that despite the extensive experience gained by the British Army in counterinsurgency during the Twentieth century, relatively little has been recorded as official doctrine in any military publications." It added: "A large amount has been written about counter-insurgency unofficially and, partly through this, military doctrine has evolved and developed."[6] The manual elucidated the evolution of its unofficial doctrine via the writings of Charles Callwell, whose book *Small Wars: Their Principles and Practice*, published in 1896, "drew together some doctrinal strands on countering insurgency and rebellion" from previous campaigns, and then it proceeded to reference the army's experience in the Easter Rising in Ireland of 1916, Charles Gwynn's *Notes on Imperial Policing* (1934), and General John Dill's *Notes on the Tactical Lessons of the Palestine Rebellion* (1937) in order to establish that Britain had a tradition of fighting insurgencies well before 1939.[7]

The British *Army Field Manual* continued this general theme, intimating that its tradition persisted into the post–World War II era and citing "counterinsurgency operations" in India and Palestine in the 1940s and the publication of documents such as the 1949 pamphlet *Imperial Policing and the Duties in Aid of the Civil Power: The Conduct of Anti-terrorist Operations in Malaya* (1952) and *A Handbook of Anti*

Mau Mau Operations (1954). Despite these and other references, the manual asserted that "very little by way of doctrine was developed" despite operations in Borneo, Cyprus, Radfan, and Aden.[8] It observed that, beyond 1969, "in the absence of any official publications on the doctrine of counter insurgency others sought to fill the gap. In the UK, Sir Robert Thompson, General Kitson, General Clutterbuck and Colonel Tugwell all recorded their experiences. In addition, they wrote doctrinal works on how insurgency and terrorism have developed and offered more up to date principles and guidelines on how to defeat these two scourges of the late twentieth century."[9]

Embedded in these statements are a set of suppositions that assume Britain has experience in countering insurgency, that counterinsurgency exists as a distinct category of conflict, and that this experience has endowed Britain with a doctrine—a set of standard procedures and understandings—that by the era of decolonization had distilled "three broad fundamentals of policy" to combat the "scourge" of insurgency: "minimum force; civil/military cooperation; and tactical flexibility." "There are some who consider," the manual proclaimed, "that by the end of the 1960s the British Army was more effective than they had ever been at countering insurgency."[10]

Subsequent commentary readily endorsed this discourse, and in response the *Field Manual* conflated a diverse range of prior experiences of conflict with a distinct "tradition" of counterinsurgency, albeit an informal one. Rather than interrogating first-order assumptions (such as whether the British Army's experience amounts to a tradition and whether counterinsurgency exists as a clearly identifiable type of war), later commentators simply reinforced the belief that British conduct regularized a set of underlying principles that "remained cornerstones" of official counterinsurgency doctrine.[11] Even negative assessments of recent British military performance have unintentionally reinforced the assumption that Britain possesses a tradition of counterinsurgency. "What has happened to our special skills at this, our particular aptitude at 'war amongst the people'?" laments Frank Ledwidge in *Losing Small Wars*, a withering deconstruction of British military shortcomings in Afghanistan and Iraq. "Britain was no stranger, historically, to insurgency and civil war in Iraq," Ledwidge claims. The "British fought dozens of small campaigns, with greater or lesser degrees of success. They developed techniques, which although sporadically applied, were to become the keynote of a 'British way' of 'counterinsurgency.'" Reflecting on his own tours of duty in Helmand and Iraq, Ledwidge recalls: "I asked myself what went wrong. Where was our supposed counter-insurgency 'inheritance'?"[12] What Ledwidge and others might more properly have asked themselves was not whether Britain had lost its inheritance of counterinsurgency, but whether it ever possessed such an inheritance in the first place.

Ledwidge's *Losing Small Wars*, in fact, captures and distils the myth of the British Army's presumed prior expertise in COIN. The book cover depicts a British soldier in Afghanistan in 2009, head in hands, despairing, it would seem, at the futility of it all. The signified content explores the cover signifier, revealing the limitations of British military conduct in Iraq and Afghanistan. The book documents the shortcomings and institutional limitations of the British armed forces, which, in Ledwidge's assessment, malfunctioned and underperformed. The book is one of a number of revisionist studies that trace, over the best part of a decade, the tale of an army with a venerated reputation for waging small wars now losing its credibility through a mixture of complacency, ineptitude, cost cutting, and laurel gazing. The product description on Amazon crystallizes the argument: "Partly on the strength of their apparent success in 'small wars' such as Malaya and Northern Ireland, the British armed forces have long been perceived as world class, if not world-beating. Yet, under British control, Basra [in southern Iraq] degenerated into a lawless city riven with militia violence and fear, while tactical mistakes and strategic incompetence in Helmand province resulted in numerous casualties and a burgeoning opium trade."[13]

It gets worse. It appeared that not only were the British armed forces underprepared for their encounters in Iraq and Afghanistan, but, when properly examined, the British Army's capacity for handling small wars is in fact largely illusory. The new revisionism revealed that what the orthodoxy considered a record of effective counterinsurgency campaigning concealed a legacy of failure and underachievement. More disturbing still, even Britain's occasional victories or partial successes were not the result of any particular style but more often the product of brute force that covered the full gamut of atrocity from massacres to gulags and even genocide, depending on whom you read.[14]

British military practice in Iraq and Afghanistan undoubtedly suffered serious limitations. Ledwidge and others rightly expose these shortcomings.[15] Our intention in this chapter is not to question either these critical accounts or the new revisionist history that shows British counterinsurgency campaigning in the twentieth century to have been more coercive and brutal than previously recognized. What this chapter argues is that the prevailing scholarship that assumes that a highly regarded tradition of small-war fighting once existed and now lies in ruins is itself recounting a myth.[16] It offers a myth because it conflates a number of different and not necessarily related analyses into a single narrative that is neither accurate nor coherent.

Ledwidge and others begin from a premise of Britain's "apparent success" in "small wars." Here, the notion of small war elides into the notion of counterinsurgency. First, therefore, it is necessary to establish what the elusive term *small wars* entails. By "small wars," commentators invariably mean those military encounters where there is a large element of discretion about whether to fight or not. They are conflicts that reside well below the existential threat that the United Kingdom confronted in World War II, where the choice of not fighting and surrendering threatened the state's continued political identity. They are wars of choice rather than necessity wherein the political decision is made to invest time and effort in causes that exist beneath this threshold and that largely reside outside national borders. They can be described, therefore, as "small wars." Counterinsurgency campaigns from the British perspective thus constitute a particular form of "small war" that involves an attempt to confound an armed challenge to established authority.[17]

Arising from an imperial history wherein British forces found themselves frequently engaged in expeditions to conquer, occupy, or pacify foreign lands, a narrative of assumed expertise easily emerged about Britain's ability to wage small wars either for territorial gain or to quell attempted insurrections against its colonial authority.[18] The blurb for Ledwidge's book on Amazon reflects this narrative. It claims: "The British armed forces have long been *perceived* as world class, if not world-beating" (added emphasis here). Problematically, the passive-voice construction fails to inform us who arrived at this perception. A straight answer to this question reveals that the British armed forces prior to the end of the Cold War rarely made this claim to expertise. Instead, it was commentators external to the British military who formed this impression. This diverse group of analysts included former British colonial civil servants, former soldiers, journalists, American academics, and serving U.S. Army officers. Explicit assertions of a distinctive tradition of counterinsurgency campaign cannot, however, be found in any British Army doctrines or documents prior to 1995. If anything, as David Ucko has suggested, the late-twentieth-century British Army eschewed any perceived tradition of counterinsurgency: "The British Army, despite repeated engagement in counterinsurgency, has historically found it difficult to internalize the lessons drawn from these campaigns, necessitating quick adaptation on the ground with each new engagement. There, the individual memory of previous notionally similar operations has flattened the learning curve, but to institutionalize this wisdom has proven an altogether more difficult proposition."[19] As Ucko's statement indicates, the British Army's lack of institutional knowledge reveals a logical difficulty in the "Where did it all go wrong?" thesis, which awkwardly conflates a commentariat's discussion of a British talent for small wars with the erroneous implication that the British armed forces had this perception of themselves. Simply because C. E. Callwell and Charles Gwynn, along with a few others, reflected on the British Army's experience in its imperial encounters *does not* constitute an official orthodoxy. There is scant evidence that the British armed forces ever internalized an understanding that they had particular skills in so-called small wars, and the little evidence that does exist is contradictory.

A Narrative, Not a Tradition

So who and what accounts for the tradition of a British proficiency in small wars? Since the end of World War II, the Malaya Emergency represented the locus classicus that influenced subsequent commentary, framing perceptions of a British flair for such encounters. The works of former Malaya Civil Service officer Sir Robert Thompson, in particular *Defeating Communist Insurgency: Experiences from Malaya and Vietnam*, provided the initial source for a British way in counterinsurgency.[20] This was not because Thompson explicitly articulated a distinctive British approach but because his five "basic principles of counterinsurgency" unambiguously drew on the British Malayan campaign. The success of these principles, moreover, contrasted dramatically with the contemporaneous American effort in South Vietnam, where a seemingly misplaced emphasis on search-and-destroy missions failed to defeat the Viet Cong. Following Thompson's work, there were remarkably few direct allusions to a distinctive British practice. The only exception perhaps was former army officer Julian Paget's 1967 account *Counter-Insurgency Campaigning*.[21]

In the early 1970s, with a sense of postimperial decline permeating the British national psyche, a different set of challenges arose that undermined any residual sense of achievement in successfully waging small wars. The year 1971 saw the publication of journalist Noel Barber's stylized account of the Malaya campaign, *War of the Running Dogs*.[22] This book, however, marked the last gasp of a late-imperial nostalgia for wars in faraway places. More significantly, 1971 also saw the publication of serving officer Brigadier Frank Kitson's *Low Intensity Operations: Subversion, Peacekeeping, and Law Enforcement*,[23] which reflected the mood of the times as national gloom descended over the United Kingdom, accompanied by rising levels of industrial unrest and seemingly irreversible economic and political decline. Significantly, Kitson's work also coincided with the onset of the most violent phase of the Northern Ireland Troubles, culminating in the Provisional IRA's concerted campaign of violence to achieve a united Ireland. Even so, in both *Low Intensity Operations* and his later ruminations on the conflicts in Kenya, Malaya, and Cyprus, *Bunch of Five*,[24] Kitson made no claim to a specifically British style of countering insurgency.

Interestingly, in September 1970 Kitson assumed command of 39 Infantry Brigade in Belfast as Northern Ireland descended into chaos. Kitson possessed a fearsome reputation in Irish Republican circles as a result of his experiences fighting in some of Britain's more prominent twentieth-century wars of colonial disengagement.[25] He certainly drew on this prior experience in Northern Ireland, notably his

Special Forces initiatives, which were based on his creation of "counter-gangs" in Kenya.[26] However, units set up under his direction, such as the Mobile Reconnaissance Force, and the various schemes it sponsored, such as the Four Square Laundry operation, were rudimentary and ephemeral, with later assessments judging such schemes amateurish at best.[27] Beyond these early and short-lived initiatives, there is little to suggest that Kitson or, indeed, any other British Army commander in Northern Ireland then or since implemented a systematic COIN plan based on a set of enduring British techniques developed in earlier small-war campaigns.[28] And indeed, as John Bew points out, to the extent that the army did employ the key "lessons" from its earlier colonial experiences—internment without trial, curfews, hard-interrogation techniques, and demonstrations of exemplary force—these lessons were associated with the most disastrous period of the army's experience in Ulster. "Rather than relying on the precedents of the past to guide the path to success," Bew notes perceptively, "it is more accurate to say the situation in Northern Ireland improved only when the Army unlearned its recent lessons from Kenya and Malaya."[29]

Here we may identify the first of a number of myths and misrepresentations about the evolution of a British COIN tradition. Commentators consistently cite the years of the Northern Ireland Troubles as a major source of Britain's small-wars expertise. Problematically, this view overlooks the fact that in Northern Ireland the army's role from the mid-1970s was primarily to support the police.[30] The army did not assume the burden of a counterinsurgency campaign. That campaign was led largely by intelligence, and the principal agency leading it was not the British Army but the Special Branch of the Royal Ulster Constabulary.[31] Throughout the 1970s and 1980s, the British Army's core focus remained planning for major battle against Warsaw Pact forces in central Europe.[32] The years of the Northern Ireland Troubles, in fact, witnessed a curious dissonance between British military thinking and the conduct of small war at the time, on the one hand, and later treatment of that thinking and conduct by scholars of counterinsurgency. It is clear that in the course of the later stages of the Cold War, the British Army and British defense thinking in general at the time were far from elaborating, let alone celebrating, some ingrained capability to deal with small-scale conflicts such as Ulster and were instead intent on ignoring or downplaying such conflict. During this period, only one work appeared that even hinted at some generalized British approach to small wars. Former army officer Colonel Michael Dewar's 1984 publication *Brush Fire Wars* offered a broad-brush account of Britain's experience in "minor wars" since 1945. Yet, even here, almost no mention is made of counterinsurgency.[33]

In sum, from the 1950s through to the end of the Cold War, there was no formulation, articulation, or enunciation in official UK publications, by the army or any other government agency or from any other serving British military figure, of a distinctly British facility for waging small wars. At most, there were hints and intimations of an underlying set of values that might have applied to British conduct in minor wars, but there is little evidence of adherence to a predetermined set of practices when it came to counterinsurgency in a decolonizing context. Paradoxically, it was only after 1990 that a systematic view developed that identified a distinctly British approach. Thus, rather than an accurately discerned historical pattern of British military activity, we have the construction of a narrative—the beginnings of a myth. More paradoxically still, this evolving narrative was created and sustained largely by American writers and thinkers. In effect, the British tradition of small-war expertise was "made in the USA." How is this paradox to be understood?

Made in America: The British Small-War Tradition

Thomas Mockaitis's 1990 study *British Counterinsurgency, 1919–1960*, began the evolution of an American narrative of British counterinsurgency experience.[34] Mockaitis produced the first systematic academic analysis of Britain's colonial campaigns via an explicit counterinsurgency framework. Although he did not propose that the British had developed a small-war-winning formula, he did suggest that the British had, over a long period of tough encounters, evolved a set of practices that accentuated the principles of minimum force and discriminate violence. It was Mockaitis's contention that the British Army had "much to teach a world increasingly challenged by the problem of internal war."[35] Later, the one hundredth anniversary republication of C. E. Callwell's classic nineteenth-century tract on the wars of imperial British expansion, *Small Wars: Their Principles and Their Practice*, in 1996 by the University of Nebraska Press reinforced this interest. The U.S. edition included an extended introduction by Douglas Porch, who noted that Callwell's tract was a repository of specialist knowledge of what "low intensity conflict" entailed.[36] These texts were influential. They provided a powerful narrative that suggested a thread of historical continuity. One consequence was that going into the mid-1990s and explicitly swayed by Mockaitis's work,[37] the British Army also began to tell a story about itself mediated through the lens of a counterinsurgency tradition. For the first time, official manuals now began to claim that the "experience of numerous 'small wars' has provided the British Army with a unique insight into this form of conflict."[38]

Early in the following decade, as earlier chapters have already discussed, John Nagl's *Learning to Eat Soup with a Knife: Counterinsurgency Lessons from Malaya and Vietnam* (2002) further embellished the view that the British possessed a unique insight into small war. Nagl's study extolled the virtues of the British Army as a learning institution that adapted its military methodology in Malaya to suit the needs of the emergency situation.[39] Nagl's thesis appeared at a propitious moment. It struck a chord in American military circles during a period that witnessed the descent of postinvasion Iraq into sectarian strife and a Sunni/al-Qaeda-sponsored uprising against the post-2003 Coalition occupation.[40] As the U.S. armed forces debated how to move from an invasion force into an effective occupying power capable of dealing with the complicated conditions of civil insurrection, Montgomery McFate's work also achieved increasing prominence. McFate, unlike Nagl, drew her inspiration from the British experience in Northern Ireland. In particular, the British Army's ability to acquire "cultural knowledge" of its enemy in the course of the Troubles impressed her.[41] According to McFate, the British "could not have built an effective strategy in Northern Ireland as they did without having a very full understanding of their enemy."[42] This hard-won knowledge, gained over years of trial and error, she maintained, had important lessons for a U.S. military attempting to operate in the complex local environments encountered in Iraq and Afghanistan.[43]

In other words, U.S. soldier-scholars, military historians, and anthropologists first identified and analyzed a tradition of British military prowess in conducting counterinsurgency. Each of the American analysts discussed so far emphasized an element of practice that they considered central to British success. They either distinguished a particularly British attitude toward small-scale military entanglements (Mockaitis and the principle of minimum force) or identified crucial lessons that could be adapted as best practice by the U.S. military (Nagl and the desirability of a flexible learning institution). British practice further afforded a sophisticated understanding of the challenges, subtleties, and potential opportunities in the specific theaters in which U.S. forces found themselves engaged, especially those characterized by complex tribal interactions (McFate and the importance of acquiring cultural knowledge).

It was this American myth of British counterinsurgency prowess that generated new COIN doctrine as well as a further paradox. Ironically, it was only after the American invention of this tradition that some sections of the British establishment consciously embraced the narrative. The initial Coalition experience in postinvasion Iraq reinforced it. Mounting intercommunal violence and attacks on Coalition forces in Iraq after 2003 seemed to demonstrate a dramatic gap between the more violent American-controlled sectors of the country and the relatively peaceful provinces to the south under British tutelage. The perception grew that the harder, more kinetic American operations created problems rather than solved them, fomenting anti-Coalition hostility and crystallizing local resistance. In comparison, in the South a lower-key British presence, where the army patrolled in soft hats and talked to the locals rather than engaged in firefights, seemed initially to characterize conditions in Basra.

The relative quiescence in the South thus corresponded with what commentators had characterized as a flexible, minimum-force approach. This characterization dovetailed with an evolving self-perception among sections of British official and academic commentary of Britain's own abilities in a defined sphere of counterinsurgency and in particular a predisposition toward the practice of restraint and the discriminate, careful application of military force. For example, according to Rod Thornton, the "uniqueness of the British approach" resided in the Victorian sensibilities of pragmatism, civic policing, and Christian sentiment as well as the romantic norms of chivalry and noblesse oblige inculcated in an officer class educated in public schools (what Americans designate as elite private schools).[44] The philosophy of "minimum force" was thus an "idea deeply rooted in the British military psyche."[45]

The Iraq Paradox

Before the invasion of Iraq, it was difficult to find any official validation of a distinctive British approach to COIN, minimum force or otherwise. Even the 1995 *Field Manual*, a somewhat prolix document, did not make clear whether the principles appropriate to counterinsurgency constituted a formal prescription of certain practices. To the extent, moreover, that it did recognize a set of principles, they were anodyne in nature (encompassing such uncontroversial positions as political primacy; coordinated government machinery; intelligence and information sharing; separating the insurgent from his support; neutralizing the insurgent; and longer-term postinsurgency planning).[46] The situation changed, however, in 2005. In that year, a House of Commons Defence Committee report on Iraq took evidence from a number of serving and former soldiers, academics, and other commentators. This expert commentary maintained that Britain possessed an inherited knowledge of "postconflict operations." Explicit references were made to prior experience in Malaya and Northern Ireland, providing insights and lessons from which others (that is, the Americans) might usefully learn.[47] The British COIN narrative was thus established and gained some traction in the public sphere and even within sections of the army.

Chief of the General Staff Mike Jackson was the most prominent adherent to the view that the British possessed small-war expertise. Jackson distinguished between the conduct of British forces around Basra and the U.S. military's harder-edged approach. He rather polemically asserted in 2004 that "we must be able to fight *with* the Americans. That does not mean that we must be able to fight *as* the Americans."[48] In 2009, after having left the army, Jackson further argued in the *Journal of Strategic Studies* that the British military experience of counterinsurgency had roots that extended from its colonial policing encounters. "There is a sense," he added, "of a real historical thread in this type of operation for the British Armed Forces."[49]

For the most part, though, formal British Army statements maintained their established viewpoint, rarely advertizing a particularly British view of counterinsurgency. When British military personnel issued statements, they were notably low key. Crucially, if they came close to acknowledging a British approach, it was invariably implied rather than overtly stated. Thus, although Brigadier Nigel Aylwin-Foster's celebrated critique of the heavy-handed tactics employed by the United States early in the occupation of Iraq in the U.S. journal *Military Review* in 2005 is often regarded as the epitome of British superior COIN condescension, it was in fact nothing of the kind. Aylwin-Foster made no specific mention of a British penchant for counterinsurgency.[50] Instead, he reiterated John Nagl's claim in *Learning to Eat Soup with a Knife* that the American army's distinctive facility for high-end war fighting arose from its institutional experience and historical origins that emphasized "the eradication of threats to national survival.'" Aylwin-Foster contrasted this emphasis with "the British Army's [purported] history as an instrument of limited war to achieve limited goals at limited cost." To the extent that Aylwin-Foster promulgated a distinctive British COIN tradition, he did so only indirectly by referring to the American narrative that the British Army's historical experience created an institutional culture that "encourages a rapid response to changing situations."[51]

As a result of such commentaries, the relative tranquility of Iraq's South began to be perceived in terms of the different military cultures of the British and American armed forces. In this context, assumptions about supposedly established British approaches to counterinsurgency came to constitute one possible explanatory variable that accounted for this apparent difference in operational outcomes. At this point, a worrying tone of self-congratulation crept into official British reports, which increasingly accepted the narrative of a British COIN tradition. The House of Commons Defence Committee report, for instance, declared: "We commend British forces for their approach to counter-insurgency in their areas of operations. We are convinced that their approach has been a contributing factor in the development of the more permissive environment in southern Iraq, which has resulted in relatively little insurgent activity."[52] Meanwhile, a Ministry of Defence report argued that the army's "positive start in Iraq" reflected prior "counter-insurgency experience from Northern Ireland" and, for good measure though somewhat bizarrely, "the Balkans" as well.[53]

At this time, official British hubris, now unquestioning in its assumption of a British COIN tradition, heavily discounted the fact that the Americans were compelled to operate in the Sunni badlands of the North rather than in the anti-Saddamite Shia South. The British-controlled areas were initially less hostile to Coalition forces after the ousting of the old regime. Yet here we encounter a further dissonance in the myth of British excellence. It was in the course of 2005 that the British force in Basra encountered serious difficulties as Sadr City fell into the hands of Iranian-backed Shia militia groups.

In this regard, Aylwin-Foster's widely reported critique of U.S. conduct represented the apogee of the myth of British counterinsurgency. His analysis certainly aroused resentment. Colonel Kevin Benson of the U.S. Army's School of Advanced Military Studies accused Aylwin-Foster of being "an insufferable British snob."[54] Yet if we disassociate Aylwin-Foster's criticism of U.S. excesses from any implicit claims of British superiority in COIN (which he did not make), his comments were in the context of the time pertinent. Given the huge problems U.S. forces encountered in securing Fallujah, for example,[55] few military professionals would have disagreed with Aylwin-Foster's main conclusion that the Coalition had "failed to capitalise on initial success" and that Iraq was in "the grip a vicious and tenacious insurgency" or that there was a desperate need to "be better prepared for Irregular Warfare and post conflict stabilisation and reconstruction operations."[56]

In fact, Aylwin-Foster's assessment did not "slam US tactics" or offer a "blistering critique,"[57] as headline writers claimed. Inflammatory headlines undoubtedly served a media purpose, creating the misleading impression of British arrogance. However, it is an impression that can be derived from Aylwin-Foster's article only by ignoring his argument. Even Colonel Benson acknowledged later that Aylwin-

Foster's piece was "pretty powerful stuff" and that "sometimes good articles do make you angry. We should publish articles like this. We are in a war and we must always be thinking of how we can improve the way we operate."[58] Aylwin-Foster's argument ultimately played an important role in refocusing Coalition military efforts in Iraq after 2005. Such counsel and other critiques like it written by American officers succeeded in realigning U.S. forces, which eventually succeeded in the relative stabilization of the country after 2007, but they did so without any ostensible reference to supposedly superior British techniques. They arose from a careful evaluation of the specific and contingent circumstances in which Coalition forces found themselves after 2005.

Bye-Bye Basra: The Fictional Decline of a Nontradition

One other insight revealed from a close reading of Aylwin-Foster's article is that it did not make invidious comparisons between the performance of the U.S. and British forces in Iraq or elsewhere. There was, however, no disguising the fact that in the two years after Aylwin-Foster's critique appeared the British themselves ran into severe difficulties in the occupation of southern Iraq, especially around the city of Basra. It was in this context of the initial success of the invasion and subsequent failure of the occupation that another false narrative affected the discourse of an alleged British approach to counterinsurgency: the myth of the decline of a once proud tradition. Some British defense circles erroneously represented the relative quiescence of the South up to 2005 as exemplifying British competence in counterinsurgency, with commentaries like the one issued by the House of Commons extolling the British Army's preference for unobtrusive patrolling in berets and their apparent willingness to work with local leaders, affording a practical demonstration of the British facility for counterinsurgency and its tradition of minimum force.

Yet the official rhetoric and the actual reality of British operations in southern Iraq begged the question whether the army was actually practicing anything that could possibly be said to resemble a counter-insurgency program at all in Iraq after 2003. The fact that the British patrolled Basra without hard hats and governed—at first—with the consent of the local population demonstrated that in the aftermath of the invasion southern Iraq *was not* in a state of insurrection. The unobtrusive approach adopted by the British, therefore, may have been entirely appropriate for the time, reflecting the specific conditions of relative stability on the ground. Why, a skeptic might ask, was any expertise in counterinsurgency required, let alone invoked by official sources and public commentators, when there was no insurgency to counter in this area? It seems more accurate to claim that British forces were engaged at that time in an occupying/peacekeeping effort, and it is this effort that subsequently failed, not any distinctively British counterinsurgency campaign—if, that is, by "counterinsurgency" we mean the attempt to suppress violent subversion.

Furthermore, it can be argued that the political decision to draw down and pull out of southern Iraq in 2007 was largely the result of the well-advertised unpopularity of the war among the British electorate. In other words, Britain never attempted a concerted suppression campaign in southern Iraq.[59] The British did not have enough troops to accomplish any such task, and it was clear that the then Labour government had no intention of increasing its commitment. The government took a political decision to reduce British forces and thus attempt to minimize the damage to its political credibility back home. In these circumstances, a counterinsurgency effort was not going to be mounted. Without the political will, there can be no such thing as a counterinsurgency program in any meaningful sense. The question therefore arises, Were the shortcomings evident in the British occupation of Basra indicative of a failure of British counterinsurgency principles or evidence of a declining COIN tradition? Operational shortcomings were certainly revealed, and the (always inaccurate) view of the British Army's capacity for rapid institutional learning was questioned, but claims that the army's reputation was jeopardized appear both exaggerated and misplaced. What was ultimately going on was that one questionable narrative was being overtaken by another—namely, that a tradition (with dubious antecedents) was now falling into disrepute.

The Revisionist Challenge

The fact that the Ministry of Defence formally sought to identify a convention of British "minimum-force" counterinsurgency by citing the examples of Northern Ireland—in fact a bruising encounter characterized by a brutal undercover intelligence war[60]—and even more curiously the Balkans (where nothing resembling a counterinsurgency campaign in any comparable sense took place) illustrated the tenuous official grasp over this supposedly deeply ingrained tradition. In the face of these claims, along with the army's failure to secure Basra, commentators understandably but misleadingly asserted the erosion of that tradition. Out of this failure grew the "Where did it all go wrong?" school of thought, which accepted the myth in order to show that the tradition had declined. In the wake of this evolving narrative, an even more serious threat to the ostensible tradition of counterinsurgency expertise emerged. This threat assumed the form of a revisionist history of the later British imperial period. The new history demonstrated, often decisively, that the examples from which the canon of inherited counterinsurgency wisdom drew, particularly the legacy of colonial withdrawal, was, as Paul Dixon contended, "actually more violent and coercive than the literature would imply."[61]

From the late 2000s, books and articles began to appear that questioned the hearts-and-minds and minimum-force precepts that had supposedly characterized the British approach to small war in places such as Malaya. The questioning of this tradition, though, was not new. In the late 1990s, Karl Hack had first exposed the coercive methods the British employed in "screwing down" the Communists in Malaya in his revisionist account of the Emergency.[62] A few years later, in 2002, John Newsinger, from a Marxist historical perspective, identified a broader critique of a brutally repressive tradition of British counterinsurgency.[63] In the later 2000s, it was the work of historians such as Huw Bennett and David French, using previously unreleased or neglected official documents, who revealed how British approaches to colonial insurgencies were often fiercely aggressive.[64] Bennett's work on the Mau Mau war in Kenya in the 1950s, for instance, presented compelling evidence that British forces committed atrocities.[65]

The revelation of draconian measures to combat insurrectionary elements in the context of the wars of decolonization cleared the way for Marxist historians such as Newsinger to contend that the record of British military success in counterinsurgency was a political distortion.[66] Rather than winning hearts and minds, British COIN was now considered a notable political failure. In an analogous vein, Douglas Porch argued that the British Army "did not have a particularly exemplary record at COIN or at any warfare, for that matter, at the time of Malaya." The evidence of "brutal COIN tactics" was sufficient, it seemed, to discount any political successes. Further, to the extent that British forces demonstrated any aptitude for institutional learning, it was a preference for learning "kinetic methods," disguised under the cloak of hearts and minds, which were "every bit as repressive—even dirty—as the French" had used in Algeria.[67]

These historians correctly drew attention to the coercive realities of Britain's imperial encounters. Such historical revisionism, however, does not necessarily undermine any assumed British capability for fighting small wars but merely reframes it in a more negative light. Strategic success, it should be recalled, assumes the attainment of political goals. The fact that the British campaigns were often extremely violent does not ipso facto mean that they failed. It simply means that such victories were just more violent and coercive than the first accounts of these campaigns claimed. What the historical revisionism exposed in its revelations of exemplary and sometimes excessive violence was that the precursor academic and journalistic literature had elaborated a myth of minimum force.

In other words, the new history presented a revised and this time more accurate critique of prior academic and journalistic interpretations of British military practice. But the counterinsurgency narrative was one that the British Army had rarely endorsed officially. Even at the height of proclamations of a British facility for small-war encounters, only a few military figures and the occasional House of Commons or Ministry of Defence report referred to a distinctive British tradition of counterinsurgency achievement based on hearts and minds and minimum force. Besides, when the odd politician and retired general did so, they merely demonstrated their lack of understanding about how the army judged its own performance in these small wars. As Bruno Reis has shown through an extensive study of British military documentation, there is no mention whatsoever of a minimum-force philosophy in British military manuals during Britain's wars of decolonization.[68] Arguably, this nescience arose from the poor institutional memory about the legacy of colonial warfare within the British Army itself, which throughout the years of the Cold War focused almost exclusively on major land battle in central Europe.[69] Once again, read in this light, the British legacy of COIN presents itself as a series of myths obscuring contending and contradictory narratives rather than any tried and tested method.[70]

What the revisionist challenge to the prevailing narrative of a British way in COIN and the subsequent scholarly debate between the detractors and defenders of a minimum-force tradition demonstrates is the highly contested nature of that historical legacy.[71] Exemplifying this debate, one of the leading academic journals in the field, *Small Wars and Insurgencies*, commissioned in 2012 a special edition to discuss "British ways of counter-insurgency." What emerged from the contributions to that volume was that the British practiced a variety of tactics in their imperial conflicts. Cases of the suppression of colonial insurrection before World War II, from the Indian Mutiny through to the Boer War and the Amritsar massacre, exhibited a preference for a "butcher and bolt" policy, using violence for moral effect.[72] Callwell's work empathized with this approach. Callwell felt that "savage" tribes must be taught "a lesson they will not forget."[73] As Daniel Whittingham remarked, such views should be regarded as "one of exemplary force, even brutality, in a 'dark age' before a more enlightened period of 'minimum force' "[74] intimated in more emollient works such as Gwynn's *Imperial Policing*.[75]

Even so, the fact that later examples of colonial warfare, for instance in Kenya and Malaya, were subsequently revealed as more pitiless than once assumed led David French to argue that minimum force was an aberration and that "coercion was always the basis of Britain's counter-insurgency campaigns."[76] By contrast, Thomas Mockaitis, also an essay contributor to the volume, highlighted that attitudes to minimum force changed over time. It would be wrong, he suggested, to set up the notion of minimum force as some absolute standard. Rather, Mockaitis claimed, it would be more accurate to suggest that Britain often achieved greater success in its campaigns in comparison to other colonial powers and that this success can be explained in part as a result of the application of "broad principles flexibly applied." In that context, he maintained, the "British military enshrined the principle of minimum force in its doctrine and in many circumstances soldiers exercised commendable restraint."[77] Plausibly, if perhaps unfalsifiably, it might be argued thereby that the appreciation of a general precept of minimum force in British practice minimized the scale of potential abuse inherent in fighting wars among the people.[78]

The debate over the British COIN legacy, veering between the extremes of coercion on the one hand and restraint on the other, arguably suggests the British approach to small war to be somewhat schizophrenic. Ledwidge, in fact, makes this point, observing that the British Army was two armies for most of the post–World War II period: one being the British Army of the Rhine that maintained an aggressive orientation, emphasizing high-intensity force concentration; the other being an army that was evolving a philosophy of minimum force arising out of the prolonged Northern Ireland crisis.[79] What the army's own dual role and split identity as well as the contestable assessments over the meaning of its historical experience illustrate above all, however, is that the British Army itself had no consistent experience of anything. Aggression and coercion coexisted with restraint and minimum force. How can a British tradition exhibit such a total contradiction: on the one hand applying the principle of minimum force and hearts and minds, on the other exhibiting coercion and exemplary force? Which one of these supposed traditions is more historically correct hardly matters (the military evidently applied practices of both restraint and coercion to suit what it saw as the requirements of the strategic situation). The clear inference of the debate, though one rarely made by pundits, is that there is no stable understanding of the British colonial experience of "small wars," no evidently discernible pattern to British practice, and therefore no coherent tradition of British counterinsurgency.

A Tradition of Political Will, Not Counterinsurgency

Freed from the distorting perspective of COIN, what the British experience of so-called small wars reveals is something altogether more prosaic—namely, the role of contingency. Daniel Whittingham observes that Callwell recognized the highly equivocal definition of the term *small war*.[80] Moreover, to the extent that Callwell's writings gained "semiofficial" status (via the publication of *Small Wars* through His Majesty's Stationary Office), the army made clear—as Chief of the General Staff Sir Neville Lyttleton's preface to the third edition emphasized—that the volume was "not to be regarded as laying down inflexible rules for guidance," nor were Callwell's views an "expression of official opinion."[81] Keith Surridge, meanwhile, noted that in the Boer War "Lords Robert and Kitchener took pragmatic approaches to the guerrilla war based on their notions of what constituted 'civilised warfare.'"[82] Even Mockaitis stressed that the minimum-force concept represents a "threshold of violence applied and interpreted in different ways in different times and places."[83] The role of contingency, not tradition, found its modern echo in the 1995 British Army *Field Manual* itself, which stressed that its broadly drawn principles were to be regarded as ideas to be "applied pragmatically and with commonsense to suit the circumstance peculiar to each campaign."[84]

If contingency, pragmatism, and common sense negate prescriptive approaches and therefore invalidate the idea of a tradition of a British approach to counterinsurgency, can anything of analytical value be said to characterize the British experience of "small war"? It is possible to point to one attribute that might constitute an explanatory variable in British practice. This attribute is, however, frequently obscured by both practitioners' and scholars' overwhelming concentration on counterinsurgency as a consequence of self-contained military doctrines and practices.[85] What is frequently missing in these assessments is the context of war, which is always an extension of political will. Past experience of so-called counterinsurgency campaigns can be comprehended only with respect to British national policy and not just by tactical and operational considerations that may have obtained on the ground. When examined in historical perspective, the British "COIN legacy" reveals that what ultimately determined military success or failure in any theater was *political will*—that is to say, the political investment in the cause that determined whether the British state stayed the course. Political will provided the time for the learning/adaptation process to occur in each contingent setting. It is this variable that holds the key to understanding the British military experience in so-called small wars. Britain, in fact, possesses no discrete tradition in counterinsurgency, not least because, as chapter 1 pointed out, COIN itself is a disputable category of war. What Britain does possess, though, is an enduring tradition of committing itself long term to a series of external and occasionally internal engagements.

Furthermore, it is possible to identify this process through the history of the British war-making experience: initial mistakes lead to learning and adaptation, which invariably lead to success in terms of the attainment of designated political goals. We can see this process in numerous historical examples from at least the Boer War to Helmand. It is a pattern that is not peculiar to Britain's small wars. It can be seen even in existential wars such as World War I and World War II.[86] The facility for "staying the course" and learning from mistakes is also evident in the cases of military action in Malaya, Kenya, Cyprus, Oman, and Northern Ireland. This practice was at work in Afghanistan as well. Here, initial operational deployments to Helmand Province went badly but were slowly remedied because the political commitment ensured the space for operational improvements to occur. There is no doubt that the original British commitment to Helmand was underresourced and poorly thought through.[87] However, British forces did not buckle under pressure and retained their presence. They recovered from their early setbacks and went on to achieve dramatic improvements in operational effectiveness.[88] In other words, they learned and adapted.

What gives the armed forces the capacity to learn and adapt is political will. The level of commitment based on considerations of the centrality of vital national interests and the broader prospects of success in contingent circumstances invariably governs the extent to which harsh, coercive measures are tolerated and sanctioned. Surridge makes the acute observation in relation to the Boer War that when Lord Roberts "opted for severe measures[,] he was supported by the British government and was told 'the new departure had been welcomed.'" Surridge shows that, "under Roberts, the British punished civilians for giving help to commandos, real or imagined. Under Kitchener, civilians were swept up and kept as virtual prisoners of war. There was little scope for winning hearts and minds beyond the dubious protection of the concentration camps." Yet, he continues, "if the attitude of the British generals was harsh then that of British politicians was hardly softer: Lord Salisbury, the prime minister, opined that 'You will not conquer these people until you have starved them out.' "[89]

In the Boer War, political determination brought strategic success. "In the end," as Surridge notes, "the British got what they wanted—the end of Boer independence and the security of the British Empire."[90] It is the successful attainment of political objectives that invariably silences any moral qualms about the means employed to reach success. Again, the same considerations were at work in the suppression of rebellion in Mesopotamia in 1920. As Peter Lieb observes in his comparison of British and German responses to insurrections in Iraq and Ukraine, respectively, the British "strategy of collective punishment was never called into question" because it was "seen as a success" despite the fact that the pacification of the Arab tribes had been "more ruthless, more indiscriminate, and more destructive than the German approach in the Ukraine had been two years earlier."[91]

The capacity to change, stay the course, and gain results, therefore, has surprisingly little to do with any historically constructed tradition of proficiency in "small wars," of either a "minimum force" or "coercive" variety. Instead, it has everything do with the political calculations of higher, elected decision makers about where the national interest ultimately resides. If that calculation has concluded that the cost of staying and fighting is worthwhile, the British have often succeeded either in whole or in part in attaining their political objectives. Conversely, where the calculation has gone the other way, an entirely different set of imperatives has come into play, which brings us to the next crucial aspect of the British tradition in small wars—that of running away.

When political will has been lacking and the calculation of the national interest deemed to lie elsewhere, the political decision has invariably been made to minimize losses and quit. Hence, in addition to committing to fighting in numerous external conflicts, which gave Britain its reputed COIN tradition, there is an equally venerable British tradition of cut-and-run withdrawals. Historical examples of this tradition are also numerous. One notable instance is Palestine in the

1940s. It has often been maintained that the "British lost" Palestine to "Jewish insurgents" when, as Matthew Hughes suggests, the British realized that all "they could rely on was force, which did not work."[92] It is possibly more accurate to say that British politicians calculated that they faced an array of forces that inhibited them from applying force in any sustained manner. As David Cesarani makes clear, Prime Minister Clement Attlee and Foreign Secretary Ernest Bevin understood that given the perilous state of the British economy after World War II, they could not crack down on Jewish insurgent groups without alienating American support, on which Britain's financial stability depended. As a consequence, the "prime minister and the Foreign Secretary constantly held the army in check and forced the high commissioner, Cunningham, to appease rather than suppress the Jewish Agency."[93] In other words, it was not that force did not work; rather, force was, for reasons based on the assessment of the British national interest, never really tried.

Cesarani argues that the "government and the army" considered Palestine "to be a major strategic asset," but one rendered increasingly unstable by Jewish emigration from Europe, rising tensions between Arabs and Jews, and concerted campaigns of violence by extremist Jewish groups.[94] Ultimately, the government probably regarded Palestine as an insignificant appendage. If it really considered Palestine a "major asset," the calculation of the national interest would likely have been very different. Instead, the government assessed the necessary political investment to retain Palestine (by 1947 a United Nations–mandated territory) and crush violent Jewish subversion to be a disproportionate use of resources given broader considerations of the national interest. Britain consequently had no intention of staying there following the agreement of a United Nations plan to partition the country.[95]

A similar political calculus leading to withdrawal applied throughout the era of decolonization. The end of the Raj and the partition of India in 1947, when Britain abandoned the jewel in its imperial crown with notable rapidity to avoid involvement in burgeoning intercommunal violence, provide another telling example.[96] So too does the Aden campaign (1963–1967). Although the British initially committed their forces to stabilize the South Arabian Federation prior to full independence following the outbreak of an insurrection in 1963, their withdrawal from Aden was hastened through a combination of the effects of the Six-Day War between the Arab powers and Israel; the closure of the Suez Canal by Nasser, which removed any residual strategic value the territory might have possessed; and financial problems at home. As a result, the political reevaluation of the British position caused the Wilson government to conclude that there was little further strategic interest in staying in order to pacify the country.[97] The British withdrew from this relatively minor conflagration having lost less than seventy military personnel over the preceding four years.[98] Perhaps the most potent example of running away—or, more accurately, staying away—was Britain's decision not to involve itself on the ground in South Vietnam despite pressure from the Johnson administration in the 1960s.[99]

The pattern of cutting and running when deemed necessary is observable in more recent conflicts as well. One of the more interesting recent cases involves British participation, or lack of it, in the multinational effort to pacify Lebanon in the 1980s. Although the British have willingly participated in peacekeeping missions, particularly in support of American initiatives, in this instance the British sent only a token force of ninety troops to Beirut. This force was, somewhat unusually, dwarfed by the thousands of American, French, and even Italian peacekeepers committed.[100] After a few months, the British government unilaterally withdrew its small force. The government assumed that persisting in a rapidly deteriorating security situation was likely to prove costly.[101] It was an astute decision. In 1983, Hezbollah-backed suicide bombers attacked the U.S. Marine and French military headquarters in the city, causing the death of hundreds of troops.[102] The attack resulted in a rapid withdrawal of the rest of the multinational force on February 26, 1984.[103]

It is in light of this alternative British tradition of cutting and running that the supposed failures of British counterinsurgency in Basra should in fact be situated. Few serious analysts consider prudential withdrawals from places such as Palestine, Aden, and Beirut as evidence of the failure of British COIN. There is no suggestion that the British failure to pacify Afghanistan in the mid–nineteenth century or quit India in 1947 demonstrated abject failure in small wars or counterinsurgency. What British external and colonial military engagement since 1945 demonstrates is the contingent character of war that requires frequent political reassessment of the investment of troops, money, and material in a particular cause.[104] Thus, alongside a legacy of hard-won and hardnosed success for British forces, there is an equally well-established tradition of strategic withdrawal. Such withdrawal is not necessarily a symptom of weakness or failure. It is, as in the case of Basra, prudential political calculation. Such calculations reflect the contingency of war for which no procrustean counterinsurgency tradition can provide a framework to order Britain's "small-war" encounters. Further, if there is any wisdom contained in the British experience of contending with small wars, perhaps knowing when not to fight—in other words, when to withdraw—is as important as committing to stay over the long term.

Any survey of the history of the British experience of small wars reveals an extensive and varied legacy of external entanglements and engagements (or in the case of Northern Ireland internal entanglement) ranging from colonial intervention to colonial withdrawal, peacekeeping, and peace enforcement. The outcome of each of these encounters has reflected the degree of political commitment to the particular case. The legacy—from the Boer War through Malaya, Dhofar, Borneo, Oman, and Kenya to Kuwait, Sierra Leone, Bosnia, Kosovo, and even Helmand—discloses a remarkable degree of operational effectiveness.[105] As Dewar notes, the "most striking feature" of these late-twentieth-century campaigns has been the "degree of success achieved by the British Army in these medium and small-scale operations."[106] No doubt the British armed forces did display at times certain tactical aptitudes that accounted in part for the "degree" of some of these successes. But, more importantly, it was when the British government sought the attainment of definable political objectives that those achievements were gained.[107] As Reis has noted, the relative success of the campaigns of decolonization came about because "Britain had a more realistic definition of victory." Invariably, this definition "allowed Britain to sometimes successfully present the violence of the insurgents as the main obstacle to self-rule, and frame successful counterinsurgency as the best way to secure independence."[108] What constituted notions of "victory" for the British was the product of political calculation, not military prowess. Moreover, whenever politics deemed the price of war too high, analogous calculations were made to withdraw from overseas entanglements if it was considered that no threat to the national interest was thereby incurred.

Thus, finally, we return to the key puzzle identified at the beginning of this chapter: Why have analysts focused on the cases of Basra and Helmand to establish a flawed argument about British operational failure within a manufactured tradition of expertise in counterinsurgency? Unpacking the evolution of this long-standing "tradition" reveals that it was invented elsewhere and for a political purpose.[109] Rarely in their historical experience have the British armed forces claimed a specific counterinsurgency expertise. This tradition has invariably been ascribed to them by others. In the United States, commentators who were keen to promote practices of minimum force or rapid institutional learning greatly facilitated the reputation of British effectiveness in "small war." However, much American commentary was not intended to achieve an accurate appreciation of the British military experience but to generate insights for domestic consumption and policy. British practices, U.S. analysts claimed, offered lessons for the American armed forces. A later generation of (mainly British) scholars came to question the historical validity of a number of these presumed lessons. They maintained instead that coercion rather than hearts and minds accounted for British success.

Such analysis filters past military commitments through the anachronistic and ahistorical lens of present commitments in Iraq and Afghanistan and the mythopoeia of a British tradition of counterinsurgency. These present-minded concerns serve as premises to make arguments that demonstrate the decline of a once unimpeachable reputation. Such an anachronistic propensity reads into the past a hypothetical completion of ideas, concepts, and practices. Purporting to explain what we currently seem to have, such abridgements of understanding are, as Conal Condren explains, "characteristically projected as an available reality and this is used to redescribe surviving evidence, so pre-empting understanding."[110] This metalanguage of explanatory modeling that conflates the past for the purposes of the present possesses a certain ideological appeal. The rhetoric of failure fitted a national mood of decline for a popular audience that possessed neither the time nor the inclination to evaluate the British Army's longer-term experience of military engagement in so-called small wars. A rigorous longer-term analysis, however, shows that the examples of Helmand (in its early phases) and Basra are exceptions, even aberrations, in relation to the majority of cases of British military intervention in wars of choice over the past fifty years. In Iraq and Afghanistan, the British Army functioned as a junior partner to the United States (though a significant partner in a broader coalition of nations) in an ambitious nation-building project. As chapter 3 demonstrated, the United States, unlike Britain, has a long tradition of armed modernization. It is in the overstretch of resources from such open-ended U.S. commitments that the limitations of late-twentieth-century and early-twenty-first-century British military commitments reveal themselves. Although this overcommitment might demand greater political realism from the United Kingdom's elected leaders, it does not of itself demonstrate any inherent failure of operational skill or inability to learn and adapt on the part of the British Army.

This chapter has distinguished the various interpretations that have been conflated to sustain the myth of a decline of a presumed tradition of British expertise in counterinsurgency. From a historical perspective, however, the British military experience cannot be categorized as a failed or failing tradition. Instead, it demonstrates great variety. The history, moreover, is a contingent one and not a metanarrative arising from an array of complex challenges that confronted a European power on its ascent and descent from empire over two centuries. This historical experience demonstrates a distinctive practice of frequent military engagement that evolved from the nineteenth-century imperial mission and the Pax Britannica that the mission demanded. The experience of empire placed a premium on acting where possible to deal with problems commensurate with the empire's perception as a major actor on the global stage, which was expressed postimperially through permanent membership in the United Nations Security Council.[111]

Over time, what the British small-war tradition demonstrates is political will. Political will determines whether Britain prevailed in its so-called counterinsurgencies. Where the political establishment invested in a cause and pursued it or defended it by force if necessary, the British armed forces stayed and fought. They made mistakes, they learned, they adapted, and more often than not they were successful. Success here means that the British armed forces' actions assisted in the attainment of political goals determined by democratically elected rulers.[112] Without the political will, a decision was often made either to withdraw the military quickly or not to contest the political space at all. Hence, running parallel to a record of prevailing in the small wars Britain chose to fight is an equally well-established tradition of cutting and running in wars where it did not.

Taking into account the multifaceted nature of the British military experience and its political ramifications, this chapter has argued that it is difficult to sustain a narrative of the implosion of a "world-beating" institution. Twentieth-century history demonstrates technical failures of leadership, doctrine, and equipment, especially when the political will to stay the course was lacking, such as the decision to withdraw from the Indian subcontinent in 1947. Nevertheless, it is possible only to claim that a venerable tradition has fallen into decay where there is evidence that the military failed to deliver despite strong political backing. With this understanding in mind, it is certainly possible to document disappointments arising from faltering political will or poor leadership (for instance, the 1956 Suez debacle, the failure to stabilize the South Arabian Federation, and the loss of control of Basra between 2006 and 2008), but it is equally difficult to pinpoint any generic failure when British forces stood and fought when they received full political support. In fact, when the "Where did it all go wrong?" argument is subject to scrutiny, we find that the narrative of a once "world-class" military disintegrating in overstretch derives from a single and, of itself, somewhat questionable case— Basra.

What emerges in fact is a variegated picture of Britain's presumed expertise in combating insurgency. It is variegated because commentators such as Ledwidge are correct, to a degree, in arguing that the narrative of a British COIN "inheritance" in part reflects the stories that the army has told about itself,[113] at various points accepting—or, more accurately, often half-accepting and partially endorsing—the view that it did indeed possess a tradition of counterinsurgency excellence. However, as this chapter has also shown, the British Army internalized an understanding of proficiency in counterinsurgency only after the end of the Cold War. For the most part, the "story" is as much about what others outside the British Army have ascribed to it. This is the case with the minimum-force philosophy: constantly repeated by scholars, commentators, and sometimes politicians, the army, or sections of it, came to believe that it actually possessed a self-evident tradition of counterinsurgency. But for soldiers and scholars alike, trying to separate that "tradition" from the contingent practices arising from the unique circumstances of every conflict was always going to prove elusive. It is too easy for analysts to read back into the past a dialectical structure that offers historical completion whenever tactical similarities present themselves. As John Bew observes in his evaluation of the British Army's experience in Northern Ireland, it is not that techniques and tactics are insignificant, but the fact that they occur and unfold in deeply dependent, unpredictable, ways. Bew tellingly concludes, "To call this COIN, however, is to look back at a complex history and pluck a method from the madness."[114]

6

The Puzzle of Counterinsurgency and Escalation

War, in its essence, is simple. It is political communication, bending an adversary to your will through violence, not an act of destruction for its own sake.[1] John Stone puts it well when he states: "Stripped down to its chassis, so to speak, almost any war emerges as an exercise in coercion. The application of force is combined with a conditional intention to stop once a desired set of political objectives is achieved."[2] The question is, How is this conditional intention to continue or cease hostilities communicated? Again, the answer is simple: through escalation or de-escalation.

The notion of escalation is also straightforward. It is, as Herman Kahn explained in 1965, "an increase in the level of conflict."[3] The point of escalation is that it is undertaken for a conscious, politically coercive purpose and not for something that happens through an involuntarily momentum of events. For Kahn, escalation is "a competition in risk taking or at least resolve."[4] It conveys intent to prosecute war until political objectives are met. But it also implies restraint—namely, the "conditional intention to stop" once those objectives are achieved. As a consequence, the simple essence of war becomes a complex calculation of escalations as its political objectives are redefined in response to events. As Stone suggests, "Even when military action is formally conducted with a view to rendering an enemy defenceless, it ceases before that state of affairs is completely achieved. Under these circumstances, the loser capitulates not because he is deprived of all means of resistance, but because the costs associated with further resistance are unlikely to produce any discernible benefits. At this stage, too, the winner stands to gain very little in relation to the costs associated with continuing hostilities."[5]

The notion of escalation as described by Stone presents an interesting addition to understandings of counterinsurgency. Counterinsurgency theorists maintain that insurgency/counterinsurgency differs from orthodox force-on-force encounters. If, following this argument, insurgency/counterinsurgency exists as a distinctive form of war, we would expect it to have its own discernible escalation dynamics. As the chapters in this volume have repeatedly shown, many COIN commentators contend that insurgent conflicts stand apart from the understandings of war enunciated by Carl von Clausewitz, who argues that war is a rational, instrumental, goal-orientated enterprise. An investigation into escalation therefore compels us to ask how the process of violent political communication is actually conducted in wars that are characterized as insurgencies/counterinsurgencies. In this manner, such an investigation can clarify a number of recurring themes in this study by considering whether insurgent-based conflict can be said to constitute something that differentiates itself from "conventional" or "regular" war. Moreover, it does so by transcending the assumption, common to most of the literature, that insurgency/counterinsurgency is a self-evident form of action based on a set of distinguishing tactics and techniques.

Stating and Restating the Question

The notion of escalation, then, can offer a practical and theoretical key to unlock the course and eventual resolution of all violent insurgent and counterinsurgent clashes. Proceeding on the premise that all war is a political dialogue, our question should therefore be, Is anything unique in insurgent/counterinsurgent clashes? To answer this question, we turn once more to the principles of strategic theory to conceptualize how the escalation process in conditions of insurgency and counterinsurgency might operate and, via examples and cases, to verify these broad observations. In contrast to what COIN commentary maintains, this theory will in fact suggest that an understanding of the features of escalation in insurgent/counterinsurgent warfare can be properly understood only within a Clausewitzian framework.

In the first instance, such an analysis requires us to revisit puzzles and questions identified in the first chapter, beginning with: Can the notion of insurgency itself be said to hold certain distinguishing characteristics in an analytical separation between insurgency and non-insurgency understandings of war? Theoretically, one way to think about a distinctive practice is to propose that insurgency denotes a mode of political communication on the part of one or more of the key protagonists that is not based on the physical denial of space and the attrition of resources through combat in order to wear down the enemy. Instead, practices in insurgent war might be understood as inflicting costs as a means of exerting influence—namely, the art of coercive persuasion, premised not on the actual destructiveness of the violent act, but on the latent threat of additional violence.[6] In other words, such a method of political communication uses violence to indicate to an adversary that the costs of not acquiescing to an opponent's political demands will outweigh the costs of concession.[7] In that manner, a process of political bargaining characterizes strategies that are terroristic in nature or practiced by rebellious nonstate political actors.[8]

These characterizations may represent a commonsense approach to the conception of the process of escalation in insurgencies and thus delineate a mode of political communication typical of this kind of war. However, given that all war—even the most physically destructive of conflicts—can be seen as political communication, it is necessary to address further first-order questions about the nature of war and escalation before evaluating whether there is anything meaningful to be said about insurgency/counterinsurgency tactics.

Because these first principles underpin the bulk of the subsequent analysis in this chapter, it will be helpful here to remind readers of the crucial premises outlined at the beginning of this book. The first essential premise is that armed force possesses an instrumental relationship with politics. In Clausewitz's classic formulation, war is an act of policy carried on with other means.[9] In its most elemental form, war is, to use Christopher Bassford's phrase, a "clash of independent wills,"[10] each seeking to prevail over the other. Each combatant's will, moreover, is determined by the combatant's social nature and the intensity and skill of effort to fulfill its political goals through violent means. These factors in turn are governed by the variables of passion, chance, and reason. For this reason, wars will always vary in "the nature of their motives" according to the unique social conditions that gave rise to them.[11] Each instance of war is thereby exclusive to its time and place, which in turn will affect its direction and duration. As Clausewitz observes, war always progresses toward its conclusion at "varying speed."[12] In other words, no two wars are ever the same and do not follow any predictable pattern.

If all war is unique, then can there in fact be any such notion as an insurgent-based war distinguishable from all other wars? According to Clausewitz, the particularity of war as just outlined is also subject to a universal dynamic, a lasting essence—to achieve goals of policy through violence. Can one, then, identify a special lasting essence of insurgent-based conflict? This question returns us to the fault line in much writing about war and strategy, initially traversed in chapter 1, which assumes, often erroneously, that in the practice of war separations can be made between the "conventional" and the "unconventional," the "regular" and the "irregular."

The case for an analytical separation of insurgent conflicts can be stated thus: each side's relative power will influence how the combatant chooses to conduct itself. For example, to maximize its advantage at any given time, a combatant may decide to avoid or delay open battle and instead prosecute operations through less-direct confrontation, using guerrilla or hit-and-run tactics or sabotage. It is this attempt to evade direct battle that forms, albeit in often unstated ways, the belief that an analytical distinction can be made between conflicts in which outright force-on-force clashes take place on battlefronts and conflicts that do not. The former are often characterized as conventional war, whereas the latter are seen as unconventional—or irregular—war. Thus, *irregular warfare* becomes a synonym for other terms that are felt to denote warfare without battles and battlefronts— namely, *insurgencies*, although, as the first chapter outlined, the lexicon of insurgency is replete with many substitutes signifying the same sort of practice: *low-intensity war*, *small war*, and *guerrilla war*, to mention only a few. A number of suppositions usually follow this assumption about the nature of particular combatants and the geopolitical circumstances in which they choose to fight. For example, much writing about irregular warfare presumes that it represents a weaker side confronting a more powerful adversary, the weaker side resorting to the irregular methods of hit-and-run tactics in order to prosecute its campaign.[13] Other assumptions follow: for example, that insurgent war signifies the involvement of nonstate groups fighting against the state and therefore is usually a characteristic of intrastate war.[14]

As the first chapter pointed out, few of these assumptions are conceptually robust. The belief that irregular war is about a weaker power confronting a superior opponent fails when one considers that in no war is there exact parity between protagonists. There exists a universal power differential where one side will always be in a theoretically weaker position than the other. Nor is it the case that irregular war connotes the presence of nonstate groups fighting the authority of an existing state.[15] Irregular tactics, if one can call them such, involving hit-and-run guerrilla actions and sabotage are a form of fighting that can be employed by any belligerent in any type of war, as the numerous tales of daring raids behind enemy lines conducted by the principal interstate combatants in major theaters of conflict, such as World War II, readily attest.[16] Neither is it possible to associate irregular/insurgent tactics with conditions of civil war. Historical examples from the English Civil War in the seventeenth century, the American Civil War in the nineteenth century, and the Chinese Civil War in the twentieth century refute any such association given that the majority of combat operations in these intrastate conflicts involved force-on-force concentrations in major battles.

If few of these characterizations of what might constitute irregular/insurgent war are intellectually credible, might it be the case that insurgencies denote a form of conflict—civil war, intrastate war— that is less prevalent than other wars and can therefore be deemed to constitute a deviation from regular, normal war? This is certainly the implication, where the terms *regular* and *conventional* denote a standard pattern or order. When applied to war, the notions of "regular" and "conventional" are taken simply to mean warfare between states. But is this really the case? Chapter 1 suggested that empirical evidence points in the other direction, statistical assessments indicating that less than one-fifth of all conflicts since the end of World War II can conceivably be classified as interstate.[17] The vast majority of wars take place within states. It is also clear that so-called irregular/insurgent wars constitute the predominant form of warfare in both the post- and pre–World War II eras[18] and as a matter of routine involve the profusion of substate political and military actors.[19] Thus, unconventional warfare represents the convention; irregular war is the regularity.[20]

Is There Anything Irregular About Insurgent Wars?

What this somewhat paradoxical situation reveals is that distinctions between forms of war are inherently arbitrary classifications. Designations, or labels, in fact reflect less the statistical predominance of certain types of conflict than political concerns that dominated Western military planning from World War II to the postwar era of Cold War confrontation. The legacy of twentieth-century total war that culminated in a titanic fight to the death between mutually exclusive ideological systems in World War II tended to fix debate in much orthodox strategic thought, implying that warfare centered around state actors, involved open battles, and could ultimately jeopardize national survival. Such wars were labeled "conventional" not because they were the convention, but because they were perceived to be more important than other "low-level," "unconventional," "irregular" wars.[21] The study and understanding of wars that might be characterized as insurgencies were consequently relegated to a low position in the pecking order of Western nations' military priorities.

This brings us to the key question: What is irregular about irregular war? The accurate response is: nothing. War is war. Whether it is described as "irregular war," "unconventional war," "small war," "low-intensity war," "insurgent," or "counterinsurgent," it follows the universal dynamic enunciated by Clausewitz: to achieve goals of policy through violence.[22] Theoretically and logically, irregular war does not exist.[23] A theatrical statement perhaps, but it compels us to address the first-order question of whether the term *irregular war* has any innate meaning: we cannot simply assume that irregular/insurgent war exists as a discrete form of war that diverges from some sort of norm. To do so is to commit the logical fallacy of petitio principii—assuming the principle you have to prove.

As suggested, when one probes into terms such as *irregular war*, they usually reveal themselves as euphemisms for unspoken denotations that imply the presence of nonstate actors involved in intrastate insurgent challenges. It has further been suggested that the manner in which the term *irregular war* has been employed in much strategic writing is not so much because it designates "irregular" phenomena, but because certain kinds of conflicts are deemed to be of lesser importance.[24] The term thus intimates a value judgment seeking to ascribe relative significance to instances of war. Hence, we observe that much strategic analysis is less to do with investigating war as a whole and more to do focusing on particular kinds of confrontation seen as more threatening to major global players. The result, as noted in chapters 4 and 5, is that, for most Western powers, insurgencies are wars that occur somewhere else and not inside their domestic jurisdictions. War involving clashes between well-armed and organized states is considered more threatening and therefore more important, hence the convention that other wars are of less significance. *Irregular war* is thus a dismissive label, or at least it functioned as such during the years of the Cold War, the implication being that "small," "minor," "less important" conflicts need not be studied with the same degree of rigor.[25] The danger, then, is that sloppy theorizing by aficionados of insurgency/counterinsurgency results in the attempt to discern the "lessons" of "irregular" war. These lessons lurk in spurious theorization, lying in wait to be "rediscovered" as timeless verities.

Is there anything of substance to be said about the notion of irregular/insurgent war? Can it be endowed with any meaningful suppositions conferring analytical utility as a category of war that can be isolated and dissected? It is possible to suggest that in its most basic inference the phrase *irregular war* is used to denote war between grossly unequal combatants. The term *asymmetric war* is also used—yet another ambiguous label because no confrontation ever takes place between exactly matched protagonists. Nevertheless, despite conceptual difficulties, it is perhaps possible to force a rough distinction between combatants where the power differential is substantial. Exactly how this differential might be quantified is beyond the scope of this volume, but the assumption that irregular war connotes a large adversarial power differential returns us to the stereotypical image of a presumably powerful state contending with an armed challenge from a materially inferior nonstate actor: an insurgent. From this assumption, we might begin to determine how the contours of escalation in such conditions might be conceived.

Escalation and Insurgency

It is not possible to talk about war and escalation of any kind without turning once again to Clausewitz's conceptual rigor and his baseline understanding of their essential features.[26] Assuming the rough definition that insurgent war denotes a conflict where there is a substantially disproportionate asymmetry in material means, is it now possible to say something novel or interesting about the escalation process? In his classic strategic formulations, Clausewitz argues that "if the enemy is to be coerced you must place him in a situation that is even more unpleasant than the sacrifice you call on him to make. The hardships of that situation must not of course be merely transient—at least not in appearance."[27] Thomas Schelling echoes this point in his writings about nuclear deterrence, describing conflicts characterized by what he called "coercive bargaining," where the "ability of one participant to gain his ends is dependent to an important degree on the choices or decisions that the other participant will make."[28]

This insight underlines the reactive environment of war. Clausewitz explains: "War is not the action of a living force upon a lifeless mass but always a collision of two living forces."[29] In analytical terms, this reactivity demands that we not only focus on what may seem logical, consistent, and efficacious from one point of view but take into account the fact that all sides have agency in war and that, as Schelling suggests, the decision-making process in war is an inherently interdependent dynamic.

Clausewitz again gives us the theoretical premise on which to develop an understanding of the philosophical essence of the decision-making process in war, which involves choices to escalate or de-escalate. "War is an act of force," he maintains, "and there is no logical limit to the application of that force. Each side, therefore, compels its opponent to follow suit; a reciprocal action is started which must lead, in theory, to extremes."[30] Clausewitz illustrates this inherent escalation dynamic by employing the analogy of two wrestlers locked in a mutual grip: as one wrestler exerts more pressure to overthrow his opponent, he compels the other to match or exceed that force, leading to a reciprocal action that sees each wrestler—or combatant—reaching a point of maximum effort.[31]

War theoretically contains an irresistible tendency to escalate toward a notional extreme. One side's ability to outescalate the other or, via Schelling's understanding of coercive bargaining, to convince the other side of one's will to escalate beyond the other's willingness or capabilities is necessary to bring war to an end. Having outlined this dynamic of escalation toward a point of utmost exertion, Clausewitz goes on to explain why of course in reality this never happens. All wars, in practice, are limited by any number of variables both tangible and intangible—time, geography, resources, organizational ability, military skill (or lack of it). However, Clausewitz reduces the basic ideas that act as a barrier to escalation to two main principles.

The first is the notion of "friction": constraints that are forever present, physical and logistical impediments that always prevent the application of maximum effort and resources at any one time.[32] For example, it may take time to mobilize forces, to transport them to where they are needed. Armed forces may suffer the slings and arrows of misfortune: they will get lost, their personnel will fall ill from disease, the enemy will assault suddenly when least expected. Indeed, all the elements of chance and luck will be at play. Second, politics constrains escalation. The goals that a social actor sets for itself and the degree of effort it is prepared to make will be subject to a means–ends calculation: the attempt to ensure that war is proportionate to the objectives sought.[33] War is thereby kept within the domains of rationality. Thus, a political actor is unlikely to escalate its activities in war toward the maximum if the cause does not necessarily threaten vital national interests—a minor territorial dispute, for example. But it may well commit everything to the fight if its very survival is threatened.

Apart from Clausewitz, most other theoretical discussions of escalation in war arose from the Cold War era, when the writings of analysts such as Kahn and Schelling predominated with an emphasis on controlling intensification of conflict as a means of stopping a slide toward all-out nuclear confrontation between the superpowers. Otherwise, as analysts such as Isabelle Duyvesteyn have noted, understandings of escalation in war below superpower conflict, especially in the realms of civil war, remain remarkably underdeveloped.[34] Cold War theorists, however, did provide a useful postulation that future superpower conflict would progress through a series of discernible boundaries—thresholds. From the outbreak of hostilities, conflict would systematically increase in intensity through an ever-expanding range of targets, geographical locations, and categories of weapons. Kahn notably visualized the spiralling conflict from peace to outright intercontinental ballistic nuclear strikes on the homelands of the United States and the Soviet Union as an escalation ladder.[35]

The point about Kahn's ladder of escalation is that it stipulated individual steps he assumed each superpower would tacitly recognize. These steps could function as putative, mutually observed limitations. As war progressed up the escalation ladder, each superpower was understood to be ever more reluctant for fear of further escalatory consequences. In this way, thresholds were perceived as the basis for implicit cooperation to restrain superpower confrontation, preventing a slide toward nuclear catastrophe.[36] Theorists such as Schelling meanwhile hypothesized that these implicit boundaries were susceptible to manipulation for political advantage. An indicated willingness to up the ante by crossing one of these targets, weapons, or geographical boundaries could demonstrate resolve. In other words, manipulating fear of thresholds would signal the intention to impose future costs on an adversary and the escalator's readiness to assume risk, with the inducement that those costs, both real and implied, will be withdrawn once an adversary has conceded.

A further elaboration of escalation thresholds is now required to understand how political communication might be said to operate in insurgent conflicts. What is a threshold? It is a prominent or salient boundary: a line in the sand. For Richard Smoke, an act of escalation is one "that crosses a saliency which defines the current limits of a war, and that occurs in a context where the actor cannot know the full consequences of his action, including particularly how his action and the opponent's potential reaction(s) may interact to generate a situation likely to induce new actions that will cross more saliences."[37] This observation introduces us to two important elements of escalation: uncertainty and risk. War is a reciprocal process of potential escalation over which you have no control. Cross a saliency, and you do not know where it all may end up.

In summary, according to Clausewitzian understandings, the restrictions on escalation are: (1) you cannot commit all of your resources, and (2) you choose not to commit all your resources. Dissecting the reasons why a political actor may or may not apply its maximum effort and resources in war is a complex amalgam of contingent factors that are impossible to systematize in any coherent manner but in one sense are likely to boil down to the unwillingness to cross certain saliences for fear of the unknown—that is, uncertain consequences on the part of the opponent and a reluctance to accept unnecessary costs or avoidable threats. Given this understanding, is it possible to posit any generalizations about the decision-making factors likely to influence whether a political actor chooses to escalate or not in any conflict involving grossly unequal combatants (our definition of irregular war)? To do this we need to consider the theoretical position confronting the decision processes of the manifestly weaker (insurgent) side and the manifestly stronger (counterinsurgent) side in turn. Once the theory has been enunciated, the assessment will illustrate the theory through a set of practical case examples drawn from the experiences of insurgent challenges in Argentina and in Northern Ireland.

Insurgent Escalation

It is possible to propose that the decision making of the weaker side, represented by an insurgent actor, in any so-called irregular war is principally going to be affected in its ability to escalate by its material inferiority. Not only is the insurgent actor likely to be outnumbered and outmatched in numerical terms, but it will also be inhibited from applying all of its potential armed capacity because it wishes to prevent a materially stronger adversary—the counterinsurgent—from bringing its full weight to bear. In other words, a central component of any combatant strategy might be to wage its campaign to avoid provoking the stronger side into escalating its action and possibly annihilating the weaker side.

Physical anxiety will in theory, therefore, lead a materially inferior opponent to try to observe constraints on its violence. How then can such an adversary wage war with any prospect of attaining its political aims? The answer is likely to reside in "coercive bargaining," an attempt to manipulate the enemy's cost–benefit calculus. Thus, the materially inferior combatant might use an armed campaign not with the primary intention of causing physical damage but of creating a more intangible effect through which its materially superior opponent can be induced to act in a manner producing favorable political outcomes for the weaker side. In effect, the inferior adversary may attempt to create a disproportionate psychological impact in order to arouse a state of widespread fear (a strategy of terrorism) or else wear away at the superior side's will to carry on (psychological attrition). Alternatively, it might seek to gnaw at the other side's morale and resources through a prolonged campaign of small-scale attacks in the hope that this will eventually erode the opponent's superior power to a point where a position of material equality is reached. This is the classic Maoist formula for guerrilla strategy practiced by Communist forces in the Chinese Civil War in the 1930s and 1940s and subsequently adopted by many insurgent forces from Nepal to Peru.

Is it possible, however, to induce moral capitulation or to foster a belief that the conflict is not worth the cost of carrying on or to reach a position of power equilibrium with a more powerful adversary without stimulating the other side to escalate its military campaign to a point where the weaker protagonist's survival is jeopardized? Although inevitably complex and speculative, any answer to this question must be premised upon the weaker side's appreciation of the contingent political environment in which it functions. In particular, the insurgent is required to possess a comprehension of the ways in which a particular target group, actor, or audience might respond to a campaign of violence. The psychological effects of small-scale attacks to produce a climate of moral collapse or a feeling of war weariness might, for example, diminish over time, and repeated attacks on similar targets will increase predictability, enabling better protection. What is to be done?

The traditional conception of escalation is to commit more resources to combat: more troops, more material, bigger formations, ever more destructive techniques. For the weaker side to apply sufficient coercive pressure, there must theoretically be more than one way to escalate, returning us to the relevance of ideas of saliency as escalation thresholds. As we have suggested, the likely intention of strategies adopted by materially inferior combatants is to exploit the wider psychological effects of violence rather than try to degrade the enemy's physical resources. This might entail a willingness, therefore, to cross a particular salient psychological boundary. A combatant might attempt to endanger the fabric of a society that attaches value to being prosperous and peaceful—for example, through a campaign of violent disturbance—but always with the prospect of diminishing returns, which increases the pressure for escalation.[38]

Widening the franchise of violence to reestablish unpredictability of threat and regenerate the psychologically disproportionate effect of a military campaign is a next step. The inferior combatant may, for instance, choose to cross a salient threshold by expanding attacks beyond the once predictable. What does this mean in practice? It entails moving the campaign toward greater levels of indiscrimination and may include people who are seen to be innocent or unconnected with any quarrel.[39] Although such an escalation may be enough to maintain the coercive impact on an opponent, it is a path that contains inherent risks, especially if the weaker side is attempting to win popular sympathy. In other words, a materially weaker actor in conditions of irregular war may seek to escalate not by committing more resources or by seeking greater physical destructiveness (through new weaponry and technological innovation), but by transcending ethical barriers.[40]

What we can deduce, then, is that widening the franchise of violence by introducing greater levels of indiscrimination is a method of escalation in irregular war. Furthermore, such an impulse conforms to the Clausewitzian notion that a reciprocal action in war will propel the combatant to intensify the level of violence, to maximize military pressure, in an attempt to coerce an opponent to accede to its will.

In summary, we have so far discussed the impetus to escalate on the part of the weaker side in terms of an attempt to sustain the coercive effect of violence, which might be eroded over time, though, as violent acts become internalized by a target population and accepted as part of the everyday risks. Once a strategic actor discerns that its military campaign is losing its capacity to influence an enemy, the potential for escalation presents itself. Such an escalation is then seen to occur as reduced discrimination regarding targets and a transcending of ethical boundaries carry a further risk of alienation for the insurgent.

Another rationale for the materially inferior side to seek escalation is that an enemy may be deemed vulnerable and that a further raising of the intensity of violence might convince that enemy once and for all to concede to its opponent's demands. Perhaps the stronger side has already made concessions, suggesting a crumbling of resolve in the face of the inferior side's attacks. Alternatively, the weaker side might perceive its stronger opponent as responding incompetently or repressively.[41] This could be a sign that the enemy is losing control of events, which the insurgent interprets as an opportunity to test its resolve with another, final push.

The common theme throughout, however, is the attempt by the weaker combatant to either forestall the more powerful side from escalating altogether or to ensure that any escalation that does occur is sufficiently inept or ineffective that it undermines the powerful side's own authority rather than dealing a blow to its opponent. Anxiety about endangering its own legitimacy, (for example, by being seen to overreact) additionally complicates the more powerful actor's response. Democratic systems of governance often face such dilemmas in relation to domestic violence—whether, for instance, they should implement tough security measures or introduce more restrictive legislation that might curb civil liberties.[42]

Counterinsurgent Escalation

The escalation dilemmas that the weaker side in irregular war hopes to impose on the stronger thus introduce us to the stronger party's decision-making processes, assuming it takes on the role of counterinsurgent in attempting to restore stability, order, and authority. We should also hold in mind that governments relying on a democratic consensus are constrained by public opinion in terms of proportionality and manageability. The main brake on escalation in irregular war on the part of the physically more powerful side thus rests on the second Clausewitzian limitation on the development of war toward a theoretical extreme, which is simply that the stronger side chooses not to use all of its might to crush an opponent.[43]

Although there is never going to be a universal template for understanding why political actors choose not to bring their full power to bear upon any enemy, we can use historical illustrations to demonstrate contingent understandings around the stronger side's escalation decisions. Let us take two instructive case studies. First, in the case of Argentina, which was subject to violent instability, as indeed were many other Latin American states in the 1970s, we can ask, Why did the Argentine military government apply the full panoply of state power in the so-called Dirty War between 1976 and 1982, effectively declaring war against one section of its population and involving massive and systematic repression in order to destroy what it perceived to be a subversive threat? Conversely, why did the British government, in its attempts to combat the threat of Irish Republican violence from the early 1970s through to the 1990s, take a different approach, sometimes even retreating from harsh measures that might be construed as "escalations"? Any understanding of these two very different cases demands both a rigorous comprehension of the historical antecedents and an appreciation, if only basic, of the worldviews of both the Argentinean and British governments at the time.

In the Argentine case, the military dictatorship that ruled the country between 1976 and 1982 conceived the violent subversion carried out by left-wing groups such as the Montoneros and Ejèrcito Revolucionario del Pueblo in terms of a Manichean struggle between the forces of Christian civilization and the forces of barbarous Marxism. This profundity is in line with the Clausewitzian stipulation that the intensity of war will vary with the passions with which the combatants fight for their respective cause. In practical terms, the regime determined the threat posed by leftist guerrilla groups to be a "social disease" that needed to be eradicated.[44] In its view, these groups were alien to the Argentine nation, prompting a senior army commander, General Roberto Viola, to declare: "Argentine citizens are not victims of the repression. The repression is against a minority that we do not consider Argentine."[45] Against this ideological backdrop, the authorities could utilize any escalatory measures they wanted, in this case state power, to obliterate all forms of dissent, including the imposition of media controls, the curtailment of civil liberties, and rule by law as opposed to the rule of law.[46] It was a process that was to lead to widespread surveillance, the secret detention of suspects, secret prisons, the systematic use of physical torture as a means of both extracting information and inflicting terror throughout society, mass executions, and the secret disposal of victims.[47]

What we can observe in the case of the Argentine government's reaction to the crisis of the 1970s is that the escalation dynamic in irregular war does under certain conditions have a propensity to widen the franchise of violence. In this case, the definition of subversion was systematically extended to embrace an ever-larger section of the population—not simply insurgent activists but also their supporters and perceived supporters. As a consequence, the regime's persecution included, in Patricia Marchak's words, "students, left-leaning intellectuals and artists, trade union leaders, journalists, liberal lawyers, and various others deemed to be enemies of the state."[48] The Argentine general Ibérico Saint-Jean explained: "First we kill all the subversives; then we will kill their collaborators; then . . . their sympathizers; then . . . those who remain indifferent; and finally we will kill the timid."[49]

Continuous redefinition of the target group thus represents a form of escalation toward the extreme in irregular war as it functions as an enabling device by which a political authority—the counterinsurgent and in this case the Argentine armed forces—can legitimize the elimination of all threats it defines as subversive.[50] In Argentina, broad categorizations of threat meant that the military government could entrap more or less any group or person it wished and justify any methods of repression, applying, in the words of the leader of the military regime, General Jorge Videla, the government's "inalienable right to exercise its legitimate defence."[51]

The Argentine military authorities were brutally effective in eliminating the perceived threat by left-wing groups. Irrespective of the damage caused to the fabric of Argentine society by the actions of the armed forces, there is no question that victory went to the stronger side, which followed an escalatory path that destroyed its opponents. Moreover, the Argentine example is merely one historical illustration among many of this approach's potency. The crucial factor here is the preparedness to cross implicit ethical barriers to prescribe discriminate targeting, a strategy used across Latin America in the same period and discernible in many other recent spheres of insurgent-based war—for example, the Algerian civil war against Islamist forces in the 1990s and the Sri Lankan regime's actions against Tamil separatists in the late 2000s.[52]

Why, therefore, do other actors *not* apply this same method? The British government, for all its initial policy mistakes in Northern Ireland, never went down the road of an Argentine-style dirty war. British policy makers chose not to crush the IRA through brute force, even though they had the theoretical capability to do so. In the words of one Irish Republican supporter, the IRA could "of course be beaten. If the British Army put the boot in they could be flattened. But will they do it?"[53]

The IRA itself in the early 1970s felt that British reluctance to "flatten" their opponents was a sign of weakness and lack of resolve that was itself to encourage the IRA down the road of escalation in mid-1972. In this case, however, critical values, resting on political calculations about how best to calm the Northern Ireland crisis without provoking more violence, underpinned the official approach to conflict. The authorities had already tried a form of escalation in August 1971 with the introduction of internment without trial, drawn—it may be noted—from Britain's supposedly classical counterinsurgency experience, but this approach had proved disastrous and merely stoked the resentment felt by Northern Ireland's Catholic nationalist population and swelled the ranks of the IRA. Realizing that such moves were in fact counterproductive, the British government repeatedly retreated from measures that were felt to alienate Northern Ireland's nationalists and prevent them from being drawn into an internal power-sharing accommodation, which the British felt, provided the best hope for ending the violence.[54]

Political calculations aside, the wider value system of the British polity also explain these restraints. Steeped in the state's liberal traditions, this system broadly adhered to the notion that the rule of law, not rule by law, should prevail. This outlook sustained a belief that any challenge to established authority should be, insofar as possible, prosecuted within the existing criminal justice system.[55] The British state's liberal-democratic outlook did not preclude the enactment of measures that might be construed as escalatory, such as the introduction of the Anti-Terrorism Act of 1974, which increased pressure on Northern Ireland's paramilitary groupings and restricted their room for operational and political maneuver. However, the emphasis on conduct within the law meant that those escalation measures that did occur were invariably employed primarily in reaction to a perceived increasing of the military pressure by the IRA (rather than proactively introduced to crush the threat) and applied only insofar as the measures would be able to recontain the conflict at what became known as "an acceptable level of violence."[56] The perception that certain degrees of violence should be tolerated within a society is interesting in its own right, underscoring as it does a liberal perception that the attempt to eradicate all forms of antistate activity may in certain circumstances simply not be worth the cost, in either material or political terms. The notion of reducing violence arising from the Northern Ireland conflict to a level that was "acceptable" was openly articulated by the British Home Secretary Reginald Maudling in December 1971 and has been widely interpreted as framing the overarching security objective in which British governments sought to deal with the Troubles thereafter.[57]

Such a political and judicial framework thus constrained the impulse to escalate toward the theoretical extreme and was in itself an expression of commitment to a set of ideological values. In other words, a governing value system acted as a brake on escalation by ensuring that the institution of measures to deal with the violence, be they of a legal or an operational nature, were seen as commensurate with the threat. Such an approach tends to emphasize that the law be applied fairly, that basic civil rights be preserved, that due process be observed, and that humanitarian treatment is extended to those detained under the law. The operation of these values is likely, therefore, to limit any escalation toward a dirty-war solution because arbitrary detentions, the use of torture, ill treatment of those in custody, and the maintenance of the right to a fair trial and appeal are prohibited.

Crucially, such a value system also implies that those who participate on the manifestly stronger side in any conflict are themselves subject to the rule of law, bound by its procedures and restraints, and liable to be punished under law for any transgressions that may overstep the boundaries of legality and proportionality.[58]

Underlying a value system of this nature is the assumption that state authority gains its legitimacy from upholding basic standards of moral and humanitarian behavior. Adherence to such standards differentiates the state from those who seek to challenge its authority by methods that violate these standards, notably through violence.[59] Should the state itself escalate toward actions that endanger these standards, then a crucial moral difference between established authority and the weaker challenger may be broken down, leading to the authority's loss of legitimacy and the right to rule. Speaking in the context of a counterterrorist campaign, Paul Wilkinson notes that the "primary objective" of any strategy "must be the protection and maintenance of a liberal democracy. It cannot be sufficiently stressed that this aim overrides in importance even the objective of eliminating terrorism and political violence."[60] With respect to British government policy in Northern Ireland, it is this understanding that facilitated the reversal of escalatory methods deemed by the courts to be unlawful or disproportionate, such as hard-interrogation techniques or the conviction of paramilitary suspects on the uncorroborated testimony of informers.[61]

Seeking Political Effects Through Escalation

The broader point of this analysis thus far is that value systems are likely to influence how a political actor conducts itself in any confrontation between manifestly unequal combatants. This includes the ideological precepts motivating the actor toward certain goals and conscious decision-making processes about how to utilize the means at its disposal to maximize its interests in given circumstances. Little of this process is predictable, and employing social scientific methodology is unlikely to yield much in the way of meaningful insight. Instead, serious engagement with social and historical forces as well as a keen understanding of motivation through a rigorous, qualitative, case study–based, historical mode of inquiry constitute best practice in plotting the course of the escalatory dynamic in any so-called irregular war.

A political actor involved in an insurgent conflict will thus take decisions about how and when to escalate a conflict based on a set of intangible calculations that reflect the quality of the actor's analysis within the fluid, mutually reactive environment of war. Evidently, a sense of liberal and humanitarian conduct constrains a theoretically more powerful actor, restricting its capacity to escalate. Such an actor, usually a state, endeavors to keep any response proportionate and tries to ensure that any actions and escalations do not compromise important political values or alienate constituencies that might be necessary to secure a long-term resolution.

At the same time, if the weaker adversary is to stand any chance of attaining some, let alone all, of its goals, it has to demonstrate political dexterity. In particular, it has to assess the impact of any escalation on its adversary to gauge whether it will succeed in maintaining coercive pressure without provoking an act of counterescalation that may impede its progress. A number of twentieth-century historical illustrations suggest that instances of nonstate groups challenging the superior power of the state often demonstrate a poor grasp of this point and are prone to overhasty acts of escalation. Such groups invariably take an initial lack of action by the state, a stumbling response or a willingness to compromise, as an indication of inward weakness and therefore as a signal to escalate a campaign of violence, heedless of the consequences. At its extreme, as in the case of Argentina, this escalation can lead to an authoritarian solution, engendering an escalatory response that, in Walter Laqueur's words, ends up meeting "indiscriminate murder with indiscriminate repression."[62]

Just as pertinently, even liberal-democratic societies are liable to take tough measures and escalate conflict if provoked beyond a certain point of tolerance, returning us to conceptions of the salient ethical boundary. On close examination, we may discern that cases such as Argentina and Northern Ireland reveal differences in degree rather than in kind. Although British conduct in Northern Ireland did not escalate through indiscriminate repression as in Argentina, it did countenance orthodox escalation solutions, including discriminate legal, policing, and intelligence measures along with the application of precision force in a new context.

In July 1972, the IRA consciously chose to escalate its campaign. The invitation to an IRA delegation to participate in talks with government had lulled the organization into a belief that violence was weakening British resolve, and, mistaking this invitation as a sign that the IRA was close to outright victory, the IRA leadership decided to "impose a sudden and severe load on the British and Unionist system."[63] In a coordinated multiple bombing, the IRA killed nine people in the center of Belfast on July 21, 1972. The attack, known as Bloody Friday, merely provoked the British government in its own act of escalation, Operation Motorman, on July 31, 1972. This was a huge demonstration of exemplary military power as more than thirty thousand troops moved in and took over the IRA-controlled districts in the cities of Belfast and Londonderry.[64] The IRA had used these "no-go" areas as bases to build up its military campaign, and the British had until that point observed restraint, being reluctant to move in for fear of inflaming sectarian tensions. Yet, as if to demonstrate the uncertain consequences of escalation, the IRA's ill-conceived attempt to raise coercive pressure brought down upon itself an overwhelming exercise in hard power.[65] Its rate of violence declined sharply (a comparison of three-week periods before and after the operation shows that recorded bomb attacks declined from 180 to 73 and shooting incidents from 2,595 to 385).[66] In a single stroke, Operation Motorman had altered the principal basis upon which the IRA's coercive bargaining position once rested.[67]

In effect, Motorman was a classic example of "surge" tactics that were to become a notable feature of military operations by U.S. forces in Iraq in 2007. The principle of escalating by "going in hard" not only runs counter to the usual canards about hearts and minds and minimum force in counterinsurgency but also establishes the point that recontaining threats and establishing the conditions for greater security are often the precursors for other forms of escalatory activity in tandem with and not instead of social and economic amelioration and the search for political reconciliation.[68] The Bloody Friday bombings demonstrate the validity of Richard Smoke's contention that escalation is a risk because the actor "cannot know the full consequences of his action."

The consequence of this escalation was that the IRA not only blew its best bargaining position but set the scene for the next twenty years, during which it withered toward a slow military defeat as British security policy moved from overt exemplary power into a more covert extension, reorientation, and escalation, leading into the shadows of intelligence-led Special Forces operations and the remorseless penetration of the IRA's ranks by security force agents and informers. Indeed, in the late 1970s, the British government rejected any further exemplary military escalations in favor of an intelligence-led campaign,[69] and by the early 1980s the intelligence war was the primary theater of British efforts to grind down the IRA.[70] Escalation occurred in the growth of counterambush operations by the Special Air Service, in which dozens of IRA members, including many of their most experienced operatives, were killed in "Find, Fix, and Finish" actions.[71] Furthermore, the British were prepared to escalate this "secret war"— via the penetration of the IRA by security forces in an extensive networks of informers and agents, comprising sometimes controversial incidents of collusion between state forces and anti-IRA loyalist paramilitary gangs[72]—to a point where the IRA almost certainly lost control over large parts its organization,[73] resulting in the collapse of its will to prosecute the armed struggle in the early 1990s.[74]

Thus, British escalation policy in regard to the IRA was not so much minimum force, on the one hand, or search and destroy, detain and torture, as in Argentina, on the other, but to spy, infiltrate, control, and kill. In this regard, there are more commonalities with the Argentinian case than a liberal-democratic polity might find comfortable, demonstrating a readiness for exemplary force and a willingness to escalate into the secret shadows. Crucially, this is not "hearts and minds" COIN as we have been led to understand it. These actions are assertive, forceful counteractions. They can be enacted brutally and indiscriminately, as in Argentina's Dirty War, or with more discrimination, as Britain's decisions in Northern Ireland, which saw the selective but no less fierce application of escalation into the realms of Special Forces and intelligence operations.

Northern Ireland demonstrates that in the end the reciprocal act of escalation in irregular wars is likely to benefit the more powerful actor, even if that actor is theoretically restrained by a liberal ethical value system. Sufficiently determined, it has the capacity to recontain any conflict with a lesser actor to a level of its choosing. In October 1970, the Canadian government did exactly this when it invoked the War Measures Act in Québec, sending out the Canadian armed forces onto the streets (a "surge," in other words) following an escalation in violence by the Front de Liberation du Québec that culminated in the kidnap and murder of hostages.[75] Similarly, in 1977 the West German government instituted severe measures against left-wing revolutionary groups such as the Red Army Faction, which escalated its campaign in the summer of 1977 by killing a well-known banker and political adviser, then kidnapping and murdering the head of the West German Employers Federation. Events reached a climax in October 1977 when members of the Red Army Faction hijacked a Lufthansa jet, killed the captain, and forced the plane to fly to Mogadishu in Somalia, where it was successfully stormed by West German commandos, resulting in the freeing of all the hostages and the death of three of the four hijackers.[76] In both the Canadian and the West German cases, liberal-democratic governments were provoked into robust acts of counterescalation that ultimately were to reduce and undermine the movements that challenged them.

Beyond recontaining an insurgent challenge through hard security measures, which include the use of surge tactics and Special Forces, covert intelligence activity rather than overt military power is thus likely to determine the more powerful actor's subsequent escalatory path. We see this pattern in events after 9/11. Stone observes that the weaker side's capacity to mount an effective challenge against its disproportionately more powerful opponent resides in its capacity to remain elusive. Remaining elusive while striking from a position of asymmetry relies on a mix of careful planning to preserve secrecy and reliance on the shelter and degree of political support among people who are prepared to help conceal the insurgents in the wider civilian populace.[77] Insurgent escalation across salient geographical and targeting thresholds, such as the al-Qaeda attacks on 9/11, thus presents the more powerful actor—the United States in the case of the 9/11 attacks—with an escalation dilemma: How can it break down the barrier of insurgent elusiveness? The stronger side has to be mindful because, as Stone explains, "too much enthusiasm for the likes of 'search and destroy' operations can inconvenience and endanger the wider population among whom they are conducted," which carries the "risk of pushing previous uncommitted individuals into the enemy camp, thereby strengthening the very thing that such operations were intended to weaken."[78]

Following the attacks on the Twin Towers and the Pentagon in September 2001, U.S. escalation took a two-tier approach according to patterns we can discern in both the Argentine and Northern Ireland cases. Escalating with overt military might to remove the Taliban in Afghanistan constituted one form of political communication to demonstrate U.S. intent and resolve. How to break al-Qaeda's more elusive terror networks around the world presented a far more difficult escalatory challenge. Speaking on September 16, 2001, Vice President Dick Cheney stated that the United States would have to work on "the dark side." "We've got to spend time in the shadows in the intelligence world," he said, "A lot of what needs to be done here will have to be done quietly, without any discussion, using sources and methods that are available to our intelligence agencies, if we're going to be successful."[79] Top Central Intelligence Agency official Buzzy Krongard echoed this sentiment, proclaiming that the campaign against al-Qaeda would be "won in large measure by forces you do not know about, in actions you will not see and in ways you may not want to know about."[80]

Both patterns of escalatory activity were in evidence in U.S.-led Coalition operations against al-Qaeda in Iraq (AQI) between 2003 and 2010. Although attention continues to focus on the Surge of U.S. forces into Iraq in 2007 as the crucial act of escalation that helped stabilize the country following its descent into civil disorder and insurgency,[81] the upscaling of activity by the Joint Special Operations Command (JSOC) is increasingly recognized as the crucial determinant in breaking AQI.[82] Overt military escalations, such as U.S. forces' attempt to dislodge insurgents from Fallujah in November–December 2004, were widely seen as costly in terms of troop losses and politically self-defeating given the extensive collateral damage inflicted and negative media coverage. The vision of the JSOC commander between 2003 and 2008, General Stanley McChrystal, however, was to wage a much more surreptitious but still relentlessly aggressive campaign of "industrial counterterrorism" that aimed to degrade AQI faster than it could regenerate itself. Utilizing the extensive intelligence resources and technologies at their disposal to keep an "unblinking eye" upon AQI insurgents, American and British Special Forces kept up a massive pace of raids against AQI operatives from 2006, particularly in and around the capital, Baghdad. JSOC's activities and the relentless grinding down of AQI operatives were eventually to crush the movement, as McChrystal had anticipated.[83]

Although intelligence-led Special Forces operations were only one facet in the decline of violence in Iraq after 2007, the contention is that they were indicative of a discernible pattern of conscious, systematic escalation on the part of the stronger side into the shadows of secret war. Reflecting patterns witnessed in Argentina, Northern Ireland, and the broader so-called global war on terror, these operations can be seen as an escalatory "blueprint" and disturbingly transcend or at least challenge many ethical barriers for liberal societies. U.S. actions against al-Qaeda after 9/11 were to include the implementation of secret renditions, black sites, enhanced interrogation, torture, and targeted killings.[84] These measures were far from the "hearts and minds," "softly softly" COIN stereotypes: they were clearly forms of hard-nosed escalation intended to bring an end to hostilities.

In the final analysis, though, even where we identify a degree of similarity in the escalation of dynamics in the waging of warfare against insurgent forces, we are still returned to vital, timeless, strategic concerns—the most pertinent being the necessity to achieve a political effect through violence. The means and preparedness to escalate are one consideration; politically acuity is another. Escalation, as has been reiterated, involves risk because the outcome is unpredictable. If escalation does not produce the required political advantage, however effective the technique, the consequences can be—and often are—lamentable. Reflecting on the mutual escalations in the era after 9/11, Stone observes: "Both sides proved rather more technically adept at applying violence than they did at generating the political effects from it."[85] Al-Qaeda raised the stakes by mounting a coordinated, highly sophisticated mass attack into the U.S. homeland. The outcome of this attack, though, was a U.S. escalation leading to the invasion and denial of al-Qaeda's sanctuary in Afghanistan. However,

U.S. unwillingness to limit the scale of retaliation led to a widening of the war on terror with the invasion of Iraq, inspiring AQI to launch its offensive against the forces of occupation. Equally, AQI's intent to escalate its campaign into a brutal sectarian war merely alienated the Shia population and Sunni tribal leaders, creating the conditions for the subsequent repression of AQI. Repetitive cycles of escalation invariably lead not to the elimination of resistance, but to recrimination, wherein the seed of further hostilities often lie.[86] For Stone, "the general point, applicable to both sides, was an old one—that it is easier to use force to kill people and break things than it is to extract any political benefit from the process. Both sides' technical capacity for escalation outstripped their ability to harness it to some politically tenable line of action."[87] Hence, the eternal strategic dilemma: You may have the capacity to escalate, but is it worth the long-term cost?

This chapter has highlighted the onus on the weaker combatant, the insurgent, to calculate the potential effects of escalatory action. The success of a violent campaign is likely to be premised upon the quality of a combatant's analysis, and it is incumbent on the weaker challenger to discern whether its campaign is based on a clear-sighted understanding of its enemy and how much violence that enemy will tolerate. Logically, this understanding should induce a further calculation of the limits of its position and whether it should "cash in" any political influence it may have secured through dialogue and compromise. Failure to do so is likely only to lead to rash escalatory decisions that may result in severe curtailment, if not annihilation, of the weaker side, as some of the examples cited earlier attest.

In one way, these insights are not novel, either in theory or practice. Clausewitz notes these dynamics at work when he observes that in situations where the "political aims are small, the motives slight and the tensions low[,] a prudent general may look for any way to avoid major crises and decisive actions, exploit any weaknesses in the opponent's political and military strategy, and reach a political settlement."[88] In other words, there are situations where a stronger side has insufficient effort or enthusiasm, and a weaker political force might do well to exploit political, social, and psychological fault lines to achieve some or all of its goals. However, war is a reciprocal phenomenon, as we have discussed, and therefore always carries the threat of escalation. Clausewitz continues, noting that if the assumptions of the prudent general who wishes to avoid major armed clashes—our theoretically weaker side challenging the power of a stronger one—prove to be "sound and promise success[,] we are not entitled to criticize him. But he must never forget that he is moving on a devious path where the god of war may catch him unawares."[89]

This chapter has endeavored to explain the puzzle of escalation in relation to counterinsurgency. It has sought to articulate a conception of the escalation process in conditions of irregular war through an understanding of the basic precepts of strategic theory. The examination went on to explore how the term *irregular war* can be construed as a situation of violent conflict that exists between manifestly unequal combatants. With this understanding, the notion of escalation could then be explored and located within the Clausewitzian understanding of war as a reactive environment in which each opponent's reciprocal actions lead to an inevitable escalation toward a theoretical extreme.

The chapter proceeded to outline how the escalatory challenges may present themselves from the perspectives of both the weaker party and the stronger party. It suggested that although the multiple and contingent factors governing behavior mean that no predictive mechanism can be formulated to forecast accurately how actors in such situations will escalate, certain broad observations may be held to be true: social values that emphasize proportionality of response, restraint of action, and the observance of the rule of law may confront more powerful actors with problems in escalation against weaker opposition, and weaker military actors invariably will have to exploit political divisions in the stronger opponent to induce a favorable reaction facilitating its objectives. Nevertheless, it has been noted that materially inferior actors are sometimes prone to escalate via increasing indiscrimination in targeting, although in most cases this approach remains unlikely to overcome a substantial power differential that will permit them to attain all their objectives. The weaker side thus has to be careful not to overestimate its capacities and provoke counterescalation that may ultimately threaten its destruction. A note of caution here, however, needs to be raised. Although we have explored the capacity to transgress ethical boundaries for tactical gain within structural parameters in the understanding that these transgressions are nevertheless also subject to fortune, the potential for insurgent ideology to become a political religion injects additional and unknowable variables—for example, martyrdom—that exceed the brief of this current work.[90]

Most importantly, it has been suggested that all sides, both weak and strong, have to engage in a continuous calculation about the political efficacy of violence and to consider carefully the effects they wish to achieve through any act of escalation. A sophisticated strategy is always likely to be premised on a careful understanding of the conditions pertaining in any instance of conflict as well as an acute appreciation of how one's adversary is likely to react. This understanding requires constant dialogue over ends and means in any actor's calculations, ensuring that the political effects sought through the actions of war are feasible and proportional to desired goals. In the final analysis, the practice of escalation in insurgent conflict corresponds to the operation of good strategic judgment in all war. Chapter 1 of this volume argued that notions such as irregular war, small wars, and insurgencies are largely artificial constructs because all conflicts take place between theoretically unequal sides. We return yet again to the wider truth of Clausewitz's observation that war is "more than a true chameleon that adapts its characteristics to any given case."[91] Wars are exclusive to time and place, and there consequently is no process unique to the escalation dynamics of insurgency/counterinsurgency. War is war whatever its individual manifestation, and as such it will always be subject to passion, chance, and reason. This explains the process of escalation regardless of the nature of the actors involved or of the social, geographical, and political conditions in which any war arises.

Conclusion

The contemporary fascination for counterinsurgency in Western military thinking and its resultant attraction for scholars of social and political science have their origins in the aftermath of the events of 9/11, in particular the ensuing occupations of Iraq and Afghanistan by Coalition forces. The costs, consequences, and controversies of this era have been immense and have preoccupied the thinking of policy makers and security analysts for the better part of a generation. In the years to come, though, the vast bulk of Western troops will have been withdrawn from major theaters of operation, with at most advisory missions remaining behind in low-profile training roles. The likelihood is that these areas of concern that once loomed so large in the popular mind will fade from view and be quickly displaced by the next set of crises on the world and domestic stages.

Although the impact of the post-9/11 era and the complex interventions in Iraq and Afghanistan have inevitably informed a backdrop for this volume, such present-minded concerns have not been the focus of this study. This book is not a commentary on those conflicts or on the foreign-policy dilemmas from which they may have arisen. The analysis in this study is instead concentrated on the lasting problems, paradoxes, and puzzles that the decade-long fascination with COIN presents for a coherent understanding of war in the modern world. After the troops are dispersed, we will be left with a residue of an intense debate about the manner in which Western nations should conceive and deal with certain kinds of conflict phenomena, specifically those often described as insurgencies and small wars. The enduring question is, What are we to make of the remaining fragments of this debate?

The analysis in this volume has been explicitly guided by the precepts of strategic theory, which we have used to derive insights for our understanding and to uncover the various dissonances that have often been submerged within the COIN discourse. Now that we have done so, what broad yet robust findings can we extract from such a study? There are, we suggest, four general themes to be highlighted as a result of the assessment contained in these pages.

The first of these durable themes concerns the elusive nature of the phenomenon that counterinsurgency is intended to counter. When placed under scrutiny, as chapter 1 revealed, notions of insurgency are extremely hard to pin down with analytical precision. The result has been a profusion of terms attempting to describe more or less the same thing: *small war, irregular war, unconventional war*, and so on. Yet that "thing" remains by degrees mysterious and intangible. These different terms have rarely succeeded in adding clarity and more often only stifle coherent meaning. Accordingly, the notion of counterinsurgency is rendered equally obscure.

Even so, when explored in detail, as chapter 2 disclosed, the resulting elasticity of the term *counterinsurgency* does suggest that the notion of COIN possesses properties not as a concrete, perceptible idea, but as a narrative. Its actual meaning may be open to question, but as an explanatory filter through which the past can be recited, it becomes a powerful tool indeed. The COIN narrative came to hold that that the awesome complexity of Iraq's postinvasion civil strife could be compressed into a single understanding—that it constituted "an insurgency" to be dealt with by bold commanders willing to "surge" U.S. forces, who would, in the enhanced conditions of security, thus apply the tried and tested tactics of classic population-centric counterinsurgency, recently rediscovered and now distilled into *The US Army/Marine Corps Counterinsurgency Field Manual*. As a consequence, the gradual decline in violence in Iraq after 2007 was seen as a vindication of the counterinsurgency school. Irrespective of whether correlation was the cause, COIN became the doctrine du jour. It was a method to be extolled in military circles and became the basis of an intellectual movement that was to advance through the corridors of power as well as the halls of academe and the world of think tanks.[1]

The power of COIN as a medium of explanation lay not simply in that it was, more by chance than design, able to narrate the decrease in violence and instability in Iraq after 2007, but that it was based on the discernment of recurrent patterns of conflict that yielded clear tactical lessons for operational conduct. The basis of this claim, as observed on numerous occasions in these pages, rested on the dissection of supposedly classic counterinsurgency encounters, most notably those of the British during the Malaya Emergency (1948–1960) and the French during the Algerian War (1954–1962). Other cases also made their appearance, either as supporting or admonishing exemplars, from the Mau Mau Rebellion in Kenya (1952–1960) to the Northern Ireland conflict (1968–1998) and Vietnam (1965–1975), among others. The problematical gathering of these conflicts under the rubric of COIN and the dubious basis for comparison have been increasingly discussed elsewhere,[2] but the historical narrative of COIN leads to the second key insight generated by this study, which is the obsession with technique.

The notion that the past yielded lessons for current and future practice was a compelling assertion for COIN theory's enduring relevance. That there was a discernible form of war that could be characterized as insurgency led, not unnaturally, to the belief that a series of palliative methods and core operational principles could be enacted that would, if correctly applied by skilled soldiers and officials well versed in the ways of COIN, always promise success. These practices invariably revolved around ideas such as securing the loyalty of the population, grievance reduction, the integration of civic action plans, along with the minimum application of military force in "clear, hold, and build" programs. As a number of chapters in this volume evinced, most notably chapter 2, this emphasis on the technical grammar of conduct came at the expense of understanding the contingent factors of politics that always give rise to war and always continuously exert their influence upon military interventions. The methodology of COIN, therefore, at one level has played to a traditional conception of military conduct that has attempted to "scientize" warfare into a series of rules to be followed.[3] However, an overriding concern for the "how" of operational conduct preempts necessary strategic questions about proportionality: What crucial political values are at stake, and what costs are worth incurring to defend them? In other words, it is not just how one fights but why one chooses to fight that is important. The "why" question is intensely political, and that is why COIN theory consequently has no answer to it.

Chapters 3 and 4 point to the third insight contained in this volume: that although COIN may eschew the making of overtly political statements, it is nonetheless highly ideological in orientation. On the surface, COIN theory purports to be apolitical and technocratic in its application. It aspires, in that sense, to become a comprehensive template for action across time and space. The timeless dynamics of insurgency are, so the thinking goes, perpetually capable of being answered by the timeless techniques of counterinsurgency.[4] The universalizing claims inherent in COIN advocacies, in other words, are symptomatic of a profoundly normative project. Paradoxically, however, as chapters 2 and 3 discovered, this project comprises an associated ideology of modernization: the unarticulated agenda that the ultimate goal of the counterinsurgency method should be to advance those societies mired in backward customs and the slough of authoritarianism along the road of socioeconomic improvement and democratic development. Whether, of course, individual societies—notably tribal in the Middle East and South Asia—were in the first instance ever amenable to such nation-building blandishments and whether it was worth the long-term costs of Western forces to attempt to engage in modernizing missions in faraway places remain open-ended questions.[5] Nevertheless, the ideology buried within the notion of Western counterinsurgency thinking, as it evolved in the 2000s, was that along the road of nation building lay the happy end of history.

This brings us to our fourth broad theme. If counterinsurgency strongly intimates an underlying end-of-history premise, its rendering in scholarly inquiry offers an entirely fictitious understanding of historical completion. Here COIN theory's capacity to mythologize the past, distort historical understanding, ignore contingency, and obscure complexity has been overwhelming. This is succinctly illustrated by the myth of British counterinsurgency recounted in chapter 5. Through constant repetition, analysts credited the British armed forces with a reputation for counterinsurgency expertise based on their experience with colonial warfare, particularly in winning over the population through techniques of minimum force and hearts and minds. Rarely was this reputation scrutinized. Commentators simply assumed the principle they had to prove.

The most pernicious aspect of the presumption of historical completion was evidenced by the fact that by the early 2000s sections of the British armed forces themselves bought into this myth concocted by others. They came to believe that they did indeed possess a core competence in counterinsurgency, even though until that point the British Army rarely ever claimed such expertise, seeing its colonial encounters mainly in terms of orthodox demonstrations of hard power to curtail rebel activity. As a consequence of buying into this myth, when shortcomings in British military interventions became evident, most notably in southern Iraq in the mid-2000s, commentators expressed dismay at the demise of this nonexistent tradition. Such mythologizing then manifested its other deleterious effect: it obscured the more prosaic but important reality of how Britain usually had prevailed in its small wars—namely, by government commitment to see these campaigns through so that stipulated political objectives could be met. Moreover, such myth making degraded the tactical proficiency that the British did possess. As evidenced in the final chapter, far from a flair for minimum force and hearts and minds, it was a talent for escalation into the dark arts of intelligence-led Special Forces operations and the penetration of rebel networks—from Malaya to Northern Ireland to the back streets of Baghdad—where Britain's capacities really lay and continues to reside.[6]

Ultimately, what do these four general findings mean for our understanding of the theory and practice of those wars grouped under the label *counterinsurgency*? Rory Stewart, the quixotic but solicitous British soldier-scholar-politician, traveler, and linguist, reflecting on his time as deputy governor of two southern Iraqi provinces under the Coalition Authority, made the following statement in early 2014:

Our entire conceptual framework was mad. All these theories—
counterinsurgency warfare, state building—were actually complete
abstract madness. They were like very weird religious systems, because they always break down into three principles, 10 functions,
seven this or that. So they're reminiscent of Buddhists who say:
"These are the four paths," or of Christians who say: "These are the
seven deadly sins." They're sort of theologies, essentially, made by
people like Buddhist monks in the eighth century—people who
have a fundamental faith, which is probably, in the end, itself completely delusional.[7]

Stewart's statement illustrates a simple but profound message echoed
throughout this volume: COIN is symptomatic of a fallacy at the heart
of much contemporary Western social inquiry, which is the attempt
to impose a structure on contingent conditions of the past that were
never present at the time and never will be in the future. COIN is,
as Stewart contends, a delusion. Counterinsurgency "theory" in this
respect is little different from many other systems of thought that attempt to read the past through an understanding of a social or political "science" as if there are patterns to be discerned, lessons to be
uncovered, and rules to be obeyed. It thus bears similarity, as Stewart
perceives, with forms of quasi-mystical religious thought. In this regard, counterinsurgency is not so much a singular false analogy but a
distorting lens that telescopes its focus, narrowing an appreciation of
the past as well as overdetermining and oversimplifying the present
and the future.

COIN is therefore a historical read back and should not be regarded
as a formula for comprehending present wars or for prescribing the
course of future ones. It might be too trite to proclaim that a study of
counterinsurgency reveals yet again the elemental truth that there are
no lessons of the past, only interpretations. But if one enduring idea
may be extracted from this study, it is that COIN-centric readings of
history should be rejected and that skepticism should be practiced toward all grand social science theorizing in general. Instead, an investigation into the puzzles and dissonances of counterinsurgency suggests
that we should, as the final chapter intimated, return to the more mod-
est but no less shrewd claims of thinkers such as Carl von Clausewitz.

His more delicate analogy that war is more than a true chameleon—always changing its surface manifestation but at heart remaining the same—offers the most stable basis for insight by conferring the one, true constant about war: all wars are unique to their time and place, conditioned as they are by the unpredictable forces of passion, chance, and reason. The analysis of the interplay of these dynamic, volatile, ever-shifting moral forces gives the study of war its vitality. In the end, therefore, it is the historical contingency of war that presents itself as much more interesting and valid than any theory of history.

Notes

Introduction

 1. Sherard Cowper-Coles, *Cables from Kabul: The Inside Story of the West's Afghan Campaign* (London: Harper, 2012), 53.

2. Ibid., 142.

 3. See David Ucko, *The New Counterinsurgency Era: Transforming the U.S. Military for Modern Wars* (Washington, D.C.: Georgetown University Press, 2009).

4. Others accounts include Ben Anderson, *No Worse Enemy: The Inside Story of the Chaotic Struggle for Afghanistan* (London: Oneworld, 2011), and Rajiv Chandrasekaran, *Little America: The War Within the War for Afghanistan* (London: Bloomsbury, 2013).

 5. See Fred Kaplan, *The Insurgents: David Petraeus and the Plot to Change the American Way of War* (New York: Simon and Schuster, 2013).

6. The literature on radicalization and deradicalization as well as, of course, on terrorism and counterterrorism more generally produced since 2001 is vast. For illustrative purposes, see Tore Bjørgo, ed., *The Roots of Terrorism: Myths, Reality, and Ways Forward* (London: Routledge, 2005); Anne Aldis and Graeme P. Herd, eds., *The Ideological War on Terror: World-Wide Strategies for Counter-Terrorism* (London: Routledge, 2007); Christopher Ankerson, ed., *Understanding Global Terror* (Cambridge, UK: Polity Press, 2007); Omar Ashour, *The De-radicalization of Jihadists: Transforming Armed Islamist Movements* (London: Routledge, 2009); Tore Bjørgo and John Horgan, eds., *Leaving Terrorism Behind: Individual and Collective Disengagement* (London: Routledge, 2009).

7. David Martin Jones and M. L. R. Smith, "Greetings from the Cybercaliphate: Some Notes on Homeland Insecurity," *International Affairs* 81, no. 5 (2005): 925–50.

8. The signpost text in this respect is John Nagl, *Learning to Eat Soup with a Knife: Counterinsurgency Lessons from Malaya and Vietnam* (Chicago: University of Chicago Press, 2002).

9. See James Pritchard and M. L. R. Smith, "Thompson in Helmand: Comparing Theory to Practice in British Counter-Insurgency Operations in Afghanistan," *Civil Wars* 12, nos. 1–2 (2010): 65–90.

10. For an important account of this period, see Rajiv Chandrasekaran, *Imperial Life in the Emerald City: Inside Bagdad's Green Zone* (London: Bloomsbury, 2007).

11. Colin H. Kahl, "COIN of the Realm: Is There a Future for Counterinsurgency?" *Foreign Affairs* 86, no. 6 (2007): 169–74.

12. Thomas E. Ricks, *The Gamble: General David Petraeus and the American Military Adventure in Iraq, 2006–2008* (New York: Penguin, 2009).

13. Kahl, "COIN of the Realm," 175–76.

14. See Oscar Ware, "Preparing for an Irregular Future Counterinsurgency," *Small Wars Journal*, July 18, 2013, http://smallwarsjournal.com/jrnl/art/preparing-for-an-irregular-future-counterinsurgency, accessed October 9, 2013; Steven Metz, "Counterinsurgency and American Strategy, Past and Future," *World Politics Review*, January 24, 2012, http://www.worldpoliticsreview.com/articles/11248/counterinsurgency-and-american-strategy-past-and-future, accessed October 10, 2013.

15. See, for example, Ken Booth, "War, Security, and Strategy: Towards a Doctrine for Stable Peace," in Ken Booth, ed., *New Thinking About International Security* (London: HarperCollins, 1991), 356, and Mary Kaldor, *New and Old Wars: Organized Violence in a Global Era* (Stanford: Stanford University Press, 1999).

16. For an analysis of this engagement, see Tim Bird and Alex Marshall, *Afghanistan: How the West Lost Its Way* (New Haven: Yale University Press, 2011).

17. See Celeste Ward Gventer, David Martin Jones, and M. L. R. Smith, eds., *The New Counter-Insurgency Era in Critical Perspective* (London: Palgrave Macmillan, 2014).

18. Cowper-Coles, *Cables from Kabul*, 279.

19. See Janine Davidson, *The Principles of American Counterinsurgency: Evolution and Debate*, Counterinsurgency and Pakistan Paper Series (Washington, D.C.: Brookings Institution Press, 2009), 3, http://www.brookings.edu/~/media/research/files/papers/2009/6/08%20counterinsurgency%20davidson/0608_counterinsurgency_davidson.pdf, accessed October 13, 2013; Octavian Manea, "Learning from Today's Crisis of Counterinsurgency," *Small Wars Journal*, October 8, 2013, http://smallwarsjournal.com/jrnl/art/learning-from-today's-crisis-of-counterinsurgency, accessed October 13, 2013.

20. See David French, *The British Way in Counter-Insurgency, 1945–1967* (Oxford: Oxford University Press, 2011); Douglas Porch, *Counterinsurgency: Exposing the Myths of the New Way of War* (Cambridge, UK: Cambridge University Press, 2013).

21. For such critiques, see Jack Fairweather, *A War of Choice: Honour, Hubris, and Sacrifice—the British in Iraq, 2003–9* (London: Vintage, 2012); Anderson, *No Worse Enemy*; Bird and Marshall, *Afghanistan*; Chandrasekaran, *Imperial Life in the Emerald City* and *Little America*.

22. As in Gian Gentile, *Wrong Turn: America's Deadly Embrace of Counterinsurgency* (New York: New Press, 2013); David H. Ucko and Robert Egnell, *Counterinsurgency in Crisis: Britain and the Challenges of Modern Warfare* (New York: Columbia University Press, 2013).

23. Karl W. Eikenberry, "The Limits of Counterinsurgency Doctrine in Afghanistan," *Foreign Affairs* 92, no. 5 (2013), http://www.foreignaffairs.com/articles/139645/karl-w-eikenberry/the-limits-of-counterinsurgency-doctrine-in-afghanistan, accessed October 14, 2013.

24. Cowper-Coles, *Cables from Kabul*, 139.

25. For such higher goals, see Colin Gray, *The Strategy Bridge: Theory for Practice* (Oxford: Oxford University Press, 2010), 15–53.

26. Michael Howard, *The Causes of Wars* (London: Counterpoint, 1983), 36.

27. M. L. R. Smith and John Stone, "Explaining Strategic Theory," *Infinity Journal* 1, no. 4 (2011): 27.

28. See, in this context, Karl Popper, *The Logic of Scientific Discovery* (London: Routledge, 2002), and Ernest Gellner, *Relativism and the Social Sciences* (Cambridge, UK: Cambridge University Press, 1987).

29. Smith and Stone, "Explaining Strategic Theory."

30. Thomas C. Schelling, *Choice and Consequence: Perspectives of an Errant Economist* (Cambridge, MA: Harvard University Press, 1984), 205.

31. See ibid., 1–26.

32. Carl von Clausewitz, *On War*, trans. and ed. Michael Howard and Peter Paret (Princeton: Princeton University Press, 1984), 75.

33. F. Lopez Alves, "Political Crises, Strategic Choices, and Terrorism: The Rise and Fall of the Uruguayan Tuparmaros," *Terrorism and Political Violence* 1, no. 2 (1989): 189–214. See also David A. Lake and Robert Powell, eds., *Strategic Choice and International Relations* (Princeton: Princeton University Press, 1999).

34. Clausewitz, *On War*, 75, emphasis in original.

35. For example, see Gary Anderson, "Counterinsurgency vs. Counterterrorism," *Small Wars Journal*, February 24, 2010, http://smallwarsjournal.com/jrnl/art/counterinsurgency-vs-counterterrorism, accessed October 10, 2013; Anthony H. Cordesman, "US Strategy in Afghanistan: The Debate We Should Be Having," Center for Strategic and International Studies, October 7, 2009, http://csis.org/publication/us-strategy-afghanistan, accessed October 2, 2013.

36. Schelling, *Choice and Consequence*, 198–99.

37. Smith and Stone, "Explaining Strategic Theory," 30.

38. Harry R. Yarger, *Strategic Theory for the 21st Century: The Little Book on Big Strategy* (Carlisle, PA: Strategic Studies Institute, 2006), 2.

1. What Is Counterinsurgency Meant to Counter? The Puzzle of Insurgency

1. See Beatrice Heuser, "The Cultural Revolution in Counter-Insurgency," *Journal of Strategic Studies* 30, no. 1 (2007): 153–71.

2. *The US Army/Marine Corps Counterinsurgency Field Manual* (Chicago: University of Chicago Press, 2007), 2.

3. Lincoln Krause, "Playing for the Breaks: Insurgent Mistakes," *Parameters* 39, no. 4 (2009): 49.

4. British Army, *Countering Insurgency*, vol. 1, part 10 (Warminster, UK: Ministry of Defence, 2009), 1-4.

5. John Nagl, "Local Security Forces," in Thomas Rid and Thomas Kearney, eds., *Understanding Counterinsurgency: Doctrine, Operations, and Challenges* (London: Routledge, 2010), 161.

6. David Kilcullen, "Counterinsurgency Redux," *Survival* 48, no. 4 (2006): 112.

7. Bard E. O'Neill, *Insurgency and Terrorism: Inside Modern Revolutionary Warfare* (Dulles, VA: Brassey's, 1990), 13.

8. Frank Kitson, *Low-Intensity Operations: Subversion, Insurgency, and Peacekeeping* (London: Faber, 1971), 48.

9. Francis Toase, introduction to Robin Corbett, ed., *Guerrilla Warfare: From 1939 to the Present Day* (London: Guild, 1986), 6–21.

10. See, for example, Richard Clutterbuck, *Guerrillas and Terrorists* (Athens: Ohio University Press, 1977), 22–32.

11. See, for example, Charles E. Callwell, *Small Wars: Their Principles and Practice* (London: His Majesty's Stationary Office, 1896; reprint, Lincoln: University of Nebraska Press and Bison Books, 1996), 21–22.

12. John Shy and Thomas Collier, "Revolutionary War," in Peter Paret, ed., *Makers of Modern Strategy: From Machiavelli to the Nuclear Age* (Oxford: Clarendon, 1986), 817.

13. Toase, introduction to Corbett, *Guerrilla Warfare*, 6.

14. Ian Beckett, "The Tradition," in John Pimlott, ed., *Guerrilla Warfare* (London: Bison, 1985), 8.

15. Carl von Clausewitz, *On War*, trans. and ed. Michael Howard and Peter Paret (Princeton: Princeton University Press, 1984), 87, 75, 88.

16. Ibid., 89.

17. Ibid., 87.

18. Ibid., 89, 88.

19. Ibid., 87.

20. Ibid., 89.

21. Colin Gray, *Categorical Confusion? The Strategic Implications of Recognizing Challenges Either as Irregular or Traditional* (Carlisle, PA: Strategic Studies Institute, 2012), 26.

22. Harry Summers, "A War Is a War Is a War Is a War," in Loren B. Thompson, ed., *Low-Intensity Conflict: The Pattern of Warfare in the Modern World* (Lexington, MA: Lexington Books, 1989), 27–45.

23. For the essentialist case, see M. L. R. Smith, "Guerrillas in the Mist: Reassessing Strategy and Low Intensity Warfare," *Review of International Studies* 29, no. 1 (2003): 19–37.

24. John A. Nagl and Brian M. Burton, "Thinking Globally and Acting Locally: Counterinsurgency Lessons from Modern Wars—a Reply to Smith and Jones," *Journal of Strategic Studies* 33, no. 1 (2010): 126.

25. Roger Trinquier, *Modern Warfare: A French View of Counterinsurgency* (London: Pall Mall, 1964; reprint, Westport, CT: Praeger, 2006), xiii, 4.

26. George Armstrong Kelly, *Lost Soldiers: The French Army and Empire in Crisis, 1945–62* (Cambridge, MA: MIT Press, 1965), 127.

27. Raoul Girardet and Jean-Pierre Thomas, *La crise militaire française, 1942–1962: Aspects sociologigques et ideologiques* (Paris: Libraire Armand Colin, 1964), 179.

28. Jacques Hogard, "Guerre révolutionnaire ou révolution dans l'art del la guerre," *Revue defénse nationale,* no. 12 (December 1956): 1498.

29. Peter Paret, *French Revolutionary Warfare from Indochina to Algeria: The Analysis of a Political and Military Doctrine* (New York: Praeger, 1964), 4.

30. Serge Chakotine, *The Rape of the Masses: The Psychology of Totalitarian Propaganda,* trans. E. W. Dickes (New York: Alliance, 1940).

31. Capt. Labignette [no first name given], "Cas concrete de guerre révolutionnaire," *Revue demilitaire l'information,* no. 281 (February–March 1957): 30.

32. Trinquier, *Modern Warfare,* 8, emphasis in original.

33. For Giáp's strategy, see Bernard Fall, *Street Without Joy* (London: Pall Mall, 1963; reprint, Mechanicsburg, PA: Stackpole, 2005), 34–35.

34. Võ Nguyên Giáp, *People's War, People's Army: The Viet Cong Insurrection Manual for Underdeveloped Countries* (New York: Praeger, 1962), 98.

35. Ibid., 48.

36. See Peter Drake Jackson, "French Ground Force Organizational Development for Counterrevolutionary Warfare Between 1945 and 1962," MA thesis, Army War College, 2005, 38–118, http://www.au.af.mil/au/awc/awcgate/army/sgsc_jackson.pdf, accessed April 14, 2013; Kelly, *Lost Soldiers,* 91; Trinquier, *Modern Warfare,* viii–ix; and Paul Aussaresses, *The Battle of the Casbah: Terrorism and Counter-Terrorism in Algeria, 1955–57* (New York: Enigma, 2002), 6.

37. See Clausewitz, *On War,* 75–77.

38. Bernard Fall, *The Vietminh Regime: Government and Administration in the Democratic Republic of Vietnam* (Ithaca, NY: Cornell University Press, 1954), 143.

39. Stanley Karnow, *Vietnam: A History* (London: Pimlico, 1994), 199.

40. Fall, *Street Without Joy,* 32.

41. Karnow, *Vietnam,* 201.

42. Kelly, *Lost Soldiers,* 211.

43. See G. D. Sheffield, "*Blitzkrieg* and Attrition: Land Operations in Europe 1914–45," in Colin McInnes and G. D. Sheffield, eds., *Warfare in the Twentieth Century: Theory and Practice* (London: Unwin Hyman, 1988), 51–79.

44. See Christopher Cradock and M. L. R. Smith, "No Fixed Values: A Reinterpretation of the Influence of the Theory of *Guerre Révolutionnaire* and the Battle of Algiers, 1956–1957," *Journal of Cold War Studies* 9, no. 4 (2007): 68–105.

45. For such strategic thinking at the time, see John J. McCuen, *The Art of Counter-Revolutionary War: The Strategy of Counter-Insurgency* (London: Faber, 1966; reprint, St. Petersburg, FL: Hailer, 2005).

46. Colin Gray, *Strategic Studies and Public Policy: The American Experience* (Lexington: University of Kentucky Press, 1982), 114, 122.

47. See tables 2.1 and 2.2 in K. J. Holsti, *The State, War, and the State of War* (Cambridge, UK: Cambridge University Press, 1996), 22–24. For further statistical evidence, see table 1 in Barbara F. Walter, "Designing Transitions from Civil War: Demobilization, Democratization, and Commitments to Peace," *International Security* 25, no. 1 (1999): 128. Other surveys indicate that the statistical prevalence of intrastate war also predates 1945; see Geoffrey Blainey, *The Causes of War* (London: Macmillan, 1988), 71, and J. David Singer and Melvin Small, *Resort to Arms: International and Civil Wars, 1816–1980* (Beverly Hills, CA: Sage, 1982).

48. Jan Willem Honig, "Strategy in a Post-Clausewitzian Setting," in Gerd de Nooy, ed., *The Clausewitzian Dictum and the Future of Western Military Strategy* (The Hague: Kluwer Law International, 1997), 118.

49. Richard K. Betts, "Should Strategic Studies Survive?" *World Politics* 50, no. 1 (1997): 7.

50. Quoted in Fall, *Street Without Joy*, 370.

51. W. Alexander Vacca and Mark Davidson, "The Regularity of Regular Warfare," *Parameters* 41, no. 2 (2011): 24.

52. Ibid., 23.

53. See, for example, Bjørn Møller, "The Faces of War," in Håkan Wiberg and Christian P. Scherrer, eds., *Ethnicity and Intra-state Conflict: Types, Causes, and Peace Strategies* (Aldershot, UK: Ashgate, 1999), 15.

54. John Keegan, *A History of Warfare* (New York: Vintage, 1994), 58.

55. Mary Kaldor, *New and Old Wars: Organized Violence in a Global Era* (Stanford: Stanford University Press, 1999), 13.

56. Martin van Creveld, *The Transformation of War* (New York: Free Press, 1991), 57–58.

57. Montgomery McFate, "The Military Utility of Understanding Adversary Culture," *Joint Forces Quarterly* 38, 3rd quarter (2005): 43.

58. Honig, "Strategy in a Post-Clausewitzian Setting," 110.

59. Clausewitz, *On War*, 87–88.

60. Gray, *Categorical Confusion?* 12.

61. Many examples across the military studies literature past and present reflect this tendency. See, for example, Donald Featherstone, *Colonial Small Wars, 1837–1901* (Newtown Abbot, UK: David and Charles, 1973), 11–13; Juliet Lodge, ed., *Terrorism: A Challenge to the State* (Oxford: Martin Robertson, 1981); Richard A. Preston, Alex Roland, and Sydney F. Wise, *Men in Arms: A History of Warfare and Its Interrelationships with Western Society* (New York: Harcourt Brace Jovanovich, 1991), 359–85.

62. William L. Shirer, *Berlin Diary: The Journal of a Foreign Correspondent, 1934–1941* (Boston: Little Brown, 1941), 556.

63. See J. F. C. Fuller, *The Second World War, 1939–45: A Strategical and Tactical History* (New York: Duell, Sloan and Pearce, 1954), 83–89, and Armand Van Ishoven, *The Luftwaffe and the Battle of Britain* (New York: Scribner, 1980).

64. Nagl and Burton, "Thinking Globally and Acting Locally," 125, 126.

65. Quoted in Roger Hilsman, *To Move a Nation: The Politics of Foreign Policy in the Administration of John F. Kennedy* (New York: Delta, 1967), 413.

66. David Galula, *Counterinsurgency Warfare: Theory and Practice* (1964; reprint, Westport, CT: Praeger, 2006), 63; British Army, *Countering Insurgency*, 3-3.

67. *US Army/Marine Corps Counterinsurgency Field Manual*, ii.

68. Michael Howard, *The Causes of War* (London: Counterpoint, 1983), 86.

69. M. L. R. Smith and John Stone, "Explaining Strategic Theory," *Infinity Journal* 1, no. 4 (2011): 27–28.

70. See Thomas C. Schelling, *The Strategy of Conflict* (New York: Oxford University Press, 1980), 83–118.

71. Summers, "A War Is a War Is a War Is a War," 44–45.

72. Vacca and Davidson, "The Regularity of Regular Warfare," 19, 23.

73. Paul Beaver, "The Threat to Israel Is Not War," *Asian Wall Street Journal*, October 24, 2000.

74. See Brendan Simms, *Unfinest Hour: Britain and the Destruction of Bosnia* (London: Penguin, 2001).

75. Edward Luttwak, "Give War a Chance," *Foreign Affairs* 78, no. 4 (1999): 36–44.

76. See Jan Willem Honig and Norbert Both, *Srebrenica: Record of a War Crime* (London: Penguin, 1996), 71–98, and James Gow, *Triumph of the Lack of Will: International Diplomacy and the Yugoslav War* (London: Hurst, 1997), 298–331.

77. See Alec Russell, "How the West Turned a Blind Eye Despite General's 'Genocide Fax,'" *Daily Telegraph*, April 6, 2004.

78. Vacca and Davidson, "The Regularity of Regular Warfare," 24.

79. For a survey of such decisions, see Alistair Horne, *A Savage War of Peace: Algeria, 1954–1962* (London: Penguin, 2002).

80. See Sherard Cowper-Coles, *Cables from Kabul: The Inside Story of the West's Afghan Campaign* (London: Harper, 2012), xxii, 53, 64–65, 120, 145, 178, 200, 223, 258.

81. See Rajiv Chandrasekaran, *Little America: The War Within the War for Afghanistan* (London, Bloomsbury, 2013), 217–35.

82. John Mackinlay, "Tackling Bin Laden: Lessons from History," *Observer*, October 28, 2001.

83. For example, see the discussion in John Bew, Martyn Frampton, and Iñigo Gurruchaga, *Talking to Terrorists: Making Peace in Northern Ireland and the Basque Country* (London: Hurst, 2009).

84. *US Army/Marines Corps Counterinsurgency Field Manual*, 18.

85. Lawrence Freedman, "Globalization and the War Against Terrorism," in Christopher Ankerson, ed., *Understanding Global Terror* (Cambridge, UK: Polity, 2007), 227.

86. Gray, *Categorical Confusion?* 48.

87. Clausewitz, *On War*, 88–89.

2. Counterinsurgency and Strategy: Problems and Paradoxes

1. Rajiv Chandrasekaran, *Little America: The War Within the War for Afghanistan* (London: Bloomsbury, 2013), 278.

2. For assessments of this alternative view, see Douglas Ollivant, *Countering the New Orthodoxy: Reinterpreting Counterinsurgency in Iraq*, National Security Studies Program Policy Paper (Washington, D.C.: New America Foundation, June 2011), http://www .newamerica.net/sites/newamerica.net/files/policydocs/Ollivant_Reinterpreting_ Counterinsurgency.pdf, accessed February 6, 2012; as well as Stephen Biddle, Jeffrey A. Friedman, and Jacob N. Schapiro, "Testing the Surge: Why Did Violence Decline in Iraq in 2007?" in Celeste Ward Gventer, David Martin Jones, and M. L. R. Smith, eds., *The New Counter-Insurgency Era in Critical Perspective* (London: Palgrave Macmillan, 2014), 201–31.

3. Chandrasekaran, *Little America*, 118.

4. Quoted in ibid., 125–26.

5. White House, "Osama bin Laden Dead: Remarks by the President on Osama bin Laden," May 2, 2011, http://www.whitehouse.gov/blog/2011/05/02/osama-bin-laden-dead, accessed November 12, 2013.

6. That the assassination of Osama bin Laden was a primary aim of U.S. policy was clear in statements by the president soon after the 9/11 attacks. In his address to Congress on September 20, 2001, President George W. Bush announced: "Our war on terror begins with al Qaeda, but it does not end there. It will not end until every terrorist group with global reach has been found, stopped and defeated" ("Text of George Bush's Speech," *Guardian*, September 21, 2001).

7. Dan Murphy, "One Year After bin Laden's Killing, al-Qaeda Is in Tatters," *Christian Science Monitor*, May 1, 2012.

8. See David Ucko, *The New Counterinsurgency Era: Transforming the US Military for Modern Wars* (Washington, D.C.: Georgetown University Press, 2009).

9. See, for example, Thomas E. Ricks, *The Gamble: General David Petraeus and the American Military Adventure in Iraq, 2006–2008* (New York: Penguin, 2009).

10. Kimberley Kagan, *The Surge: A Military History* (New York: Encounter, 2009), 202. See also Peter R. Mansoor, *Surge: My Journey with General David Petraeus and the Remaking of the Iraq War* (New Haven: Yale University of Press, 2013).

11. Ralph Wipfli and Steven Metz, "COIN of the Realm: US Counterinsurgency Strategy," colloquium brief, U.S. Army War College and 21st Century Defense Initiative of the Brookings Institution, Strategic Studies Institute, c. 2008, http://www .strategicstudiesinstitute.army.mil/pdffiles/pub846.pdf, accessed December 26, 2011.

12. Chris McGreal and Jon Boone, "US Launches New Afghan Counterinsurgency Strategy," *Guardian*, September 24, 2009, http://www.guardian.co.uk/world/2009/sep/24/ us-adopts-new-afghan-plan, accessed December 26, 2011.

13. Peter Baker and Elisabeth Bumiller, "Obama Considers Strategy Shift in Afghan War," *New York Times*, September 22, 2009, http://www.nytimes.com/2009/09/23/world/ asia/23policy.html, accessed March 29, 2012.

14. On the logical incoherence of concept stretching, see John Kadvany, *Imre Lakatos and the Guises of Reason* (Durham, NC: Duke University Press, 2001), 85–88.

15. *The US Army/Marine Corps Counterinsurgency Field Manual* (Chicago: University of Chicago Press, 2007), 2.

16. Ibid., ii.

17. Michael Howard, *The Causes of War* (London: Counterpoint, 1983), 36.

18. Basil Liddell Hart, *Strategy: The Indirect Approach* (London: Faber, 1967), 335.

19. On the notion of strategy as maximizing power and outcome, see Lawrence Freed-man, *Strategy: A History* (Oxford: Oxford University Press, 2013), 575–629.

20. Antulio J. Echevarria, "Reconsidering War's Logic and Grammar," *Infinity Journal* 1, no. 2 (2011): 4.

21. US Department of Defense, *Dictionary of Military and Associate Terms* (Washington, D.C.: US Department of Defense, November 8, 2010), http://www.dtic.mil/doctrine/dod_dictionary/data/d/3840.html, accessed February 7, 2012.

22. For the latter, see, for example, Air Staff, *AP 3000: British Air and Space Power Doctrine* (London: UK Ministry of Defence, 2009); Zachary Fryer-Biggs, "DoD's New Cyber Doctrine: Panetta Defines Deterrence, Preempting Strategy," *Defensenews.com*, October 13, 2012, http://www.defensenews.com/article/20121013/DEFREG02/310130001/DoD-8217-s-New-Cyber-Doctrine, accessed March 5, 2013.

23. Carl von Clausewitz, *On War*, trans. and ed. Michael Howard and Peter Paret (Princeton: Princeton University Press, 1984), 89.

24. Ibid., 87.

25. Ibid., 89.

26. John A. Nagl and Brian M. Burton, "Thinking Globally and Acting Locally: Counterinsurgency Lessons from Modern Wars—a Reply to Smith and Jones," *Journal of Strategic Studies* 33, no. 1 (2010): 125.

27. Ibid., 126.

28. Bernard Fall, "Counterinsurgency: The French Experience," speech to the Industrial College of the Armed Forces, Washington, D.C., January 18, 1963.

29. Harry Eckstein, "On the Etiology of Internal Wars," *History and Theory* 4, no. 2 (1965): 133.

30. Steven R. David, "Review Article: Internal War, Causes and Cures," *World Politics* 49, no. 4 (1997): 568.

31. David Galula, *Counterinsurgency Warfare: Theory and Practice* (1964; reprint, Westport, CT: Praeger, 2006); Robert Trinquier, *Modern Warfare: A French View of Counterinsurgency* (London: Pall Mall, 1964; reprint, Westport, CT: Praeger, 2006); Robert Thompson, *Defeating Communist Insurgency: Experiences from Malaya and Vietnam* (London: Chatto and Windus, 1966); Frank Kitson, *Low Intensity Operations: Subversion, Insurgency, and Peacekeeping* (London: Faber, 1971).

32. Thomas Rid, "The Nineteenth Century Origins of Counterinsurgency Doctrine," *Journal of Strategic Studies* 33, no. 5 (2010): 727–58.

33. William A. Hosington, *Lyautey and the French Conquest of Morocco* (London: Palgrave Macmillan, 1995); Michael P. M. Finch, *A Progressive Occupation? The Gallieni–Lyautey Method of Colonial Pacification in Tonkin and Madagascar, 1885–1900* (Oxford: Oxford University Press, 2013).

34. Charles Callwell, *Small Wars: Their Principles and Practice* (London: His Majesty's Stationary Office, 1896; reprint, Lincoln: University of Nebraska Press and Bison Books, 1996); Charles Gwynn, *Imperial Policing* (London: Macmillan, 1934).

35. H. R. McMaster, *Dereliction of Duty: Lyndon Johnson, Robert McNamara, the Joint Chiefs of Staff, and the Lies That Led to Vietnam* (New York: HarperCollins, 1997); John Nagl, *Learning to Eat Soup with a Knife: Counterinsurgency Lessons from Malaya and Vietnam* (Chicago: University of Chicago Press, 2002); Peter R. Mansoor, *Baghdad at Sunrise: A Brigade Commander's War in Iraq* (New Haven: Yale University Press, 2009); David Kilcullen, *The Accidental Guerrilla: Fighting Small Wars in the Midst of a Big One* (London: Hurst, 2009), and *Counterinsurgency* (Oxford: Oxford University Press, 2010).

36. For an analysis of COIN thinking along these lines, see Gian Gentile, *Wrong Turn: America's Deadly Embrace of Counterinsurgency* (New York: New Press, 2013), 34–58.

37. Andrew F. Krepenivich, *The Army and Vietnam* (Baltimore: Johns Hopkins University Press, 1986); McMaster, *Dereliction of Duty*.

38. Richard Clutterbuck, *The Long, Long War: The Emergency in Malaya, 1948–1960* (London: Cassell, 1966).

39. See, for example, Wade Markel, "Draining the Swamp: The British Strategy of Population Control," *Parameters* 36, no. 1 (2006): 35–48; Walter C. Ladwig, "Managing Counterinsurgency: Lessons from Malaya," *Military Review*, May–June 2007, 56–66; Maj. Michael D. Sullivan, "Leadership in Counterinsurgency: A Tale of Two Leaders," *Military Review*, September–October 2007, 119–23.

40. Clutterbuck, *The Long Long War*, 131.

41. See U.S. Army, *PRT Playbook: Tactics, Techniques, and Procedures* (Fort Leavenworth, KS: Center for Army Lessons Learned, 2007). For an assessment of the role of Provincial Reconstruction Teams in Afghanistan, see James Pritchard and M. L. R. Smith, "Thompson in Helmand: Comparing Theory to Practice in British Counter-Insurgency Operations in Afghanistan," *Civil Wars* 12, nos. 1–2 (2010): 65–90.

42. Karl Hack, "'Iron Claws on Malaya': The Historiography of the Malayan Emergency," *Journal of Southeast Asian Studies* 30, no. 1 (1999): 102.

43. In particular, see the work of Huw Bennett, who argues that the British Army perceived harsh methods as a necessary precursor to "hearts and minds" operations: "Minimum Force in British Counter-Insurgency," *Small Wars and Insurgencies* 21, no. 3 (2010): 459–75; "The Other Side of the COIN: Minimum and Exemplary Force in British Army Counter-Insurgency in Kenya," *Small Wars and Insurgencies* 18, no. 4 (2007): 638–64; and "'A Very Salutary Effect': The Counter-Terror Strategy in the Early Malayan Emergency, June 1948 to December 1949," *Journal of Strategic Studies* 32, no. 3 (2009): 414–44.

44. David Martin Jones and M. L. R. Smith, "The Perils of Hyper-vigilance: The War on Terrorism and the Surveillance State in South-East Asia," *Intelligence and National Security* 17, no. 4 (2002): 31–54.

45. The example of Malaya is referenced at various points in *The US Army/Marine Corps Counterinsurgency Field Manual* and the British Army's manual *Countering Insurgency*, vol. 1, part 10 (Warminster, UK: Ministry of Defence, 2009). No mention is made of the broader legal and military context in which British operations were conducted.

In the *Counterinsurgency Field Manual*, the main allusion to the Malayan Emergency is to the effectiveness of the British in developing a civilian police force to function alongside the military (see 234–35).

46. See Karl Hack, "The Malayan Emergency as a Counter-Insurgency Paradigm," *Journal of Strategic Studies* 32, no. 3 (2009): 394–96.

47. An explicit relationship between grievance settlement and counterinsurgency is made in British Army, *Countering Insurgency*, 2-3 and 2-4.

48. John Mackinlay, *Globalisation and Insurgency*, Adelphi Paper no. 352 (London: International Institute for Strategic Studies and Oxford University Press, 2002), 33.

49. David Kilcullen, "Twenty-Eight Articles: Fundamentals of Company Level Counterinsurgency," *Small Wars Journal*, March 29, 2006, 8, smallwarsjournal.com/documents/28articles.pdf, accessed November 17, 2013.

50. Nagl and Burton, "Thinking Globally and Acting Locally," 135–36.

51. See, in this context, David Martin Jones, "Politics, Statecraft, and the Art of War," *Infinity Journal* 4, no. 2 (2014): 18–24.

52. The deeper reasons why military professionals, notably those in countries such as the United States and the United Kingdom, eschew politics fall outside the scope of this study, but C. Wright Mills perhaps provides an explanation: "Inside their often trim bureaucracy, where everything seems under neat control, army officers have felt that 'politics' is a dirty, uncertain, and ungentlemanly kind of game; and in terms of their status code, they have often felt that politicians were unqualified creatures inhabiting an uncertain world" (*The Power Elite* [New York: Oxford University Press, 1956], 174).

53. Michael Oakeshott, *Rationalism in Politics and Other Essays* (London: Methuen, 1981) 88.

54. Ibid.

55. Ibid.

56. KCL Insurgency Group, "Reviewing UK Army Countering Insurgency," meeting, June 20, 2007, King's College London, notes taken by the group's chair and circulated internally.

57. Montgomery McFate, "The Military Utility of Understanding Adversary Culture," *Joint Forces Quarterly* 38, 3rd quarter (2005): 43.

58. For such a misunderstanding, see, among other sources, Martin Van Creveld, *The Transformation of War* (New York: Free Press, 1991), 33–62; K. J. Holsti, *The State, War, and the State of War* (Cambridge, UK: Cambridge University Press, 1996), 1–18; Mary Kaldor, *New and Old Wars: Organized Violence in the Global Era* (Stanford: Stanford University Press, 1999), 20–23; John Keegan, *A History of Warfare* (New York: Vintage, 1994), 13–30; John Mueller, "The Banality of Ethnic War," *International Security* 25, no. 1 (2000): 42–70; Ralph Peters, "The New Strategic Trinity," *Parameters* 28, no. 4 (1998–1999): 73–79.

59. Clausewitz, *On War*, 89.

60. Ibid., 87.

61. Colin S. Gray, *The Strategy Bridge: Theory for Practice* (Oxford: Oxford University Press, 2010), 29.

62. Helmuth von Moltke, *Moltke on the Art of War: Selected Writings*, ed. Daniel J. Hughes (New York: Presidio, 1993), 45.

63. See John Stone, *Military Strategy: The Politics and Technique of War* (London: Continuum, 2011), 4–13.

64. The original U.S. document was US Department of the Army, *Counterinsurgency*, FM3-24/MCWP 3-33.5 (Washington, D.C.: US Department of the Army, Headquarters, 2006), followed in 2007 by the *Counterinsurgency Field Manual*.

65. Geoffrey Till, "The Evolution of Strategy in the New World Order," in Craig A. Snyder, ed., *Contemporary Security and Strategy* (London: Palgrave Macmillan, 2008), 97.

66. British Army, *Army Doctrine Publication: Operations* (Swindon, UK: Defence, Concepts, and Doctrine Centre and Ministry of Defence, 2010), 2, https://www.gov.uk/government/uploads/system/uploads/attachment_data/file/33695/ADPOperationsDec10.pdf, accessed November 19, 2013.

67. See British Army, *Countering Insurgency*, 3-3, and Galula, *Counterinsurgency Warfare*, 63.

68. Quoted in British Army, *Countering Insurgency*, 3-3, 3-4

69. For a survey of the situation in Afghanistan, see Tim Bird and Alex Marshall, *Afghanistan: How the West Lost Its Way* (New Haven: Yale University Press, 2010).

70. Office of the President of the United States, *National Security Strategy* (Washington, D.C.: Office of the President of the United States, 2010), 21.

71. Again, the British counterinsurgency manual superficially appears to recognize the role of ideology, but in tactically instrumental terms as a "mechanism of motivation" employed by insurgent leaders to mobilize followers (British Army, *Countering Insurgency*, 2-5).

72. Nagl and Burton, "Thinking Globally and Acting Locally," 126.

73. Gian Gentile, "A Strategy of Tactics: Population-Centric COIN and the Army," *Parameters* 39, no. 3 (2009): 5–7.

74. Celeste Ward Gventer, "Interventionism Run Amok," *Foreign Policy*, August 10, 2011, http://www.foreignpolicy.com/articles/2011/08/10/interventionism_run_amok, accessed November 19, 2013.

75. Gentile, "A Strategy of Tactics," 5–9.

76. Gentile, *Wrong Turn*, 85–110.

77. This narrative theme is explored in Joshua Rovner, "The Heroes of COIN," *Orbis* 52, no. 2 (2012): 215–32.

78. Fred Barnes, "How Bush Decided on the Surge," *Weekly Standard*, February 4, 2008, http://www.weeklystandard.com/Content/Public/Articles/000/000/014/658dwgrn.asp, accessed May 14, 2014.

79. Michael Barone, "Lessons from the Surge," *Townhall.com*, December 29, 2007, http://townhall.com/columnists/michaelbarone/2007/12/29/lessons_from_the_surge/page/full, accessed May 14, 2014.

80. Peter D. Feaver, "Anatomy of the Surge," *Commentary*, April 1, 2008, http://www.commentarymagazine.com/article/anatomy-of-the-surge/, accessed May 14, 2014.

81. See Sullivan, "Leadership in Counterinsurgency," 119–23.

82. Lewis Sorley, *A Better War: The Unexamined Victories and Final Tragedy of America's Last Years in Vietnam* (Orlando, FL: Harcourt, 1999).

83. See Max Boot, "The War Over the Vietnam War: A New Biography Puts an End to the Idea That We Could Not Win," *Wall Street Journal*, October 4, 2011, http://online.wsj.com/article/SB10001424052970204422404576595011469382894.html, accessed March 26, 2012. Such a view is countered in Gentile, *Wrong Turn*, 59–84.

84. Gentile, *Wrong Turn*, 85.

85. See Tom Englehardt, *The End of Victory Culture: Cold War America and the Disillusioning of a Generation* (Amherst: University of Massachusetts Press, 1995), 234–41.

86. *The Legacy of Lawrence of Arabia*, BBC2, Episode 1, January 16, 2010, and Episode 2, January 23, 2010.

87. See, for example, Tarak Barkawi and Mark Laffey, "The Post-colonial Moment in Security Studies," *Review of International Studies* 32, no. 2 (2006): 329.

88. See John Nagl, "Let's Win the Wars We're In," *Joint Forces Quarterly* 52, 1st quarter (2009): 20–26.

89. Nagl, *Learning to Eat Soup with a Knife*, 18.

90. Ibid., 35–55.

91. Colin Gray, "Thinking Asymmetrically in Times of Terror," *Parameters* 32, no. 1 (2002): 13.

92. *US Army/Marine Corps Counterinsurgency Field Manual*, liii.

93. The British Army's manual *Countering Insurgency* also stipulates a set of "ten [self-evident] principles for counterinsurgency": "1. Primacy of political purpose. 2. Unity of effort. 3. Understand the human terrain. 4. Secure the population. 5. Neutralise the insurgent. 6. Gain and maintain popular support. 7. Operate in accordance with the law. 8. Integrate intelligence. 9. Prepare for the long term. 10. Learn and adapt" (1-2, 3-2).

94. Sarah Sewall, "Introduction to the University of Chicago Press Edition: A Radical Field Manual," in *US Army/Marine Corps Counterinsurgency Field Manual*, xxxiii.

95. Quoted in John Nagl, "Constructing the Legacy of Field Manual 3-24," *Joint Forces Quarterly* 58, 3rd quarter (2010): 118.

96. See, for example, Gentile, *Wrong Turn*, 89–94.

3. Counterinsurgency and the Ideology of Modernization

1. Thomas E. Ricks, *Fiasco: The American Military Adventure in Iraq* (New York: Penguin, 2006), 228–32.

2. John Nagl, "Foreword to the University of Chicago Press Edition," in *The US Army/ Marine Corps Counterinsurgency Field Manual* (Chicago: University of Chicago Press, 2007), xv.

3. Eric Voegelin, *Modernity Without Restraint: Political Religions; The New Science of Politics; and Science, Politics, and Gnosticism*, vol. 5 of *The Collected Works of Eric Voegelin* (Columbia: University of Missouri Press, 2000).

4. Sherard Cowper-Coles, *Cables from Kabul: The Inside Story of the West's Afghan Campaign* (London: Harper, 2012), 277–78.

5. Gian Gentile, *Wrong Turn: America's Deadly Embrace of Counterinsurgency* (New York: Free Press, 2013), 7.

6. Thomas E. Ricks, *The Gamble: General David Petraeus and the American Military Adventure in Iraq, 2006–2008* (New York: Penguin, 2009); Victor Davis Hanson, *The Savior Generals: How Five Great Commanders Saved Wars That Were Lost—from Ancient Greece to Iraq* (London: Bloomsbury 2013).

7. Rajiv Chandrasekaran, *Little America: The War Within the War for Afghanistan* (London: Bloomsbury, 2013), 118.

8. *US Army/Marine Corps Counterinsurgency Field Manual*, 200.

9. David Kilcullen, "Twenty-Eight Articles: Fundamentals of Company Level Counterinsurgency," *Small Wars Journal*, March 29, 2006, 2, smallwarsjournal.com/documents/28articles.pdf, accessed November 17, 2013.

10. *US Army/Marine Corps Counterinsurgency Field Manual*, 37.

11. Quoted in Nils Gilman, *Mandarins of the Future: Modernization Theory in Cold War America* (Baltimore: Johns Hopkins University Press, 2003), 1.

12. Ibid., 16.

13. Samuel P. Huntington, "The Change to Change: Modernization, Development, and Politics," *Comparative Politics* 3, no. 3 (1971): 284, 285.

14. Charles Lindblom, "Political Science in the 1940s and 1950s," *Daedalus* 126, no. 1 (1997): 230.

15. Leonard Binder, "The Natural History of Development Theory," *Comparative Studies in Society and History* 28, no. 1 (1986): 10.

16. Talcott Parsons, *The Social System* (New York: Free Press, 1951); Edward Shils, *Tradition* (London: Faber and Faber, 1981).

17. Talcott Parsons, *On Institutions and Social Evolution* (Chicago: University of Chicago Press, 1982), 24.

18. Ibid., 48.

19. Karl Deutsch, *The Nerves of Government: Models of Political Communication and Control* (New York: Free Press 1963), 145.

20. Ibid., 241.

21. Binder, "The Natural History of Development Theory," 11.

22. Huntington, "The Change to Change," 287–88.

23. Ibid., 288.

24. See Gilman, *Mandarins of the Future*, 155–202.

25. Marion J. Levy, *Modernization: Latecomers and Survivors* (New York: Free Press, 1972), 3, 136.

26. Dankwart A. Rustow, *A World of Nations: Problems of Political Modernization* (Washington, D.C.: Brookings Institution Press, 1972), 6.

27. David E. Apter, *The Politics of Modernization* (Chicago: University of Chicago Press, 1965), 9–10, 43.

28. Huntington, "The Change to Change," 289–90.

29. Ibid.
30. Daniel Lerner, *The Passing of Traditional Society: Modernizing the Middle East* (New York: Free Press, 1958).
31. Gabriel Almond and James S. Coleman, eds., *The Politics of the Developing Areas* (Princeton: Princeton University Press, 1960).
32. Huntington, "The Change to Change," 314.
33. Samuel P. Huntington, *Political Order in Changing Societies* (New Haven: Yale University Press, 1968), 6.
34. Lucian W. Pye and Sidney Verba, introduction to Lucian W. Pye and Sidney Verba, eds., *Political Culture and Political Development* (Princeton: Princeton University Press, 1965), 11.
35. Leonard Binder, James S. Colman, Joseph LaPalombara, Lucian W. Pye, Sidney Verba, and Myron Weiner, *Crises and Sequences in Political Development* (Princeton: Princeton University Press, 1971).
36. Rustow, *A World of Nations*.
37. Gunnar Myrdal, *Asian Drama: An Inquiry Into the Poverty of Nations* (London: Allen Lane and Penguin, 1968), 20.
38. W. W. Rostow, *Politics and the Stages of Economic Growth* (Cambridge, UK: Cambridge University Press, 1971), 50–53, 65.
39. Ibid., 96.
40. Huntington, *Political Order in Changing Societies*, 11.
41. Ibid., 35.
42. Ibid., 35, 36.
43. Ibid., 41.
44. Ibid., 55.
45. Ibid., 87.
46. Seymour Martin Lipset, "Some Social Requisites of Democracy: Economic Development and Political Legitimacy," *American Political Science Review* 53, no. 1 (1959): 75.
47. Johanna Bockman, review of Nils Gilman, *Mandarins of the Future: Modernization Theory in Cold War America*, *Journal of Cold War Studies* 8, no. 2 (2006): 141.
48. Walter A. McDougall, *Promised Land, Crusader State: The American Encounter with the World Since 1776* (New York: Houghton Mifflin, 1997), 4–5.
49. See Andrew Hurrell and Ngaire Woods, "Globalization and Inequality," *Millennium* 24, no. 3 (1995): 447–70.
50. Francis Fukuyama, *The End of History and the Last Man* (London: Penguin, 1992), 287–340.
51. McDougall, *Promised Land*, 173.
52. See Andrew J. Bacevich and Elizabeth H. Prodromou, "God Is Not Neutral: Religion and US Foreign Policy After 9/11," *Orbis* 48, no. 1 (2001): 43–54; Garry Dorrien, *Imperial Designs: Neoconservatism and the New Pax Americana* (New York: Routledge, 2005), 203–35; Michael Hardt and Antonio Negri, *Empire* (Cambridge, MA: Harvard University Press, 2000).

53. *US Army/Marine Corps Counterinsurgency Field Manual*, 2.

54. Sarah Sewall, "Introduction to the University of Chicago Press Edition: A Radical Field Manual," in *US Army/Marine Corps Counterinsurgency Field Manual*, xxx.

55. Kilcullen, "Twenty-Eight Articles," 8.

56. See Philip A. Brown and M. L. R. Smith, "The Rise of Gulf War Paradigm 2.0," *Orbis* 58, no. 1 (2013): 83–103.

57. For example, K. J. Holsti's statistical assessment indicates that 75 percent of the 164 cases of warfare identified since the end of World War II involved armed conflict within state boundaries, and only 18–20 percent of cases can accurately be termed "interstate wars" (*The State, War, and the State of War* [Cambridge, UK: Cambridge University Press, 1996], 22–24).

58. Lt. Gen. Sir John Kiszley, "Learning About Counterinsurgency," *Military Review*, March–April 2007, 10.

59. See Walter LaFeber, "The Rise and Fall of Colin Powell," *Political Science Quarterly* 124, no. 1 (2009): 71–93.

60. Quoted in Nagl, "Foreword," xiv.

61. David Ucko, "Innovation or Inertia? The US Military and the Learning of Counterinsurgency," *Orbis* 52, no. 2 (2008): 291.

62. David C. Hendrickson and Robert W. Tucker, "Revisions in Need of Revising: What Went Wrong in the Iraq War," *Survival* 47, no. 2 (2005): 7–32.

63. See, for example, Ahmed S. Hashem, "The Insurgency in Iraq," *Small Wars and Insurgencies* 14, no. 3 (2003): 1–22; Alistair Finlan, "Trapped in the Dead Ground: US Counter-Insurgency Strategy in Iraq," *Small Wars and Insurgencies* 16, no. 1 (2005): 1–21; Robert Tomes, "Schlock and Blah: Counter-Insurgency Realities in a Rapid Dominance Era," *Small Wars and Insurgencies* 16, no. 1 (2005): 37–56; Jeffrey Record, "Why the Strong Lose," *Parameters* 35, no. 4 (2005–2006): 16–31.

64. Nagl, "Foreword," xv.

65. See, for example, Lt. Gen. David Petraeus, "Learning Counterinsurgency: Observations from Soldiering in Iraq," *Military Review*, January–February 2006, 2–11.

66. Ucko, "Innovation or Inertia?" 294.

67. In particular, see Nigel Aylwin-Foster, "Changing the Army for Counterinsurgency Operations," *Military Review*, November–December 2005, 2–15.

68. Frank G. Hoffman, "Neo-classical Insurgency?" *Parameters* 37, no. 2 (2007): 71–87.

69. Examples of this literature include: Jonathan Stevenson, *"We Wrecked the Place": Contemplating an End to Northern Ireland's Troubles* (New York: Free Press, 1996); Malachi O'Doherty, *The Trouble with Guns: Republican Strategy and the Provisional IRA* (Belfast: Blackstaff, 1998); Michael Page, *Prisons, Peace, and Terrorism: Penal Policy and the Reduction of Terrorism in Northern Ireland, Italy, and the Basque Country, 1968–97* (Basingstoke, UK: Macmillan, 1998); Ed Moloney, *A Secret History of the IRA* (London: Penguin, 2002); Peter Neumann, *Britain's Long War: British Strategy in the Northern Ireland Conflict, 1969–98* (Basingstoke, UK: Palgrave Macmillan, 2003).

70. For more on McFate, see Matthew B. Stannard, "Montgomery McFate's Mission," *San Francisco Chronicle*, April 29, 2007.

71. Montgomery McFate, "The Military Utility of Understanding Adversary Culture," *Joint Forces Quarterly* 38, 3rd quarter (2005): 42.

72. Montgomery McFate, "Iraq: The Social Context of IEDs," *Military Review*, May–June 2005, 37–40.

73. Montgomery McFate and Andrea Jackson, "An Organizational Solution for DOD's Cultural Knowledge Needs," *Military Review*, July–August 2005, 18.

74. *US Army/Marine Corps Counterinsurgency Field Manual*, 27.

75. For a survey of this area, see Col. Clinton J. Ancker, "Doctrine for Asymmetric Warfare," *Military Review*, July–August 2003, 18–25; Patrick Porter, "Shadow Wars: Asymmetric Warfare in the Past and Future," *Security Dialogue* 37, no. 4 (2006): 551–61.

76. Rupert Smith's *The Utility of Force: The Art of War in the Modern World* (London: Allen Lane, 2005) is the seminal work in this developing field, although Mary Kaldor's *New and Old Wars: Organized Violence in a Global Era* (Stanford: Stanford University Press, 1999) also foreshadowed much of this debate.

77. See, for example, Andrew Dorman, Matthew Uttley, and M. L. R. Smith, eds., *The Changing Face of Military Power: Joint Warfare in an Expeditionary Era* (Basingstoke, UK: Palgrave, 2002).

78. John Nagl, *Learning to Eat Soup with a Knife: Lessons from Malaya and Vietnam* (Chicago: University of Chicago Press, 2002), 51.

79. Montgomery McFate and Andrea V. Jackson, "The Object of War: Counterinsurgency and the Four Tools of Political Competition," *Military Review*, January–February 2006, 13–16.

80. Nagl, *Learning to Eat Soup with a Knife*, 216.

81. Quoted in Stannard, "Montgomery McFate's Mission."

82. Quoted in ibid.

83. See, for example, Eliot Cohen, Conrad Crane, Jan Horvath, and John Nagl, "Principles, Imperatives, and Paradoxes of Counterinsurgency," *Military Review*, March–April 2006, 49–53.

84. Nagl, "Foreword," xiii–xx.

85. Montgomery McFate, "Anthropology and Counterinsurgency: The Strange Story of Their Curious Relationship," *Military Review*, March–April 2005, 24, 27.

86. Beatrice Heuser, "The Cultural Revolution in Counter-Insurgency," *Journal of Strategic Studies* 30, no. 1 (2007): 165.

87. Ucko, "Innovation or Inertia?" 308.

88. See, for example, Lt. Col. Robert M. Cassidy, "The Savage Wars of Peace," *Military Review*, November–December 2004, 76–77, and "Winning the War of the Flea," *Military Review*, September 2004, 41–46; Lt. Col. Wade M. Markel, "Draining the Swamp: The British Strategy of Population Control," *Parameters* 36, no. 1 (2006): 35–48, and "Winning Our Own Hearts and Minds: Promotion in Wartime," *Military Review*, November–December 2004, 25–30; Lt. Col. James D. Campbell, "French Algeria and British Northern Ireland: Legitimacy and the Rule of Law in Low-Intensity Conflict," *Military Review*, March–April 2005, 2–5; Lou DiMarco, "Losing the Moral Compass: Torture and *Guerre Revolutionnaire* in the Algerian War," *Parameters* 36, no. 2 (2006): 63–76;

Brian A. Jackson, "Counterinsurgency Intelligence in a 'Long War': The British Experience in Northern Ireland," *Military Review*, January–February 2007, 74–85; Walter C. Ladwig, "Managing Counterinsurgency: Lessons from Malaya," *Military Review*, May–June 2007, 56–66; Maj. Michael D. Sullivan, "Leadership in Counterinsurgency: A Tale of Two Leaders," *Military Review*, September–October 2007, 119–23.

89. See David Galula, *Counterinsurgency Warfare: Theory and Practice* (1964; reprint, Westport, CT: Praeger, 2006), and *Pacification in Algeria, 1956–1958* (1963; reprint, Santa Monica, CA: RAND, 2006); Roger Trinquier, *Modern Warfare: A French View of Counterinsurgency* (London: Pall Mall, 1964; reprint, Westport, CT: Praeger, 2006); Bernard Fall, *Street Without Joy: The French Debacle in Indochina* (London: Pall Mall, 1963; reprint, Mechanicsburg, PA: Stackpole, 2005); John J. McCuen, *The Art of Counter-Revolutionary War: The Strategy of Counterinsurgency* (London: Faber, 1966; reprint, St. Petersburg, FL: Hailer 2005).

90. There was, of course, always a residual academic interest in matters of insurgency even during the years of the Cold War, as represented by the writings of academics such as Charles Townshend, I. F. W. Beckett, and others located ostensibly around the British Army's officer training and staff college at Camberley, Surrey. See, for example, Ian F. W. Beckett, *The Roots of Counterinsurgency: Armies and Guerrilla Warfare* (London: Blanford, 1988); Ian F. W. Beckett and John Pimlott, eds., *Armed Forces and Modern Counterinsurgency* (New York: St. Martin's Press, 1985); Charles Townshend, *Britain's Civil Wars: Counterinsurgency in the Twentieth Century* (London: Faber & Faber, 1986). In the United States, the study of insurgency/counterinsurgency also retained a marginal following. On the one hand, a handful of scholars such as the historian Thomas Mockaitis showed an interest in the British experience of counterinsurgency, and other analysts produced studies on the subject framed within the context of conducting inquests into the American performance in Vietnam. See, for example, Thomas R. Mockaitis, *British Counter-Insurgency, 1919–1960* (London: Macmillan, 1990), and Andrew Krepenevich, *The Army and Vietnam* (Baltimore: Johns Hopkins University Press, 1986).

91. Colin Gray, "Thinking Asymmetrically in Times of Terror," *Parameters* 32, no. 1 (2002): 13.

92. There are too many examples to enumerate, but for a selection see Kalev I. Sepp, "Best Practices in Counterinsurgency," *Military Review*, May–June 2005, 8–12; Col. Thomas X. Hammes, "Countering Evolved Insurgent Networks," *Military Review*, July–August 2006, 18–26; and Jan S. Breemer, "Statistics, Real Estate, and the Principles of War: Why There Is No Unified Theory of War," *Military Review*, September–October 2006, 84–89.

93. Sarah Sewall, "Modernizing US Counterinsurgency Practice: Rethinking Risk and Developing a National Strategy," *Military Review*, September–October 2006, 103.

94. Ibid., 104.

95. John A. Lynn, "Patterns of Insurgency and Counterinsurgency," *Military Review*, July–August 2005, 27.

96. Ibid.

97. See Col. James K. Greer, "Operation Knockout: COIN in Iraq," *Military Review*, November–December 2005, 16–19; Petraeus, "Learning Counterinsurgency." For a broader survey of the effects of this learning process, see Frederick W. Kagan and Kimberly Kagan, "The Patton of Counterinsurgency," *Weekly Standard*, October 3, 2008.

98. Lt. Col. Chris Gibson, "Battlefield Victories and Strategic Success: The Path Forward in Iraq," *Military Review*, September–October 2006, 49.

99. Capt. Travis Patriquin, "Using Occam's Razor to Connect the Dots: The Ba'ath Party and the Insurgency in Tal Afar," *Military Review*, January–February 2007, 16–25.

100. This is not to say that the efforts to make the U.S. Army embrace COIN thinking did not encounter resistance. For the contending positions, see the debate between John Nagl and Gian Gentile: John Nagl, "Let's Win the Wars We're In," *Joint Forces Quarterly* 52, 1st quarter (2009): 20–26, and Gian Gentile, "Let's Build an Army to Win *All* Wars," *Joint Forces Quarterly*, 52, 1st quarter (2009): 27–33.

101. See also Carter Malkasian, "The Role of Perceptions and Political Reform in Counterinsurgency: The Case of Western Iraq, 2004–05," *Small Wars and Insurgencies* 17, no. 3 (2006): 367–94; Warren Chin, "Examining the Application of British Counterinsurgency Doctrine by the American Army in Iraq," *Small Wars and Insurgencies* 18, no. 1 (2007): 1–26; James Corum, "Rethinking US Army Counter-Insurgency Doctrine," *Contemporary Security Policy* 28, no. 1 (2007): 127–42.

102. Of the many possible contributions in this respect, see Maj. Morgan Mann, "The Power Equation: Using Tribal Politics in Counterinsurgency," *Military Review*, May–June 2007, 104–8; Col. Joseph D. Celeski, "Attacking Insurgent Space: Sanctuary Denial and Border Interdiction," *Military Review*, November–December 2006, 51–57; Col. Gregory Wilson, "Anatomy of a Successful COIN Operation: OEF-Philippines and the Indirect Approach," *Military Review*, November–December 2006, 2–12; Michael R. Melillo, "Outfitting a Big-War Military with Small-War Capabilities," *Parameters* 36, no. 3 (2006): 22–35; David M. Tressler, *Negotiation in the New Strategic Environment: Lessons from Iraq* (Carlisle, PA: Strategic Studies Institute, 2007); James Clancy and Chuck Crossett, "Measuring Effectiveness in Irregular Warfare," *Parameters* 37, no. 2 (2007): 88–100; Brian Reed, "A Social Network Approach to Understanding an Insurgency," *Parameters* 37, no. 2 (2007): 19–30; Jeffrey Record, "External Assistance: Enabler of Insurgent Success," *Parameters* 36, no. 3 (2006): 36–49; Jim Baker, "Systems Thinking and Counterinsurgencies," *Parameters* 36, no. 4 (2006–2007): 26–43; Raymond Millen, "The Hobbesian Notion of Self-Preservation Concerning Human Behavior During an Insurgency," *Parameters* 36, no. 4 (2006–2007): 4–13.

103. See, for example, Christopher M. Ford, "Speak No Evil: Targeting a Population's Neutrality to Defeat an Insurgency," *Parameters* 35, no. 4 (2005): 51–66; Lt. Col. Douglas A. Ollivant and Lt. Eric D. Chewing, "Producing Victory: Rethinking Conventional Forces in COIN Operations," *Military Review*, July–August 2006, 50–59; David Betz, "Redesigning Land Forces for 'Wars Amongst the People,'" *Contemporary Security Policy* 28, no. 2 (2007): 221–43; Major Mark P. Krieger, "We the People Are Not the Center of Gravity," *Military Review*, July–August 2007, 96–100; Col. Peter R. Mansoor and

Maj. Mark S. Ulrich, "Linking Doctrine to Action: A New Center-of-Gravity Analysis," *Military Review*, September–October 2007, 45–51.

104. *US Army/Marine Corps Counterinsurgency Field Manual*, i.

105. Colin Jackson, "Government in a Box? Counter-Insurgency, State Building, and the Technocratic Conceit," in Celeste Ward Gventer, David Martin Jones, and M. L. R. Smith, eds., *The New Counter-Insurgency Era in Critical Perspective* (London: Palgrave Macmillan, 2014), 92.

106. Ibid., 82.

107. Ibid., 82–105.

108. On the idea of the Leviathan state as the basis of security and the decline of violence, see Steven Pinker, *The Better Angels of Our Nature: A History of Violence and Humanity* (London: Penguin, 2011).

109. Jackson, "Government in a Box?" 82–83.

110. Kilcullen, "Twenty-Eight Articles," 1.

111. *US Army/Marine Corps Counterinsurgency Field Manual*, 55.

112. Sewall, "Introduction," xxxvii.

113. Ibid., xli.

114. Ibid., xxxvii.

115. Michael Oakeshott, *Rationalism in Politics and Other Essays* (London: Methuen, 1981), 101.

116. Jacques Ellul, *The Technological Society* (London: Jonathan Cape, 1964), 24–25.

117. *US Army/Marine Corps Counterinsurgency Field Manual*, 35.

118. For this division of the population into three groups, see figure 1.1, "Example Logical Lines of Operations for a Counterinsurgency," in *US Army/Marines Corps Counterinsurgency Field Manual*, 155.

119. Ibid, ix–xi.

120. The International Security Assistance Force statement formally claims its mission to be: "In support of the Government of the Islamic Republic of Afghanistan, ISAF conducts operations in Afghanistan to reduce the capability and will of the insurgency, support the growth in capacity and capability of the Afghan National Security Forces (ANSF), and facilitate improvements in governance and socio-economic development in order to provide a secure environment for sustainable stability that is observable to the population." See http://www.isaf.nato.int/mission.html, accessed November 5, 2011.

121. Gentile, *Wrong Turn*, 119.

122. Rostow, *Politics and the Stages of Growth*, 135.

123. Ibid., 276.

124. Rostow cited in Robert S. McNamara, *In Retrospect: The Tragedy and Lessons of Vietnam* (New York: Vintage, 1996), 38.

125. Ibid., 48.

126. See Jason Thomas, "Romancing the COIN," *Small Wars Journal*, March 13, 2012, http://smallwarsjournal.com/jrnl/art/romancing-the-coin, accessed March 30, 2012.

127. Hans Morgenthau, "Vietnam and the National Interest," in Marvin E. Gettleman, ed., *Vietnam: History, Documents, and Opinions on a Major Crisis* (London: Penguin, 1965), 391.

128. See, among other sources, Anthony H. Cordesman, *"Shape, Clear, Hold, Build, and Transfer": The Full Metrics of the Afghan War* (Washington, D.C.: Center for Strategic and International Studies, February 18, 2010), http://csis.org/files/publication/100302_afghan_metrics_combined.pdf, accessed March 30, 2012.

129. James A. Gavrilis, "A Model for Population-Centered Warfare: A Conceptual Framework for Analyzing and Understanding the Theory and Practice of Insurgency and Counterinsurgency," *Small Wars Journal*, May 10, 2009, http://smallwarsjournal.com/jrnl/art/a-model-for-population-centered-warfare, accessed March 26, 2012.

130. *US Army/Marine Corps Counterinsurgency Field Manual*, 51.

131. Alex Marshall, "Imperial Nostalgia, the Liberal Lie, and the Perils of Postmodern Counterinsurgency," *Small Wars and Insurgencies* 21, no. 2 (2010): 235.

132. Ambassador Robert D. Blackwill, "Afghanistan and the Uses of History: Insights from Ernest May," Second Annual Ernest May Memorial Lecture, Aspen Strategy Group, August 2010, http://www.aspeninstitute.org/policy-work/aspen-strategy-group/programs-topic/other-events/afghan-history, accessed December 26, 2011.

133. Michael Oakeshott, *The Politics of Faith and the Politics of Scepticism*, ed. Timothy Fuller (New Haven: Yale University Press, 1996), 45–67.

134. See Jeffrey H. Michaels and Matthew Ford, "Bandwagonistas: Rhetorical Re-description, Strategic Choice, and the Politics of Counter-Insurgency," *Small Wars and Insurgencies* 22, no. 2 (2011): 352–84.

4. The Paradoxes of Counterinsurgency and Globalization

1. *The US Army/Marine Corps Counterinsurgency Field Manual* (Chicago: University of Chicago Press, 2007), 38–50.

2. Ibid., 37, 45.

3. Anthony Giddens, The *Consequences of Modernity* (Cambridge, UK: Cambridge University Press, 1991), 64.

4. John Baylis and Steve Smith, introduction to John Baylis and Steve Smith, eds., *The Globalization of World Politics: An Introduction to International Relations* (Oxford: Oxford University Press, 2001), 9.

5. Anthony G. McGrew, "Conceptualizing Global Politics," in Anthony G. McGrew and Paul G. Lewis, eds., *Global Politics, Globalization, and the Nation-State* (Cambridge, UK: Polity, 1992), 23.

6. Thomas Larsonn, *The Race to the Top: The Real Story of Globalization* (Washington, D.C.: Cato Institute, 2001), 9.

7. Francis Fukuyama, *The End of History and the Last Man* (London: Penguin, 1992); Thomas L. Friedman, *The Lexus and the Olive Tree* (New York: Anchor Books, 2000).

8. Jan Nederveen Pieterse, "Globalization as Hybridization," in Mike Featherstone, Scott Lash, and Roland Robertson, eds., *Global Modernities* (London: Sage, 1995), 99–100.

9. David Held and Anthony McGrew, "The End of the Old Order? Globalization and the Prospects for World Order," *Review of International Studies* 24, no. 3 (1998), 232.

10. Colin Hay and David Marsh, "Introduction: Demystifying Globalization," in Colin Hay and David Marsh, eds., *Demystifying Globalization* (London: Macmillan, 2000), 3.

11. See Jeffrey S. Juris, *Networking Futures: The Movements Against Corporate Globalization* (Durham, NC: Duke University Press, 2008), 2.

12. For example, see Bernard-Henri Lévy, *Left in Dark Times: A Stand Against the New Barbarism* (New York: Random House, 2008), and Naomi Klein, *No Logo* (New York: Picador, 2000).

13. Tarak Barkawi and Mark Laffey, "The Post-colonial Moment in Security Studies," *Review of International Studies* 32, no. 2 (2006): 329.

14. For the classic exposition of this thesis, see Edward Gibbon, *The History of the Decline and Fall of the Roman Empire*, 12 vols., ed. J. B. Bury (New York: Fred de Fau, 1904), vol. 4, chap. 38, parts I–III.

15. Ernest Gellner, *Muslim Society* (Cambridge, UK: Cambridge University Press, 1981).

16. Ernest Gellner, *Conditions of Liberty: Civil Society and Its Rivals* (London: Hamish Hamilton, 1994), 199.

17. See Kemal H. Karpat, *The Politicization of Islam: Reconstructing Faith, States, and Community in the Late Ottoman Empire* (Oxford: Oxford University Press, 1981), 18.

18. See Elie Kedourie, *Afghani and Adud: An Essay on Religious Unbelief and Political Activism in Modern Islam* (London: Cass, 1966); Nikki R. Keddie, *An Islamic Response to Imperialism: Political and Religious Writings of Jamal a-Din "al-Afghani"* (Berkeley: University of California Press, 1998).

19. Natana J. Delong-Bas, *Wahabi Islam: From Revival to Reform to Global Jihad* (London: I. B. Tauris, 2004).

20. Sayyid Qutb, *Milestones* (New York: Mother Mosque Foundation, 1979), 81, 94.

21. William E. Shepherd, *Sayyid Qutb and Islamic Activism* (Leiden: Brill, 1996).

22. Qutb, *Milestones*, 63–70.

23. Ayman Muhammad Rabi al-Zawahiri, quoted in Nimrod Raphaeli, *Radical Islamist Profiles*, 3. *Ayman Muhammad Rabi al Zawahiri: The Making of an Arch Terrorist* (Berlin: Middle East Research Institute, 2003), 10.

24. "Declaration of Jihad Against the Country's Tyrants" ("Al-Qaeda Training Manual"), n.d., 5. Recovered by police in Manchester, UK, in 1998, translated from Arabic to English, and presented as evidence in the trial of Richard Reid in 2003, the "Al-Qaeda Training Manual" is available at http://www.thetulsan.com/manual.html, accessed December 26, 2013.

25. Ibid., 3.

26. Johannes J. G. Jansen, *The Neglected Duty: The Creed of Sadat's Assassins and Islamic Resurgence in the Middle East* (London: Macmillan, 1986).

27. Quoted in Raphaeli, *Radical Islamist Profiles*, 10.

28. John Mackinlay, "Tackling bin Laden: Lessons from History," *Observer*, October 28, 2001.

29. See John Mackinlay, *The Insurgent Archipelago* (London: Hurst, 2009), 1–8.

30. Ibid., 4–6.

31. In fact, David Kilcullen and Montgomery McFate shared a writing platform in *Anthropology Today*, defending themselves and the role of anthropologists in facilitating the writing of FM 3-24, whom Roberto González had attacked for allegedly allowing themselves to become tools of "US imperial power" ("Towards Mercenary Anthropology? The New US Army Counterinsurgency Manual FM 3-24 and the Military Anthropology Complex," *Anthropology Today* 23, no. 3 [2007]: 17; see also David Kilcullen, "Ethics, Politics, and Non-state Warfare," *Anthropology Today* 23, no. 3 (2007): 20, and Montgomery McFate, "Building Bridges or Burning Heretics," *Anthropology Today* 23, no. 3 [2007]: 21).

32. David Kilcullen, "Twenty-Eight Articles: Fundamentals of Company-Level Counterinsurgency," *Small Wars Journal*, March 29, 2006, 6, smallwarsjournal.com/documents/28articles.pdf, accessed November 17, 2013.

33. David Kilcullen, "Counterinsurgency Redux," *Survival* 48, no. 4 (2006): 111, 112.

34. *US Army/Marine Corps Counterinsurgency Field Manual*, 8.

35. Sarah Sewall, "Introduction to the University of Chicago Press Edition: A Radical Field Manual," in *US Army/Marine Corps Counterinsurgency Field Manual*, xlii.

36. Ibid., xliii.

37. Frank Hoffman, "Neo-classical Insurgency?" *Parameters* 37, no. 2 (2007): 71.

38. See Jonathan Masters and Zachary Laub, "Al-Qaeda in Iraq (a.k.a. Islamic State in Iraq and Greater Syria," Council on Foreign Relations, October 29, 2013, http://www.cfr.org/iraq/al-qaeda-iraq-k-islamic-state-iraq-greater-syria/p14811, accessed December 27, 2013.

39. David Betz, "Redesigning Land Forces for 'Wars Amongst the People,'" *Contemporary Security Policy* 28, no. 2 (2007): 225.

40. Hoffman, "Neo-classical Insurgency?" 71.

41. Quoted in Montgomery McFate, "Iraq: The Social Context of IEDs," *Military Review*, May–June 2005, 40.

42. See, for example, *US Army/Marine Corps Counterinsurgency Field Manual*, 11–15.

43. Hoffman, "Neo-classical Insurgency?" 71.

44. Steven Metz, *Rethinking Insurgency* (Carlisle, PA: Strategic Studies Institute, 2007), 36.

45. Robert Taber, *War of the Flea: The Classic Study of Guerrilla Warfare* (New York: L. Stuart, 1965).

46. For a counterpoint to Steven Metz, see Lt. Col. Robert M. Cassidy, "The British Army and Counterinsurgency: The Salience of Military Culture," *Military Review*, May–June 2005, 56.

47. For an assessment of David Galula and his influence on COIN thinking, see Douglas Porch, "David Galula and the Revival of COIN in the US Military," in Celeste Ward Gventer, David Martin Jones, and M. L. R. Smith, eds., *The New Counter-Insurgency Era in Critical Perspective* (London: Palgrave Macmillan, 2014), 173–98.

48. See Christopher Cradock and M. L. R. Smith, " 'No Fixed Values': A Reinterpretation of the Influence of the Theory of *Guerre Révolutionnaire* and the Battle of Algiers, 1956–1957," *Journal of Cold War Studies* 9, no. 4 (2007): 68–105.

49. See Jameel Jaffar and Amrit Singh, *Administration of Torture: A Documentary Record from Washington to Abu Ghraib* (New York: Columbia University Press, 2007).

50. See, for example, John Mackinlay's discussion of Britain's uncertain domestic counterterrorist/counterinsurgency policy after 9/11 in *The Insurgent Archipelago*, 117–219.

51. David Kilcullen, "Countering Global Insurgency," *Journal of Strategic Studies* 28, no. 4 (2005): 609.

52. Ibid., 610.

53. See Mackinlay, *The Insurgent Archipelago*, 77–121.

54. Hoffman, "Neo-classical Insurgency?" 77.

55. *US Army/Marine Corps Counterinsurgency Field Manual*, 25, 26.

56. Richard Jackson, "An Analysis of EU Counterterrorism Discourse Post–September 11," *Cambridge Review of International Affairs* 20, no. 2 (2007): 243.

57. Hoffman, "Neo-classical Insurgency?" 78. It would be more accurate to say the jihadist aspires to something founded in the seventh century.

58. David Kilcullen, "Subversion and Counter Subversion in the Campaign Against Terrorism in Europe," *Studies in Conflict and Terrorism* 30, no. 8 (2007): 649, 652.

59. Quoted in George Packer, "Knowing the Enemy: Can Social Scientists Redefine the 'War on Terror'?" *New Yorker*, December 18, 2006.

60. See in this context Barry Cooper, *New Political Religions, or An Analysis of Modern Terrorism* (Columbia: Missouri University Press, 2004).

61. See Mackinlay, *The Insurgent Archipelago*, 5.

62. KCL Insurgency Group, "Reviewing UK Army Countering Insurgency," meeting, King's College London, June 20, 2007, notes taken by the group's chair and circulated internally.

63. Raymond Aron, *On War: Atomic Weapons and Global Diplomacy*, trans. Terence Kilmartin (London: Secker and Warburg, 1958), 63.

64. Carl von Clausewitz, *On War*, trans. and ed. Michael Howard and Peter Paret (Princeton: Princeton University Press, 1984), 87–88.

65. Ibid., 87.

66. John Mackinlay, for instance, believes Clausewitz embodies this concern with interstate war; he suggested in 2001 that the "coalition of likeminded states to 'wage the War on Terrorism' is an old-fashioned emergency structure that would address a Clausewitzian threat to security" ("Tackling bin Laden"). Again, this interpretation is erroneous. Clausewitz never wrote about what constituted "threats to security," and to the extent that it is possible to discern a Clausewitzian understanding of threat, it is one that arises from the complex social and political conditions of individual societies— that is, the source of *all* war. Therefore, Mackinlay's statement is a tautology.

67. Jan Willem Honig, "Strategy in a Post-Clausewitzian Setting," in Gerd de Nooy, ed., *The Clausewitzian Dictum and the Future of Western Military Strategy* (The Hague: Kluwer Law International, 1997), 110.

68. Kilcullen, "Counterinsurgency Redux," 116, emphasis in original.
69. Honig, "Strategy in a Post-Clausewitzian Setting," 118.
70. Lawrence Freedman, "Globalisation and the War Against Terrorism," in Christopher Ankerson, ed., *Understanding Global Terror* (Cambridge, UK: Polity, 2007), 227.
71. Kilcullen, "Countering Global Insurgency," 606, 605.
72. John Mackinlay, *Globalisation and Insurgency*, Adelphi Paper no. 352 (London: International Institute for Strategic Studies and Oxford University Press, 2002), 33.
73. Kilcullen, "Countering Global Insurgency," 611–12.
74. *US Army/Marine Corps Counterinsurgency Field Manual*, 54.
75. Mackinlay, "Tackling bin Laden."
76. See, for example, Cooper, *New Political Religions*, 147, as well as Samuel L. Berger and Mona Sutphen, "Commandeering the Palestinian Cause: Bin Laden's Belated Concern," in James F. Hoge and Gideon Rose, eds., *How Did This Happen? Terrorism and the New War* (New York: Public Affairs, 2001), 123.
77. Mackinlay, "Tackling bin Laden."
78. Kilcullen, "Countering Global Insurgency," 612.
79. Richard Jackson, "Security, Democracy, and the Rhetoric of Counter-Terrorism," *Democracy and Security* 1, no. 2 (2005): 152.
80. Paul Rogers, *Global Security and the War on Terror: Elite Power and the Illusion of Control* (London: Routledge, 2008), 82, 99.
81. Joseba Zulaika and William A. Douglass, "The Terrorist Subject: Terrorism Studies and the Absent Subjectivity," *Critical Studies on Terrorism* 1, no. 1 (2008): 33.
82. Ken Booth, "The Human Faces of Terror: Reflections in a Cracked Looking-Glass," *Critical Studies on Terrorism* 1, no. 1 (2008): 75.
83. Barkawi and Laffey, "The Post-colonial Moment in Security Studies," 329. See also Taraq Barkawi, "On the Pedagogy of 'Small Wars,'" *International Affairs* 80, no. 1 (2004): 28.
84. Rogers, *Global Security and the War on Terror*, 33.
85. Mackinlay, "Tackling bin Laden."
86. Freedman, "Globalisation and the War Against Terrorism," 227.
87. Sewall, "Introduction to the University of Chicago Press Edition," xlii.
88. Kilcullen, "Countering Global Insurgency," 609.
89. "Full Text of MI5 Director-General's Speech," *Daily Telegraph*, November 5, 2007.
90. See John Naughton, "Stephen Pinker: Fighting Talk from the Prophet of Peace," *Observer*, October 15, 2011.
91. See, for example, Anthony Glees and Chris Pope, *When Students Turn to Terror: Terrorist and Extremist Activity on British University Campuses* (London: Social Affairs Unit, 2005).
92. Peter Clarke, *Learning from Experience: Counter-Terrorism in the UK Since 9/11*, Colin Cramphorn Memorial Lecture (London: Policy Exchange, 2007), 18.
93. See Jonathan Sacks, *The Home We Build Together: Recreating Society* (London: Continuum, 2008). Mackinlay also recognizes this point in *The Insurgent Archipelago*, 199.

94. See Thomas Harding, "Public Support for Afghanistan Is Vital," *Daily Telegraph*, November 13, 2008; Michael Evans, "Army Chief Predicts a 'Generation of Conflict,'" *London Times*, August 28, 2007.

95. Clausewitz, *On War*, 88–89.

5. The Illusion of Tradition: Myths and Paradoxes of British Counterinsurgency

1. Sarah Sewall, "Introduction to the University of Chicago Press Edition: A Radical Field Manual," in *The US Army/Marine Corps Counterinsurgency Field Manual* (Chicago: University of Chicago Press, 2007), xxiv.

2. British Army, *Army Field Manual*, vol. 5: *Operations Other Than War* (London: Ministry of Defence, 1995), 1-1, http://www.scribd.com/doc/28438057/11709-AFM-Vol-v-Operations-Other-Than-War, accessed January 5, 2013.

3. As summarized in Ian F. W. Beckett, "British Counter-Insurgency: A Historical Reflection," *Small Wars and Insurgencies* 23, nos. 4–5 (2012): 783.

4. British Army, *Countering Insurgency*, vol. 1, part 10 (Warminster, UK: Ministry of Defence, 2009).

5. Raul Girardet, *Mythes et mythologies politiques* (Paris: Éditions de Seuil: 1986), 17.

6. British Army, *Army Field Manual*, IV-1.

7. Ibid., VI-10 to VI-17. See Charles Callwell, *Small Wars: Their Principles and Practice* (London: His Majesty's Stationary Office, 1896; reprint, Lincoln: University of Nebraska Press and Bison Books, 1996); Charles Gwynn, *Notes on Imperial Policing* (London: Macmillan, 1934); and General John Dill, *Notes on the Tactical Lessons of the Palestine Rebellion* (London: War Office, 1937).

8. British Army, *Army Field Manual*, VI-20.

9. Ibid., IX-24.

10. Ibid., IX-26.

11. See, for example, Peter Lieb, "Suppressing Insurgencies in Comparison: The German in the Ukraine, 1918, and the British in Mesopotamia," *Small Wars and Insurgencies* 23, nos. 4–5 (2012): 628.

12. Frank Ledwidge, *Losing Small Wars: British Military Failure in Iraq and Afghanistan* (New Haven: Yale University Press, 2011), 3, 16, 151, 5.

13. Description of Ledwidge's *Losing Small Wars* on Amazon at http://www.amazon.co.uk/Losing-Small-Wars-Military-Afghanistan/dp/0300166710, accessed January 16, 2013.

14. See, for example, David Anderson, *History of the Hanged: Britain's Dirty War and the End of Empire* (London: Weidenfeld and Nicolson, 2005); Caroline Elkins, *Imperial Reckoning: The Untold Story of Britain's Gulag in Kenya* (New York: Henry Holt, 2005).

15. Numerous accounts by journalists, former soldiers, and academics retail the problems encountered by British forces in Iraq and Afghanistan. See, for example, James

Fergusson, *A Million Bullets: The Real Story of the British Army in Afghanistan* (London: Bantam, 2008); Stephen Grey, *Operation Snakebite* (London: Penguin, 2009); Patrick Bury, *Callsign Hades* (London: Simon and Schuster, 2010); Jack Fairweather, *A War of Choice: Honour, Hubris, and Sacrifice—the British in Iraq, 2003–9* (London: Vintage, 2012); Tim Bird and Alex Marshall, *Afghanistan: How the West Lost Its Way* (New Haven: Yale University Press, 2011); Ben Anderson, *No Worse Enemy: The Inside Story of the Chaotic Struggle for Afghanistan* (London: Oneworld, 2011); Toby Harnden, *Dead Men Risen: The Welsh Guards and the Defining Story of Britain's War in Afghanistan* (London: Bloomsbury, 2011); Sandy Gall, *The War Against the Taliban: Why It All Went Wrong in Afghanistan* (London: Bloomsbury, 2012). For the most penetrating scholarly dissection of leadership shortcomings in Iraq, see Huw Bennett, "The Reluctant Counter-Insurgents: Britain's Absent Surge in Southern Iraq," in Celeste Ward Gventer, David Martin Jones, and M. L. R. Smith, eds., *The New Counter-Insurgency Era in Critical Perspective* (London: Palgrave Macmillan, 2008), 278–96.

16. See, for example, David Betz and Anthony Cormack, "Iraq, Afghanistan, and British Strategy," *Orbis* 53, no. 2 (2009): 321.

17. British Army, *Countering Insurgency*, 1–4.

18. See Gwynn, *Imperial Policing*; Donald Featherstone, *Colonial Small Wars, 1837–1901* (Newtown Abbott, UK: David and Charles, 1973).

19. David Ucko, "Innovation and Inertia? The US Military and the Learning of Counterinsurgency," *Orbis* 52, no. 2 (2008): 291.

20. Robert Thompson, *Defeating Communist Insurgency: Experiences from Malaya and Vietnam* (London: Chatto and Windus, 1966), 50–62.

21. Julian Paget, *Counter-Insurgency Campaigning* (London: Faber, 1967).

22. Noel Barber, *War of the Running Dogs: How Malaya Defeated the Communist Guerrillas* (London: Collins, 1971).

23. Frank Kitson, *Low Intensity Operations: Subversion, Insurgency, and Peacekeeping* (London: Faber, 1971).

24. Frank Kitson, *Bunch of Five* (London: Faber, 1977).

25. John McGuffin, *The Guinea Pigs* (Harmondsworth, UK: Penguin, 1974).

26. See Frank Kitson, *Gangs and Counter-Gangs* (London: Barrie and Rockliff, 1960).

27. Mark Urban, *Big Boys Rules: The Secret Struggle Against the IRA* (London: Faber, 1992), 35–9.

28. See Peter Neumann, *Britain's Long War: British Strategy in the Northern Ireland Conflict, 1969–98* (London: Palgrave Macmillan, 2003).

29. John Bew, "Mass, Methods, and Means: The Northern Ireland 'Model' of Counter-Insurgency," in Gventer, Jones, and Smith, *The New Counter-Insurgency Era in Critical Perspective*, 160.

30. Desmond Hamill, *Pig in the Middle: The Army in Northern Ireland, 1969–1984* (London: Methuen, 1984), 159–223.

31. Chris Ryder, *The RUC: A Force Under Fire* (London: Methuen, 1989), 226–372.

32. See Colin McInnes, *Hot War, Cold War: The British Army's Way in Warfare, 1945–95* (London: Brassey's, 1996).

33. Michael Dewar, *Brush Fire Wars: Campaigns of the British Army Since 1945* (London: Robert Hale, 1984), esp. 180–85.

34. Thomas R. Mockaitis, *British Counter-Insurgency, 1919–1990* (London: Macmillan, 1990).

35. Thomas R. Mockaitis, *British Counter-Insurgency in the Post-imperial Era* (Manchester, UK: Manchester University Press, 1995), 12.

36. Douglas Porch, introduction to Callwell, *Small Wars*, v.

37. See British Army, *Army Field Manual*, IV-1.

38. Ibid., 2-1-1.

39. John A. Nagl, *Learning to Eat Soup with a Knife: Counterinsurgency Lessons from Malaya and Vietnam* (Chicago: University of Chicago Press, 2002), 59–111.

40. Lt. Gen. David Petraeus, "Learning Counterinsurgency: Observations from Soldiering in Iraq," *Military Review*, January–February 2006, 2–11.

41. Montgomery McFate, "The Military Utility of Understanding Adversary Culture," *Joint Forces Quarterly* 38, 3rd quarter (2005): 42.

42. Quoted in Matthew B. Stannard, "Montgomery McFate's Mission," *San Francisco Chronicle*, April 29, 2007.

43. Montgomery McFate, "Iraq: The Social Context of IEDs," *Military Review*, May–June 2005, 37–40; Montgomery McFate and Andrea V. Jackson, "An Organizational Solution for DOD's Cultural Knowledge Needs," *Military Review*, July–August 2005, 18.

44. Rod Thornton, "The British Army and the Origins of Its Philosophy of Minimum Force," *Small Wars and Insurgencies* 15, no. 1 (2006): 85.

45. Rod Thornton, "'Minimum Force': A Reply to Huw Bennett," *Small Wars and Insurgencies* 20, no. 1 (2009): 215.

46. British Army, *Army Field Manual*, 3-2.

47. UK House of Commons, Defence Committee, *Iraq: An Initial Assessment of Post-conflict Operations*, Sixth Report of Session 2004–2005, vol. 1 (London: Her Majesty's Stationary Office, 2005), 27–35.

48. Quoted in Richard Norton-Taylor, "General Hits Out at US Tactics," *Guardian*, April 21, 2004.

49. Mike Jackson, "British Counter-Insurgency," *Journal of Strategic Studies* 32, no. 3 (2009): 347.

50. Nigel Aylwin-Foster, "Changing the Army for Counterinsurgency Operations," *Military Review*, November–December 2005, 2–15.

51. Ibid., 8, 9.

52. UK House of Commons, Defence Committee, *Iraq*, 4.

53. UK Ministry of Defence, *Stability Operations in Iraq (Op Telic 2-5): An Analysis from a Land Perspective* (London: Ministry of Defence, 2005), 14, http://download.cable-drum.net/wikileaks_archive/file/uk-stbility-operations-in-iraq-2006.pdf, accessed July 11, 2006.

54. Quoted in Matthew Davis, "UK Officer Slams US Iraq Tactics," *BBC News*, January 11, 2006, http://news.bbc.co.uk/1/hi/world/middle_east/4603136.stm, accessed June 21, 2012.

55. For accounts of the U.S. experience in Fallujah, see Dick Camp, *Operation Phantom Fury: The Assault and Capture of Fallujah, Iraq* (Minneapolis: Zenith, 2009); David Bellavia, *House to House: An Epic Memoir of War* (London: Simon and Schuster, 2007); and Richard S. Lowry, *New Dawn: The Battles for Fallujah* (New York: Savas Beatie, 2010).

56. Aylwin-Foster, "Changing the Army for Counterinsurgency Operations," 4.

57. Davis, "UK Officer Slams US Iraq Tactics"; Richard Norton-Taylor and Jamie Wilson, "US Army in Iraq Institutionally Racist, Claims British Officer," *Guardian*, January 12, 2006.

58. Quoted in Davis, "UK Officer Slams US Iraq Tactics."

59. Thomas Waldman, "British 'Post-conflict' Operations: Into the Heart of Strategic Darkness," *Civil Wars* 9, no. 1 (2007): 61–86.

60. On Northern Ireland, see, for example, Jack Holland and Susan Phoenix, *Phoenix: Policing the Shadows. The Secret War Against Terrorism in Northern Ireland* (London: Hodder and Stoughton, 1996); Sean O'Callaghan, *The Informer* (London: Corgi, 1998); Ed Moloney, *A Secret History of the IRA* (London: Penguin, 2002); Henry McDonald, *Gunsmoke and Mirrors: How Sinn Féin Dressed Up Defeat as Victory* (Dublin: Gill and Macmillan, 2008).

61. Paul Dixon, "'Hearts and Minds?' British Counter-Insurgency from Malaya to Iraq," *Journal of Strategic Studies* 32, no. 3 (2009): 366.

62. Karl Hack, "'Iron Claws on Malaya': The Historiography of the Malayan Emergency," *Journal of Southeast Asian Studies* 30, no. 1 (1999): 102. See also Karl Hack, "The Malayan Emergency as Counter-Insurgency Paradigm," *Journal of Strategic Studies* 32, no. 3 (2009): 383–414.

63. John Newsinger, *British Counter-Insurgency: From Palestine to Northern Ireland* (London: Palgrave, 2002).

64. Huw Bennett, "'A Very Salutary Effect': The Counter-Terror Strategy in the Early Malayan Emergency, June 1948 to December 1949," *Journal of Strategic Studies* 32, no. 3 (2009): 415–44, and "Minimum Force in British Counterinsurgency," *Small Wars and Insurgencies* 21, no. 3 (2010): 459–75; David French, *The British Way in Counter-Insurgency, 1945–1967* (Oxford: Oxford University Press, 2011).

65. Huw Bennett, "Soldiers in the Court Room: The British Army's Part in the Kenya Emergency Under the Legal Spotlight," *Journal of Imperial and Commonwealth History* 39, no. 5 (2011): 717–30.

66. Karl Hack identified "a herd mentality" in the denunciation of British COIN methods, exemplified in Benjamin Grob-Fitzgibbons's *Imperial Endgame*, which argued that Britain "self-consciously deployed 'dirty wars' and related tactics to shape a postcolonial world tied to the West and capitalism" (*Imperial Endgame: Britain's Dirty Wars and the End of Empire* [London: Palgrave Macmillan, 2011], quoted in Karl Hack, "Everyone Lived in Fear: Malaya and the British War in Counter-Insurgency," *Small Wars and Insurgencies* 23, nos. 4–5 [2012]: 678).

67. Douglas Porch, "The Dangerous Myth and Dubious Promise of COIN," *Small Wars and Insurgencies* 22, no. 2 (2011): 249.

68. Bruno Reis, "The Myth of British Minimum Force in Counterinsurgency Campaigns During Decolonisation (1945–1970)," *Journal of Strategic Studies* 34, no. 2 (2011): 245–79.

69. For example, see Frank Kitson's principal work on the British Army, *Warfare as a Whole* (London: Faber, 1987). Only one chapter is dedicated to "activities outside the NATO area" (60–81), and even here no mention whatsoever is made of any predilection for counterinsurgency operations.

70. For one interpretation of such narrative changes, see Jonathan Gumz, "Reframing the Historical Problematic of Insurgency: How the Professional Military Literature Created a New History and Missed the Past," *Journal of Strategic Studies* 32, no. 4 (2009): 553–88.

71. See, for example, Huw Bennett, "The Other Side of COIN: Minimum and Exemplary Force in British Army Counter-Insurgency in Kenya," *Small Wars and Insurgencies* 18, no. 4 (2007): 638–64; Thornton, "'Minimum Force'"; Reis, "The Myth of British Minimum Force."

72. Daniel Whittingham, "'Savage Warfare': C. E. Callwell, the Roots of Counter-Insurgency, and the Nineteenth Century Context," *Small Wars and Insurgencies* 23, nos. 4–5 (2012): 592.

73. Callwell, *Small Wars*, 395, quoted in ibid., 594.

74. Whittingham, "'Savage Warfare,'" 592.

75. Lieb, "Suppressing Insurgencies in Comparison," 627–28.

76. David French, "Nasty Not Nice: British Counter-Insurgency Doctrine and Practice, 1945–1967," *Small Wars and Insurgencies* 23, nos. 4–5 (2012): 757.

77. Thomas R. Mockaitis, "The Minimum Force Debate: Contemporary Sensibilities Meet Imperial Practice," *Small Wars and Insurgencies* 23, nos. 4–5 (2012): 773, 774.

78. Matthew Hughes, "Introduction: British Ways of Counter-Insurgency, a Historical Perspective," *Small Wars and Insurgencies* 23, nos. 4–5 (2012): 581.

79. See Ledwidge, *Losing Small Wars*, 141, 163, 174.

80. Whittingham, "'Savage Warfare,'" 592.

81. Quoted in ibid., 593.

82. Keith Surridge, "An Example to Be Followed or a Warning to Be Avoided? The British, Boers, and Guerrilla Warfare, 1900–1902," *Small Wars and Insurgencies* 23, nos. 4–5 (2012): 609.

83. Mockaitis, "The Minimum Force Debate," 766.

84. British Army, *Army Field Manual*, 3-2.

85. See Hughes, "Introduction," 585.

86. See, for example, John Terraine, *The Smoke and the Fire: Myths and Anti-myths of War, 1861–1945* (London: Sidgwick and Jackson, 1980); G. D. Sheffield, *The Chief: Douglas Haig and the British Army* (London: Aurum, 2011).

87. See James Pritchard and M. L. R. Smith, "Thompson in Helmand: Comparing Theory to Practice in British Counter-Insurgency Operations in Afghanistan," *Civil Wars* 12, nos. 1–2 (2010): 65–90.

88. See Theo Farrell, "A Good War Gone Wrong?" *RUSI Journal* 156, no. 5 (2011): 60–64.

89. Surridge, "An Example to Be Followed or a Warning to Be Avoided?" 614, 622.

90. Ibid., 623.

91. Lieb, "Suppression of Insurgencies in Comparison," 637.

92. Hughes, "Introduction," 586.

93. David Cesarani, "The War on Terror That Failed: British Counter-Insurgency in Palestine 1945–1947 and the 'Farran Affair,'" *Small Wars and Insurgencies* 23, nos. 4–5 (2012): 663.

94. Ibid.

95. Dewar, *Brush Fire Wars*, 17–26.

96. In August 1946, British viceroy Archibald Wavell wrote home to the Labour government that British rule in India "was on the point of dissolution" (quoted in Christopher Bayly and Tim Harper, *Forgotten Wars: The End of Britain's Asian Empire* [London: Penguin, 2007], 251).

97. For an assessment of the Aden campaign, see Jonathan Walker, *Aden Insurgency: The Savage War in South Arabia 1962–1967* (Staplehurst, UK: Spellmount, 2005).

98. Dewar, *Brush Fire Wars*, 113–36.

99. For an assessment of Britain's noninvolvement in Vietnam, see Stephen Benedict Dyson, "Alliances, Domestic Politics, and Leader Psychology: Why Did Britain Stay Out of Vietnam and Go Into Iraq?" *Political Psychology* 28, no. 6 (2007): 647–66.

100. See "Lebanon: The Multinational Force," *Country-data.com*, n.d., http://www .country-data.com/cgi-bin/query/r-8078.htm, accessed July 18, 2012.

101. For an account of the situation in Lebanon, see Robert Fisk, *Pity the Nation: Lebanon at War* (Oxford: Oxford University Press, 1990), 443–92.

102. See Eric M. Hammel, *The Root: The Marines in Beirut, August 1982–February 1984* (New York: Harcourt Brace Jovanovich, 1985).

103. See "On This Day" (February 26, 1984), *BBC News* online, n.d., http://news.bbc .co.uk/onthisday/hi/dates/stories/february/26/newsid_4153000/4153013.stm, accessed January 3, 2014.

104. Gian P. Gentile, "A Strategy Without Tactics: Population-centric COIN and the Army," *Parameters* 39, no. 3 (2009): 5–6.

105. Dewar, *Brush Fire Wars*, 180.

106. Ibid., 180–85.

107. For one notable account in this regard, see Andrew M. Dorman, *Blair's Successful War: British Military Intervention in Sierra Leone* (Farnham, UK: Ashgate, 2009).

108. Reis, "The Myth of British Minimum Force," 274.

109. In this context of inventing tradition, see the classic study Eric Hobsbawm and Terence Ranger, eds., *The Invention of Tradition: Essays on Invented Traditions Throughout the World* (Cambridge, UK: Cambridge University Press, 1983).

110. Conal Condren, *Argument and Authority in Early Modern England: The Presupposition of Oaths and Engagements* (Cambridge, UK: Cambridge University Press, 2006), 26–27.

111. For a survey of such imperial actions, see John Dickie, *The New Mandarins: How British Foreign Policy Works* (London: I. B. Tauris, 2004); Christopher Meyer, *Getting*

Our Way: 500 Years of Adventure and Intrigue. The Inside Story of British Diplomacy (London: Weidenfeld and Nicolson, 2009); Douglas Hurd, Choose Your Weapons: The British Foreign Secretary, Two Centuries of Conflict and Personalities (London: Weidenfeld and Nicolson, 2010).

112. Carl von Clausewitz, On War, trans. and ed. Michael Howard and Peter Paret (Princeton: Princeton University Press, 1984), 88.

113. Ledwidge, Losing Small Wars, 148.

114. Bew, "Mass, Methods, and Means," 169.

6. The Puzzle of Counterinsurgency and Escalation

1. Brian Jenkins, Terrorism: A New Mode of Conflict (Los Angeles: Crescent, 1975), 1.

2. John Stone, "Escalation and the War on Terror," Journal of Strategic Studies 35, no. 5 (2012): 639.

3. Herman Kahn, On Escalation: Metaphors and Scenarios (New York: Praeger, 1965), 3.

4. Ibid., 289–90.

5. Stone, "Escalation and the War on Terror," 639.

6. Thomas C. Schelling, Choice and Consequence: Perspectives of an Errant Economist (Cambridge, MA: Harvard University Press, 1984), 268–90.

7. Lawrence Freedman, "Terrorism and Strategy," in Lawrence Freedman, Christopher Hill, Adam Roberts, R. J. Vincent, Paul Wilkinson, and Philip Windsor, Terrorism and International Order (London: Routledge and Kegan Paul, 1986), 61.

8. See R. D. Crelinsten, "Terrorism as Political Communication: The Relationship Between the Controller and Controlled," in Paul Wilkinson and A. M. Stewart, eds., Contemporary Research on Terrorism (Aberdeen, Scotland: Aberdeen University Press, 1987), 6–7.

9. Carl von Clausewitz, On War, trans. and ed. Michael Howard and Peter Paret (Princeton: Princeton University Press, 1984), 87.

10. Christopher Bassford, "John Keegan and the Grand Tradition of Trashing Clausewitz: A Polemic," War in History 1, no. 3 (1994): 329.

11. Clausewitz, On War, 88.

12. Ibid., 87.

13. See Charles E. Callwell, Small Wars: Their Principles and Practice (London: His Majesty's Stationary Office, 1896; reprint, Lincoln: University of Nebraska Press and Bison Books, 1996), 21–22.

14. John Shy and Thomas Collier, "Revolutionary War," in Peter Paret, ed., Makers of Modern Strategy: From Machiavelli to the Nuclear Age (Oxford: Clarendon Press, 1986), 817.

15. Ian F. W. Beckett, "The Tradition," in John Pimlott, ed., Guerrilla Warfare (London: Bison Books, 1985), 8.

16. Francis Toase, introduction to Robin Corbett, ed., Guerrilla Warfare: From 1939 to the Present Day (London: Guild, 1986), 6.

17. K. J. Holsti, *The State, War, and the State of War* (Cambridge, UK: Cambridge University Press, 1996), tables 2.1 and 2.2, 22–24. See also table 1 in Barbara F. Walter, "Designing Transitions from Civil War: Demobilization, Democratization, and Commitments to Peace," *International Security* 25, no. 1 (1999): 128.

18. See Geoffrey Blainey, *The Causes of War* (London: Macmillan, 1988), 71, as well as J. David Singer and Melvin Small, *Resort to Arms: International and Civil Wars, 1816–1980* (Beverly Hills, CA: Sage, 1982).

19. See Peter Janke, *Guerrilla and Terrorist Organisations: A World Directory and Bibliography* (Brighton, UK: Harvester, 1983). Janke identified the existence of 569 violent substate groupings.

20. W. Alexander Vacca and Mark Davidson, "The Regularity of Regular Warfare," *Parameters* 41, no. 2 (2011): 18–28.

21. Richard Betts, "Should Strategic Studies Survive?" *World Politics* 50, no. 1 (1997): 7.

22. Harry Summers, "A War Is a War Is a War Is a War," in Loren B. Thompson, ed., *Low Intensity Conflict: The Pattern of Warfare in the Modern World* (Lexington, MA: Lexington Books, 1989), 27–45.

23. M. L. R. Smith, "Guerrillas in the Mist: Reassessing Strategy and Low Intensity Warfare," *Review of International Studies* 29, no. 1 (2003): 20–23.

24. Ibid., 30.

25. Ibid.

26. See Colin Gray, *The Strategy Bridge: Theory for Practice* (Oxford: Oxford University Press, 2010), 1–9.

27. Clausewitz, *On War*, 77.

28. Thomas C. Schelling, *The Strategy of Conflict* (Cambridge, MA : Harvard University Press, 1980), 5.

29. Clausewitz, *On War*, 77.

30. Ibid.

31. Ibid., 75.

32. Ibid., 119–21.

33. See ibid., 90–99.

34. Isabelle Duyvesteyn, "The Escalation and De-escalation of Irregular War: Setting Out the Problem," *Journal of Strategic Studies* 35, no. 5 (2012): 602.

35. Summarized in ibid., 604.

36. Stone, "Escalation and the War on Terror," 641.

37. Richard Smoke, *War: Controlling Escalation* (Cambridge, MA: Harvard University Press, 1977), 35.

38. Ernest Evans, *Calling a Truce to Terror* (Westport, CT: Greenwood Press, 1979), 29.

39. J. Bowyer Bell, *The Myth of the Guerrilla* (New York: Knopf, 1971), 51–52.

40. Charles Russell, Leon Banker, and Bowman Miller, "Out-Inventing the Terrorist," in Yonah Alexander, David Carlton, and Paul Wilkinson, eds., *Terrorism: Theory and Practice* (Boulder, CO: Westview, 1979), 12–13.

41. N. O. Berry, "Theories on the Efficacy of Terrorism," in Wilkinson and Stewart, *Contemporary Research on Terrorism*, 293–305.

42. Peter Neumann and M. L. R. Smith, *The Strategy of Terrorism: How It Works and Why It Fails* (London: Routledge, 2008), 39–46.

43. Ibid., 82–83.

44. Donald C. Hodges, *Argentina's Dirty War: An Intellectual History* (Austin: University of Texas Press, 1981), 182.

45. Gen. Roberto Viola and Brig. Gen. L. A. Jáuregui, press conference, April 1977, quoted in Daniel Frontalini and María Cristana Caiati, *El Mito de la guerra sucia* (Buenos Aires: Centro de Estudios Legales y Sociales, 1984), 75.

46. M. L. R. Smith and Sophie Roberts, "War in the Gray: Exploring the Concept of Dirty War," *Studies in Conflict and Terrorism* 31, no. 5 (2008): 385–87.

47. Paul H. Lewis, *Guerrillas and Generals: Dirty War in Argentina* (Greenwood, CT: Praeger, 2002), 147–57; Richard Gillespie, "A Critique of the Urban Guerrilla: Argentina, Uruguay, and Brazil," *Conflict Quarterly*, no. 1 (1980): 39–53.

48. Patricia Marchak, *God's Assassins: State Terrorism in Argentina in the 1970s* (Montreal: McGill-Queens University Press, 1999), 112.

49. Quoted in Richard Gillespie, *Soldiers of Peron: Argentina's Montoneros* (Oxford: Oxford University Press, 1983), 250.

50. Smith and Roberts, "War in the Gray," 389.

51. Quoted in David Pion-Berlin and George A. Lopez, "Of Victims and Executioners: Argentine State Terror, 1975–1979," *International Studies Quarterly* 35, no. 1 (1991): 70.

52. See, for example, Luis Martinez, *The Algerian Civil War, 1990–1998* (New York: Columbia University Press, 2000); S. D. Selvadurai and M. L. R. Smith, "Black Tigers, Bronze Lotus: The Evolution and Dynamics of Sri Lanka's Strategies of Dirty War," *Studies in Conflict and Terrorism* 36, no. 7 (2013): 547–72.

53. Myles Shevlin, quoted in Gerard McKnight, *The Mind of the Terrorist* (London: Michael Joseph, 1974), 74.

54. A power-sharing arrangement as the long-term solution had been the British government's policy position since early 1972. See Peter Neumann, *Britain's Long War: British Strategy in the Northern Ireland Conflict, 1969–1998* (London: Palgrave, 2003), 43–69.

55. See R. D. Crelinsten, "Analysing Terrorism and Counter-Terrorism: A Communication Model," *Terrorism and Political Violence* 14, no. 2 (2002): 77–122.

56. A phrase derived from Secretary of State for Northern Ireland William Whitelaw, who stated that the government's objective was to reduce the violence to an "acceptable level" (quoted in J. Bowyer Bell, *The Secret Army: The IRA* [Dublin: Poolbeg, 1989], 384).

57. "Acceptable Level of Violence," in *A Glossary of Terms Related to the Conflict*, Conflict and Politics in Northern Ireland Web Service, last updated July 2005, http://cain.ulst.ac.uk/othelem/glossary.htm, accessed May 15, 2014.

58. See James Salt and M. L. R. Smith, "Reassessing Military Assistance to the Civil Powers: Are Traditional British Anti-terrorist Responses Still Effective?" *Low Intensity Conflict and Law Enforcement* 13, no. 3 (2005): 227–49.

59. Paul Wilkinson, *Terrorism and the Liberal State* (New York: New York University Press, 1986), 3–22.

60. Ibid., 125–26.
61. See Peter Taylor, *Beating the Terrorists: Interrogation at Omagh, Gough, and Castlereagh* (London: Penguin, 1980).
62. Walter Laqueur, "Terrorism—a Balance Sheet," in Walter Laqueur, ed., *The Terrorism Reader* (Philadelphia: Temple University Press, 1978), 264.
63. The then IRA chief of staff quoted in Séan McStiofain, *Memoirs of a Revolutionary* (Edinburgh: Cremonesi, 1975), 295.
64. M. L. R. Smith, *Fighting for Ireland? The Military Strategy of the Irish Republican Movement* (London: Routledge, 1995), 109–12.
65. Ibid., 110.
66. Peter Chippindale, "Motorman's Slow Drive," *Guardian*, August 26, 1972.
67. See M. L. R. Smith and Peter R. Neumann, "Motorman's Long Journey: Changing the Strategic Setting in Northern Ireland," *Contemporary British History* 19, no. 4 (2005): 413–14.
68. David Martin Jones, M. L. R. Smith, and John Stone, "Counter-COIN: Counterinsurgency and the Preemption of Strategy," *Studies in Conflict and Terrorism* 35, no. 9 (2012): 606–7.
69. See John Bew, "Mass, Methods, and Means: The Northern Ireland 'Model' of Counter-Insurgency," in Celeste Ward Gventer, David Martin Jones, and M. L. R. Smith, eds., *The New Counter-Insurgency Era in Critical Perspective* (London: Palgrave Macmillan, 2014), 165–66.
70. See John Newsinger, "From Counter-Insurgency to Internal Security: Northern Ireland, 1962–1992," *Small Wars and Insurgencies* 6, no. 1 (1995): 88–111.
71. See UK Chief of the General Staff, *Operation Banner: An Analysis of Military Operations in Northern Ireland*, Army Code 71842 (London: Ministry of Defence, July 2006), 8-8-11, and Mark Urban, *Big Boys Rules: The Secret Struggle Against the IRA* (London: Faber, 1992).
72. See Nicholas Davies, *Dead Men Talking* (Edinburgh: Mainstream, 2004), 11–42.
73. See, for example, Jack Holland and Susan Phoenix, *Phoenix: Policing the Shadows. The Secret War Against Terrorism in Northern Ireland* (London: Hodder and Stoughton, 1996), 391–94; Allen Barker, *Shadows: Inside Northern Ireland's Special Branch* (Edinburgh: Mainstream, 2004); Martin Ingram and Greg Harkin, *Stakeknife: Britain's Secret Agents in Ireland* (Dublin: O'Brien Press, 2004), 255–64; and George Clark, *Border Crossings: The Stories of the RUC Special Branch, the Garda Special Branch, and the IRA Moles* (Dublin: Gill and Macmillan, 2009), 184.
74. See, for example, Henry McDonald, *Gunsmoke and Mirrors: How Sinn Féin Dressed Up Defeat as Victory* (Dublin: Gill and Macmillan, 2008).
75. See Crelinsten, "Terrorism as Political Communication."
76. See Stephan Aust, *The Baader-Meinhof Complex* (London: Bodley Head, 2008), 305–431.
77. Stone, "Escalation and the War on Terror," 642.
78. Ibid.
79. Quoted in Jeremy Scahill, *Dirty Wars: The World Is a Battlefield* (London: Serpent's Tail, 2013), 20.

80. Quoted in ibid., 27.

81. See Fred Kaplan, *The Insurgents: David Petraeus and the Plot to Change the American Way of War* (New York: Simon and Schuster, 2013); Peter R. Mansoor, *Surge: My Journey with General David Petraeus and the Remaking of the Iraq War* (New Haven: Yale University Press, 2013).

82. See, for example, Mark Urban, *Task Force Black: The Explosive True Story of the SAS and the Secret War in Iraq* (London: Abacus, 2011), 259–78.

83. Ibid., 33–43, 163–76.

84. See, among other works, James Risen, *State of War: The Secret History of the CIA and the Bush Administration* (New York: Free Press, 2007); Christopher H. Pyle, *Getting Away with Torture: Secret Government, War Crimes, and Rule of Law* (Washington, D.C.: Potomac Books, 2009); and Scahill, *Dirty Wars*.

85. Stone, "Escalation and the War on Terror," 649.

86. M. L. R. Smith, "Quantum Strategy: The Interior World of War," *Infinity Journal* 3, no. 1 (2012): 10–13.

87. Stone, "Escalation and the War on Terror," 649.

88. Clausewitz, *On War*, 99.

89. Ibid., 99.

90. For an exploration of this issue, see David Martin Jones and M. L. R. Smith, *Sacred Violence: Political Religion in a Secular Age* (London: Palgrave Macmillan, 2014).

91. Clausewitz, *On War*, 89.

Conclusion

1. Jeffrey H. Michaels and Matthew Ford, "Bandwagonistas: Rhetorical Re-description, Strategic Choice, and the Politics of Counter-Insurgency," *Small Wars and Insurgencies* 22, no. 2 (2011): 352–84.

2. See, for example, Douglas Porch, *Counterinsurgency: Exposing the Myths of the New Way of War* (Cambridge, UK: Cambridge University Press, 2013).

3. See David Martin Jones and M. L. R. Smith, "Grammar but No Logic: Technique Is Not Enough—a Reply to Nagl and Burton," *Journal of Strategic Studies* 33, no. 3 (2010): 430–41.

4. John A. Nagl and Brian Burton, "Thinking Globally and Acting Locally: Counterinsurgency Lessons from Modern Wars—a Reply to Smith and Jones," *Journal of Strategic Studies* 33, no. 1 (2010): 123–38.

5. Joshua Rovner, "Questions About COIN After Iraq and Afghanistan," in Celeste Ward Gventer, David Martin Jones, and M. L. R. Smith, *The New Counter-Insurgency Era in Critical Perspective* (London: Palgrave Macmillan, 2014), 299–318.

6. For example, Mark Urban's study of Special Operations in Iraq notes General David Petraeus's observation in 2006 that "the UK brings considerable assets to this [the fight against al-Qaeda in Baghdad] in the intelligence world and other areas." These "other areas" were almost certainly a reference to the capacities of the Special Air

Services, which were especially esteemed by the Americans. Later, in comments to the *London Times* in August 2008, Petraeus stated that the regiment "helped immensely in the Baghdad area, in particular to take down the al-Qaeda car bomb networks and other al-Qaeda operations in Iraq's capital city, so they have done a phenomenal job . . . they have exceptional initiative, exceptional skill, exceptional courage and, I think, exceptional savvy. I can't say enough about how impressive they are in thinking on their feet" (quoted in Mark Urban, *Task Force Black: The Explosive True Story of the SAS and the Secret War in Iraq* [London: Abacus, 2011], 218, 274).

7. Quoted in Decca Aitkenhead, "Rory Stewart: 'The Secret of Modern Britain Is That There Is No Power Anywhere,'" *Guardian*, January 3, 2014.

Bibliography

"Acceptable Level of Violence." In *A Glossary of Terms Related to the Conflict*. Conflict and Politics in Northern Ireland Web Service, last updated July 2005. http://cain.ulst.ac.uk/othelem/glossary.htm.

Air Staff. *AP 3000: British Air and Space Power Doctrine*. London: Ministry of Defence, 2009.

Aitkenhead, Decca. "Rory Stewart: 'The Secret of Modern Britain Is That There Is No Power Anywhere.'" *Guardian*, January 3, 2014.

Aldis, Anne, and Graeme P. Herd, eds. *The Ideological War on Terror: World-Wide Strategies for Counter-Terrorism*. London: Routledge, 2007.

Alexander, Yonah, David Carlton, and Paul Wilkinson. *Terrorism: Theory and Practice*. Boulder, CO: Westview, 1979.

Almond, Gabriel, and James S. Coleman, eds. *The Politics of the Developing Areas*. Princeton: Princeton University Press, 1960.

Alves, F. Lopez. "Political Crises, Strategic Choices, and Terrorism: The Rise and Fall of the Uruguayan Tuparmaros." *Terrorism and Political Violence* 1, no. 2 (1989): 189–214.

Ancker, Col. Clinton J. "Doctrine for Asymmetric Warfare." *Military Review*, July–August 2003, 18–25.

Anderson, Ben. *No Worse Enemy: The Inside Story of the Chaotic Struggle for Afghanistan*. London: Oneworld, 2011.

Anderson, David. *History of the Hanged: Britain's Dirty War and the End of Empire*. London: Weidenfeld and Nicolson, 2005.

Anderson, Gary. "Counterinsurgency vs. Counterterrorism." *Small Wars Journal*, February 24, 2010. http://smallwarsjournal.com/jrnl/art/counterinsurgency-vs-counterterrorism.

Ankerson, Christopher, ed. *Understanding Global Terror*. Cambridge, UK: Polity Press, 2007.

Apter, David E. *The Politics of Modernization*. Chicago: University of Chicago Press, 1965.

Aron, Raymond. *On War: Atomic Weapons and Global Diplomacy.* Translated by Terence Kilmartin. London: Secker and Warburg, 1958.

Ashour, Omar. *The De-radicalization of Jihadists: Transforming Armed Islamist Movements.* London: Routledge, 2009.

Aussaresses, Paul. *The Battle of the Casbah: Terrorism and Counter-Terrorism in Algeria, 1955–57.* New York: Enigma, 2002.

Aust, Stephan. *The Baader-Meinhof Complex.* London: Bodley Head, 2008.

Aylwin-Foster, Nigel. "Changing the Army for Counterinsurgency Operations." *Military Review*, November–December 2005, 2–15.

Bacevich, Andrew J., and Elizabeth H. Prodromou. "God Is Not Neutral: Religion and US Foreign Policy After 9/11." *Orbis* 48, no. 1 (2001): 43–54.

Baker, Jim. "Systems Thinking and Counterinsurgencies." *Parameters* 36, no. 4 (2006–2007): 26–43.

Baker, Peter, and Elisabeth Bumiller. "Obama Considers Strategy Shift in Afghan War." *New York Times*, September 22, 2009. http://www.nytimes.com/2009/09/23/world/asia/23policy.html.

Barber, Noel. *War of the Running Dogs: How Malaya Defeated the Communist Guerrillas.* London: Collins, 1971.

Barkawi, Taraq. "On the Pedagogy of 'Small Wars.'" *International Affairs* 80, no. 1 (2004): 19–37.

Barkawi, Tarak, and Mark Laffey, "The Post-colonial Moment in Security Studies." *Review of International Studies* 32, no. 2 (2006): 329–52.

Barker, Allen. *Shadows: Inside Northern Ireland's Special Branch.* Edinburgh: Mainstream, 2004.

Barnes, Fred. "How Bush Decided on the Surge." *Weekly Standard*, February 4, 2008. http://www.weeklystandard.com/Content/Public/Articles/000/000/014/658dwgrn.asp.

Barone, Michael. "Lessons from the Surge." *Townhall.com*, December 29, 2007. http://townhall.com/columnists/michaelbarone/2007/12/29/lessons_from_the_surge/page/full.

Bassford, Christopher. "John Keegan and the Grand Tradition of Trashing Clausewitz: A Polemic." *War in History* 1, no. 3 (1994): 319–36.

Baylis, John, and Steve Smith, eds. *The Globalization of World Politics: An Introduction to International Relations.* Oxford: Oxford University Press, 2001.

——. Introduction to John Baylis and Steve Smith, eds., *The Globalization of World Politics: An Introduction to International Relations*, 1–14. Oxford: Oxford University Press, 2001.

Bayly, Christopher, and Tim Harper. *Forgotten Wars: The End of Britain's Asian Empire.* London: Penguin, 2007.

Beaver, Paul. "The Threat to Israel Is Not War." *Asian Wall Street Journal*, October 24, 2000.

Beckett, Ian F. W. "British Counter-Insurgency: A Historical Reflection." *Small Wars and Insurgencies* 23, nos. 4–5 (2012): 781–98.

——. *The Roots of Counterinsurgency: Armies and Guerrilla Warfare.* London: Blanford, 1988.

——. "The Tradition." In John Pimlott, ed., *Guerrilla Warfare*, 8–29. London: Bison Books, 1985.

Beckett, Ian F. W., and John Pimlott, eds. *Armed Forces and Modern Counterinsurgency.* New York: St. Martin's Press, 1985.

Bell, J. Bowyer. *The Myth of the Guerrilla.* New York: Knopf, 1971.

——. *The Secret Army: The IRA.* Dublin: Poolbeg, 1989.

Bellavia, David. *House to House: An Epic Memoir of War.* London: Simon and Schuster, 2007.

Bennett, Huw. "Minimum Force in British Counterinsurgency." *Small Wars and Insurgencies* 21, no. 3 (2010): 459–75.

——. "The Other Side of the COIN: Minimum and Exemplary Force in British Army Counter-Insurgency in Kenya." *Small Wars and Insurgencies* 18, no. 4 (2007): 638–64.

——. "The Reluctant Counter-Insurgents: Britain's Absent Surge in Southern Iraq." In Celeste Ward Gventer, David Martin Jones, and M. L. R. Smith, eds., *The New Counter-Insurgency Era in Critical Perspective*, 278–96. London: Palgrave Macmillan, 2014.

——. "Soldiers in the Court Room: The British Army's Part in the Kenya Emergency Under the Legal Spotlight." *Journal of Imperial and Commonwealth History* 39, no. 5 (2011): 717–30.

——. "'A Very Salutary Effect': The Counter-Terror Strategy in the Early Malayan Emergency, June 1948 to December 1949." *Journal of Strategic Studies* 32, no. 3 (2009): 414–44.

Berger, Samuel L., and Mona Sutphen. "Commandeering the Palestinian Cause: Bin Laden's Belated Concern." In James F. Hoge and Gideon Rose, eds., *How Did This Happen? Terrorism and the New War*, 123–28. New York: Public Affairs, 2001.

Berry, N. O. "Theories on the Efficacy of Terrorism." In Paul Wilkinson and A. M. Stewart eds., *Contemporary Research on Terrorism*, 293–305. Aberdeen, Scotland: Aberdeen University Press, 1987.

Betts, Richard K. "Should Strategic Studies Survive?" *World Politics* 50, no. 1 (1997): 7–33.

Betz, David. "Redesigning Land Forces for '*Wars Amongst the People*.'" *Contemporary Security Policy* 28, no. 2 (2007): 221–43.

Betz, David, and Anthony Cormack. "Iraq, Afghanistan, and British Strategy." *Orbis* 53, no. 2 (2009): 319–36.

Bew, John. "Mass, Methods, and Means: The Northern Ireland 'Model' of Counter-Insurgency." In Celeste Ward Gventer, David Martin Jones, and M. L. R. Smith, eds., *The New Counter-Insurgency Era in Critical Perspective*, 156–72. London: Palgrave Macmillan, 2014.

Bew, John, Martyn Frampton, and Iñigo Gurruchaga. *Talking to Terrorists: Making Peace in Northern Ireland and the Basque Country.* London: Hurst, 2009.

Biddle, Stephen, Jeffrey A. Friedman, and Jacob N. Schapiro. "Testing the Surge: Why Did Violence Decline in Iraq in 2007?" In Celeste Ward Gventer, David Martin Jones, and M. L. R. Smith, eds., *The New Counter-Insurgency Era in Critical Perspective*, 201–31. London: Palgrave Macmillan, 2014.

Binder, Leonard. "The Natural History of Development Theory." *Comparative Studies in Society and History* 28, no. 1 (1986): 3–33.

Binder, Leonard, James S. Colman, Joseph LaPalombara, Lucian W. Pye, Sidney Verba, and Myron Weiner. *Crises and Sequences in Political Development.* Princeton: Princeton University Press, 1971.

Bird, Tim, and Alex Marshall. *Afghanistan: How the West Lost Its Way*. New Haven: Yale University Press, 2011.

Bjørgo, Tore, ed. *The Roots of Terrorism: Myths, Reality, and Ways Forward*. London: Routledge, 2005.

Bjørgo, Tore, and John Horgan, eds. *Leaving Terrorism Behind: Individual and Collective Disengagement*. London: Routledge, 2009.

Blackwill, Ambassador Robert D. "Afghanistan and the Uses of History: Insights from Ernest May." Second Annual Ernest May Memorial Lecture, Aspen Strategy Group, August 2010. http://www.aspeninstitute.org/policy-work/aspen-strategy-group/programs-topic/other-events/afghan-history.

Blainey, Geoffrey. *The Causes of War*. London: Macmillan, 1988.

Bockman, Johanna. Review of Nils Gilman, *Mandarins of the Future: Modernization Theory in Cold War America*. *Journal of Cold War Studies* 8, no. 2 (2006):141–44.

Boot, Max. "The War Over the Vietnam War: A New Biography Puts an End to the Idea That We Could Not Win." *Wall Street Journal*, October 4, 2011. http://online.wsj.com/article/SB10001424052970204422404576595011469382894.html.

Booth, Ken. "The Human Faces of Terror: Reflections in a Cracked Looking-Glass." *Critical Studies on Terrorism* 1, no. 1 (2008): 65–79.

——, ed. *New Thinking About International Security*. London: HarperCollins, 1991.

——. "War, Security, and Strategy: Towards a Doctrine for Stable Peace." In Ken Booth, ed., *New Thinking About International Security*, 335–76. London: HarperCollins, 1991.

Breemer, Jan S. "Statistics, Real Estate, and the Principles of War: Why There Is No Unified Theory of War." *Military Review*, September–October 2006, 84–89.

British Army. *Army Doctrine Publication: Operations*. Swindon, UK: Defence, Concepts, and Doctrine Centre and Ministry of Defence, 2010. https://www.gov.uk/government/uploads/system/uploads/attachment_data/file/33695/ADPOperationsDec10.pdf.

——. *Army Field Manual*. Vol. 5: *Operations Other Than War*. London: Ministry of Defence, 1995. http://www.scribd.com/doc/28438057/11709-AFM-Vol-v-Operations-Other-Than-War.

——. *Countering Insurgency*. Vol. 1, Part 10. Warminster, UK: Ministry of Defence, 2009.

Brown, Philip A., and M. L. R. Smith. "The Rise of Gulf War Paradigm 2.0." *Orbis* 58, no. 1 (2013): 83–103.

Bury, Patrick. *Callsign Hades*. London: Simon and Schuster, 2010.

Callwell, Charles E. *Small Wars: Their Principles and Practice*. London: His Majesty's Stationary Office, 1896. Reprint. Lincoln: University of Nebraska Press and Bison Books, 1996.

Camp, Dick. *Operation Phantom Fury: The Assault and Capture of Fallujah, Iraq*. Minneapolis: Zenith, 2009.

Campbell, Lt. Col. James D. "French Algeria and British Northern Ireland: Legitimacy and the Rule of Law in Low-Intensity Conflict." *Military Review*, March–April 2005, 2–5.

Cassidy, Lt. Col. Robert M. "The British Army and Counterinsurgency: The Salience of Military Culture." *Military Review*, May–June 2005, 53–59.

——. "The Savage Wars of Peace." *Military Review*, November–December 2004, 76–77.

——. "Winning the War of the Flea." *Military Review*, September 2004, 41–46.

Celeski, Joseph D. "Attacking Insurgent Space: Sanctuary Denial and Border Interdiction." *Military Review*, November–December 2006, 51–57.

Cesarani, David. "The War on Terror That Failed: British Counter-Insurgency in Palestine 1945–1947 and the 'Farran Affair.'" *Small Wars and Insurgencies* 23, nos. 4–5 (2012): 648–70.

Chakotine, Serge. *The Rape of the Masses: The Psychology of Totalitarian Propaganda.* Translated by E. W. Dickes. New York: Alliance, 1940.

Chandrasekaran, Rajiv. *Imperial Life in the Emerald City: Inside Bagdad's Green Zone.* London: Bloomsbury, 2007.

——. *Little America: The War Within the War for Afghanistan.* London: Bloomsbury, 2013.

Chin, Warren. "Examining the Application of British Counterinsurgency Doctrine by the American Army in Iraq." *Small Wars and Insurgencies* 18, no. 1 (2007): 1–26.

Chippindale, Peter. "Motorman's Slow Drive." *Guardian*, August 26, 1972.

Clancy, James, and Chuck Crossett. "Measuring Effectiveness in Irregular Warfare." *Parameters* 37, no. 2 (2007): 88–100.

Clark, George. *Border Crossings: The Stories of the RUC Special Branch, the Garda Special Branch, and the IRA Moles.* Dublin: Gill and Macmillan, 2009.

Clarke, Peter. *Learning from Experience: Counter-Terrorism in the UK Since 9/11.* Colin Cramphorn Memorial Lecture. London: Policy Exchange, 2007.

Clausewitz, Carl von. *On War.* Translated and edited by Michael Howard and Peter Paret. Princeton: Princeton University Press, 1984.

Clutterbuck, Richard. *Guerrillas and Terrorists.* Athens: Ohio University Press, 1977.

——. *The Long, Long War: The Emergency in Malaya, 1948–1960.* London: Cassell, 1966.

Cohen, Eliot, Conrad Crane, Jan Horvath, and John Nagl. "Principles, Imperatives, and Paradoxes of Counterinsurgency." *Military Review*, March–April 2006, 49–53.

Condren, Conal. *Argument and Authority in Early Modern England: The Presupposition of Oaths and Engagements.* Cambridge, UK: Cambridge University Press, 2006.

Cooper, Barry. *New Political Religions, or An Analysis of Modern Terrorism.* Columbia: Missouri University Press, 2004.

Corbett, Robin, ed. *Guerrilla Warfare: From 1939 to the Present Day.* London: Guild, 1986.

Cordesman, Anthony H. *"Shape, Clear, Hold, Build, and Transfer": The Full Metrics of the Afghan War.* Washington, D.C.: Center for Strategic and International Studies, February 18, 2010. http://csis.org/files/publication/100302_afghan_metrics_combined.pdf.

——. "US Strategy in Afghanistan: The Debate We Should Be Having." Center for Strategic and International Studies, October 7, 2009. http://csis.org/publication/us-strategy-afghanistan.

Corum, James. "Rethinking US Army Counter-Insurgency Doctrine." *Contemporary Security Policy* 28, no. 1 (2007): 127–42.

Cowper-Coles, Sherard. *Cables from Kabul: The Inside Story of the West's Afghan Campaign.* London: Harper, 2012.

Cradock, Christopher, and M. L. R. Smith. "'No Fixed Values': A Reinterpretation of the Influence of the Theory of *Guerre Révolutionnaire* and the Battle of Algiers, 1956–1957." *Journal of Cold War Studies* 9, no. 4 (2007): 68–105.

Crelinsten, R. D. "Analysing Terrorism and Counter-Terrorism: A Communication Model." *Terrorism and Political Violence* 14, no. 2 (2002): 77–122.

——. "Terrorism as Political Communication: The Relationship Between the Controller and Controlled." In Paul Wilkinson and A. M. Stewart, eds., *Contemporary Research on Terrorism*, 427–41. Aberdeen, Scotland: Aberdeen University Press, 1987.

David, Steven R. "Review Article: Internal War, Causes and Cures." *World Politics* 49, no. 4 (1997): 552–76.

Davidson, Janine. *The Principles of American Counterinsurgency: Evolution and Debate.* Counterinsurgency and Pakistan Paper Series. Washington, D.C.: Brookings Institution Press, 2009. http://www.brookings.edu/~/media/research/files/papers/2009/6/08%20counterinsurgency%20davidson/0608_counterinsurgency_davidson.pdf.

Davies, Nicholas. *Dead Men Talking.* Edinburgh: Mainstream, 2004.

Davis, Matthew. "UK Officer Slams US Iraq Tactics." *BBC News*, January 11, 2006. http://news.bbc.co.uk/1/hi/world/middle_east/4603136.stm.

"Declaration of Jihad Against the Country's Tyrants" ("Al-Qaeda Training Manual"). N.d. http://www.thetulsan.com/manual.html.

Delong-Bas, Natana J. *Wahabi Islam: From Revival to Reform to Global Jihad.* London: I. B. Tauris, 2004.

Deutsch, Karl. *The Nerves of Government: Models of Political Communication and Control.* New York: Free Press, 1963.

Dewar, Michael. *Brush Fire Wars: Campaigns of the British Army Since 1945.* London: Robert Hale, 1984.

Dickie, John. *The New Mandarins: How British Foreign Policy Works.* London: I. B. Tauris, 2004.

Dill, General John. *Notes on the Tactical Lessons of the Palestine Rebellion.* London: War Office, 1937.

DiMarco, Lou. "Losing the Moral Compass: Torture and *Guerre Revolutionnaire* in the Algerian War." *Parameters* 36, no. 2 (2006): 63–76.

Dixon, Paul. "'Hearts and Minds?' British Counter-Insurgency from Malaya to Iraq." *Journal of Strategic Studies* 32, no. 3 (2009): 353–81.

Dorman, Andrew M. *Blair's Successful War: British Military Intervention in Sierra Leone.* Farnham, UK: Ashgate, 2009.

Dorman, Andrew, Matthew Uttley, and M. L. R. Smith, eds. *The Changing Face of Military Power: Joint Warfare in an Expeditionary Era.* Basingstoke, UK: Palgrave, 2002.

Dorrien, Garry. *Imperial Designs: Neoconservatism and the New Pax Americana.* New York: Routledge, 2005.

Duyvesteyn, Isabelle. "The Escalation and De-escalation of Irregular War: Setting Out the Problem." *Journal of Strategic Studies* 35, no. 5 (2012): 601–11.

Dyson, Stephen Benedict. "Alliances, Domestic Politics, and Leader Psychology: Why Did Britain Stay out of Vietnam and Go Into Iraq?" *Political Psychology* 28, no. 6 (2007): 647–66.

Echevarria, Antulio J. "Reconsidering War's Logic and Grammar." *Infinity Journal* 1, no. 2 (2011): 4–7.

Eckstein, Harry. "On the Etiology of Internal Wars." *History and Theory* 4, no. 2 (1965): 133–63.

Eikenberry, Karl W. "The Limits of Counterinsurgency Doctrine in Afghanistan." *Foreign Affairs* 92, no. 5 (2013). http://www.foreignaffairs.com/articles/139645/karl-w-eikenberry/the-limits-of-counterinsurgency-doctrine-in-afghanistan.

Elkins, Caroline. *Imperial Reckoning: The Untold Story of Britain's Gulag in Kenya*. New York: Henry Holt, 2005.

Ellul, Jacques. *The Technological Society*. London: Jonathan Cape, 1964.

Englehardt, Tom. *The End of Victory Culture: Cold War America and the Disillusioning of a Generation*. Amherst: University of Massachusetts Press, 1995.

Evans, Ernest. *Calling a Truce to Terror*. Westport, CT: Greenwood Press, 1979.

Evans, Michael. "Army Chief Predicts a 'Generation of Conflict.'" *London Times*, August 28, 2007.

Fairweather, Jack. *A War of Choice: Honour, Hubris, and Sacrifice—the British in Iraq, 2003–9*. London: Vintage, 2012.

Fall, Bernard. "Counterinsurgency: The French Experience." Speech to the Industrial College of the Armed Forces, Washington, D.C., January 18, 1963.

——. *Street Without Joy: The French Debacle in Indochina*. London: Pall Mall, 1963. Reprint, Mechanicsburg, PA: Stackpole, 2005.

——. *The Vietminh Regime: Government and Administration in the Democratic Republic of Vietnam*. Ithaca, NY: Cornell University Press, 1954.

Farrell, Theo. "A Good War Gone Wrong?" *RUSI Journal* 156, no. 5 (2011): 60–64.

Featherstone, Donald. *Colonial Small Wars, 1837–1901*. Newtown Abbot, UK: David and Charles, 1973.

Featherstone, Mike, Scott Lash, and Roland Robertson, eds. *Global Modernities*. London: Sage, 1995.

Feaver, Peter D. "Anatomy of the Surge." *Commentary*, April 1, 2008. http://www.commentarymagazine.com/article/anatomy-of-the-surge.

Fergusson, James. *A Million Bullets: The Real Story of the British Army in Afghanistan*. London: Bantam, 2008.

Finch, Michael P. M. *A Progressive Occupation? The Gallieni–Lyautey Method of Colonial Pacification in Tonkin and Madagascar, 1885–1900*. Oxford: Oxford University Press, 2013.

Finlan, Alistair. "Trapped in the Dead Ground: US Counter-Insurgency Strategy in Iraq." *Small Wars and Insurgencies* 16, no. 1 (2005): 1–21.

Fisk, Robert. *Pity the Nation: Lebanon at War*. Oxford: Oxford University Press, 1990.

Ford, Christopher M. "Speak No Evil: Targeting a Population's Neutrality to Defeat an Insurgency." *Parameters* 35, no. 4 (2005): 51–66.

Freedman, Lawrence. "Globalisation and the War Against Terrorism." In Christopher Ankerson, ed., *Understanding Global Terror*, 217–39. Cambridge, UK: Polity, 2007.

——. *Strategy: A History*. Oxford: Oxford University Press, 2013.

——. "Terrorism and Strategy." In Lawrence Freedman, Christopher Hill, Adam Roberts, R. J. Vincent, Paul Wilkinson, and Philip Windsor, *Terrorism and International Order*, 56–82. London: Routledge and Kegan Paul, 1986.

Freedman, Lawrence, Christopher Hill, Adam Roberts, R. J. Vincent, Paul Wilkinson, and Philip Windsor. *Terrorism and International Order*. London: Routledge and Kegan Paul, 1986.

French, David. *The British Way in Counter-Insurgency, 1945–1967*. Oxford: Oxford University Press, 2011.

———. "Nasty Not Nice: British Counter-Insurgency Doctrine and Practice, 1945–1967." *Small Wars and Insurgencies* 23, nos. 4–5 (2012): 744–61.

Friedman, Thomas L. *The Lexus and the Olive Tree*. New York: Anchor Books, 2000.

Frontalini, Daniel, and María Cristana Caiati. *El Mito de la guerra sucia*. Buenos Aires: Centro de Estudios Legales y Sociales, 1984.

Fryer-Biggs, Zachary. "DoD's New Cyber Doctrine: Panetta Defines Deterrence, Preempting Strategy." *Defensenews.com*, October 13, 2012. http://www.defensenews.com/article/20121013/DEFREG02/310130001/DoD-8217-s-New-Cyber-Doctrine.

Fukuyama, Francis. *The End of History and the Last Man*. London: Penguin, 1992.

Fuller, J. F. C. *The Second World War, 1939–45: A Strategical and Tactical History*. New York: Duell, Sloan and Pearce, 1954.

"Full Text of MI5 Director-General's Speech." *Daily Telegraph*, November 5, 2007.

Gall, Sandy. *The War Against the Taliban: Why It All Went Wrong in Afghanistan*. London: Bloomsbury, 2012.

Galula, David. *Counterinsurgency Warfare: Theory and Practice*. 1964. Reprint. Westport, CT: Praeger, 2006.

———. *Pacification in Algeria, 1956–1958*. 1963. Reprint. Santa Monica, CA: RAND, 2006.

Gavrilis, James A. "A Model for Population-Centered Warfare: A Conceptual Framework for Analyzing and Understanding the Theory and Practice of Insurgency and Counterinsurgency." *Small Wars Journal*, May 10, 2009. http://smallwarsjournal.com/jrnl/art/a-model-for-population-centered-warfare.

Gellner, Ernest. *Conditions of Liberty: Civil Society and Its Rivals*. London: Hamish Hamilton, 1994.

———. *Muslim Society*. Cambridge, UK: Cambridge University Press, 1981.

———. *Relativism and the Social Sciences*. Cambridge, UK: Cambridge University Press, 1987.

Gentile, Gian. "Let's Build an Army to Win *All* Wars." *Joint Forces Quarterly* 52, 1st quarter (2009): 27–33.

———. "A Strategy Without Tactics: Population-centric COIN and the Army." *Parameters* 39, no. 3 (2009): 5–17.

———. *Wrong Turn: America's Deadly Embrace of Counterinsurgency*. New York: New Press, 2013.

Gettleman, Marvin E., ed. *Vietnam: History, Documents, and Opinions on a Major Crisis*. London: Penguin, 1965.

Gibbon, Edward. *The History of the Decline and Fall of the Roman Empire*. 12 vols. Edited by J. B. Bury. New York: Fred de Fau, 1904.

Gibson, Lt. Col. Chris. "Battlefield Victories and Strategic Success: The Path Forward in Iraq." *Military Review*, September–October 2006, 49–55.

Giddens, Anthony. *The Consequences of Modernity*. Cambridge, UK: Cambridge University Press, 1991.

Gillespie, Richard. "A Critique of the Urban Guerrilla: Argentina, Uruguay, and Brazil." *Conflict Quarterly*, no. 1 (1980): 39–53.

——. *Soldiers of Peron: Argentina's Montoneros*. Oxford: Oxford University Press, 1983.

Gilman, Nils. *Mandarins of the Future: Modernization Theory in Cold War America*. Baltimore: Johns Hopkins University Press, 2003.

Girardet, Raoul. *Mythes et mythologies politiques*. Paris: Éditions de Seuil, 1986.

Girardet, Raoul, and Jean-Pierre Thomas. *La crise militaire française, 1942–1962: Aspects sociologigques et ideologiques*. Paris: Libraire Armand Colin, 1964.

Glees, Anthony, and Chris Pope. *When Students Turn to Terror: Terrorist and Extremist Activity on British University Campuses*. London: Social Affairs Unit, 2005.

González, Roberto J. "Towards Mercenary Anthropology? The New US Army Counterinsurgency Manual FM 3-24 and the Military Anthropology Complex." *Anthropology Today* 23, no. 3 (2007): 14–19.

Gow, James. *Triumph of the Lack of Will: International Diplomacy and the Yugoslav War*. London: Hurst, 1997.

Gray, Colin. *Categorical Confusion? The Strategic Implications of Recognizing Challenges Either as Irregular or Traditional*. Carlisle, PA: Strategic Studies Institute, 2012.

——. *Strategic Studies and Public Policy: The American Experience*. Lexington: University Press of Kentucky, 1982.

——. *The Strategy Bridge: Theory for Practice*. Oxford: Oxford University Press, 2010.

——. "Thinking Asymmetrically in Times of Terror." *Parameters* 32, no. 1 (2002): 5–14.

Greer, Col. James K. "Operation Knockout: COIN in Iraq." *Military Review*, November–December 2005, 16–19.

Grey, Stephen. *Operation Snakebite*. London: Penguin, 2009.

Grob-Fitzgibbon, Benjamin. *Imperial Endgame: Britain's Dirty Wars and the End of Empire*. London: Palgrave Macmillan, 2011.

Gumz, Jonathan. "Reframing the Historical Problematic of Insurgency: How the Professional Military Literature Created a New History and Missed the Past." *Journal of Strategic Studies* 32, no. 4 (2009): 553–88.

Gventer, Celeste Ward. "Interventionism Run Amok." *Foreign Policy*, August 10, 2011. http://www.foreignpolicy.com/articles/2011/08/10/interventionism_run_amok.

Gventer, Celeste Ward, David Martin Jones, and M. L. R. Smith, eds. *The New Counter-Insurgency Era in Critical Perspective*. London: Palgrave Macmillan, 2014.

Gwynn, Charles. *Imperial Policing*. London: Macmillan, 1934.

Hack, Karl. "Everyone Lived in Fear: Malaya and the British War in Counter-Insurgency." *Small Wars and Insurgencies* 23, nos. 4–5 (2012): 671–99.

——. " 'Iron Claws on Malaya': The Historiography of the Malayan Emergency." *Journal of Southeast Asian Studies* 30, no. 1 (1999): 99–125.

——. "The Malayan Emergency as a Counter-Insurgency Paradigm." *Journal of Strategic Studies* 32, no. 3 (2009): 383–414.

Hamill, Desmond. *Pig in the Middle: The Army in Northern Ireland, 1969–1984*. London: Methuen, 1984.

Hammel, Eric M. *The Root: The Marines in Beirut, August 1982–February 1984.* New York: Harcourt Brace Jovanovich, 1985.

Hammes, Col. Thomas X. "Countering Evolved Insurgent Networks." *Military Review,* July–August 2006, 18–26.

Hanson, Victor Davis. *The Savior Generals: How Five Great Commanders Saved Wars That Were Lost—from Ancient Greece to Iraq.* London: Bloomsbury, 2013.

Harding, Thomas. "Public Support for Afghanistan Is Vital." *Daily Telegraph,* November 13, 2008.

Hardt, Michael, and Antonio Negri. *Empire.* Cambridge, MA: Harvard University Press, 2000.

Harnden, Toby. *Dead Men Risen: The Welsh Guards and the Defining Story of Britain's War in Afghanistan.* London: Bloomsbury, 2011.

Hart, Basil Liddell. *Strategy: The Indirect Approach.* London: Faber, 1967.

Hashem, Ahmed S. "The Insurgency in Iraq." *Small Wars and Insurgencies* 14, no. 3 (2003): 1–22.

Hay, Colin, and David Marsh, eds. *Demystifying Globalization.* London: Macmillan, 2000.

——. "Introduction: Demystifying Globalization." In Colin Hay and David Marsh, eds., *Demystifying Globalization,* 1–19. London: Macmillan, 2000.

Held, David, and Anthony McGrew. "The End of the Old Order? Globalization and the Prospects for World Order." *Review of International Studies* 24, no. 3 (1998): 219–45.

Hendrickson, David C., and Robert W. Tucker. "Revisions in Need of Revising: What Went Wrong in the Iraq War." *Survival* 47, no. 2 (2005): 7–32.

Heuser, Beatrice. "The Cultural Revolution in Counter-Insurgency." *Journal of Strategic Studies* 30, no. 1 (2007): 153–71.

Hilsman, Roger. *To Move a Nation: The Politics of Foreign Policy in the Administration of John F. Kennedy.* New York: Delta, 1967.

Hobsbawm, Eric, and Terence Ranger, eds. *The Invention of Tradition: Essays on Invented Traditions Throughout the World.* Cambridge, UK: Cambridge University Press, 1983.

Hodges, Donald C. *Argentina's Dirty War: An Intellectual History.* Austin: University of Texas Press, 1981.

Hoffman, Frank G. "Neo-classical Insurgency?" *Parameters* 37, no. 2 (2007): 71–87.

Hogard, Jacques. "Guerre révolutionnaire ou révolution dans l'art del la guerre." *Revue defénse nationale,* no. 12 (December 1956): 1498–1504.

Hoge, James F., and Gideon Rose, eds. *How Did This Happen? Terrorism and the New War.* New York: Public Affairs, 2001.

Holland, Jack, and Susan Phoenix. *Phoenix: Policing the Shadows. The Secret War Against Terrorism in Northern Ireland.* London: Hodder and Stoughton, 1996.

Holsti, K. J. *The State, War, and the State of War.* Cambridge, UK: Cambridge University Press, 1996.

Honig, Jan Willem. "Strategy in a Post-Clausewitzian Setting." In Gerd de Nooy, ed., *The Clausewitzian Dictum and the Future of Western Military Strategy,* 109–23. The Hague: Kluwer Law International, 1997.

Honig, Jan Willem, and Norbert Both. *Srebrenica: Record of a War Crime.* London: Penguin, 1996.

Horne, Alistair Horne. *A Savage War of Peace: Algeria, 1954–1962.* London: Penguin, 2002.

Hosington, William A. *Lyautey and the French Conquest of Morocco.* London: Palgrave Macmillan, 1995.

Howard, Michael. *The Causes of War.* London: Counterpoint, 1983.

Hughes, Matthew. "Introduction: British Ways of Counter-Insurgency, a Historical Perspective." *Small Wars and Insurgencies* 23, nos. 4–5 (2012): 580–90.

Huntington, Samuel P. "The Change to Change: Modernization, Development, and Politics." *Comparative Politics* 3, no. 3 (1971): 283–322.

——. *Political Order in Changing Societies.* New Haven: Yale University Press, 1968.

Hurd, Douglas. *Choose Your Weapons: The British Foreign Secretary, Two Centuries of Conflict and Personalities.* London: Weidenfeld and Nicolson, 2010.

Hurrell, Andrew, and Ngaire Woods. "Globalization and Inequality." *Millennium* 24, no. 3 (1995): 447–70.

Ingram, Martin, and Greg Harkin. *Stakeknife: Britain's Secret Agents in Ireland.* Dublin: O'Brien Press, 2004.

Jackson, Brian A. "Counterinsurgency Intelligence in a 'Long War': The British Experience in Northern Ireland." *Military Review,* January–February 2007, 74–85.

Jackson, Colin. "Government in a Box? Counter-Insurgency, State Building, and the Technocratic Conceit." In Celeste Ward Gventer, David Martin Jones, and M. L. R. Smith, eds., *The New Counter-Insurgency Era in Critical Perspective,* 82–110. London: Palgrave Macmillan, 2014.

Jackson, Mike. "British Counter-Insurgency." *Journal of Strategic Studies* 32, no. 3 (2009): 347–51.

Jackson, Peter Drake. "French Ground Force Organizational Development for Counterrevolutionary Warfare Between 1945 and 1962." MA thesis, Army War College, 2005. http://www.au.af.mil/au/awc/awcgate/army/sgsc_jackson.pdf.

Jackson, Richard. "An Analysis of EU Counterterrorism Discourse Post–September 11." *Cambridge Review of International Affairs* 20, no. 2 (2007): 233–47.

——. "Security, Democracy, and the Rhetoric of Counter-Terrorism." *Democracy and Security* 1, no. 2 (2005): 147–71.

Jaffar, Jameel, and Amrit Singh. *Administration of Torture: A Documentary Record from Washington to Abu Ghraib.* New York: Columbia University Press, 2007.

Janke, Peter. *Guerrilla and Terrorist Organisations: A World Directory and Bibliography.* Brighton, UK: Harvester, 1983.

Jansen, Johannes J. G. *The Neglected Duty: The Creed of Sadat's Assassins and Islamic Resurgence in the Middle East.* London: Macmillan, 1986.

Jenkins, Brian. *Terrorism: A New Mode of Conflict.* Los Angeles: Crescent, 1975.

Jones, David Martin. "Politics, Statecraft, and the Art of War." *Infinity Journal* 4, no. 2 (2014): 18–24.

Jones, David Martin, and M. L. R. Smith. "Grammar but No Logic: Technique Is Not Enough—a Reply to Nagl and Burton." *Journal of Strategic Studies* 33, no. 3 (2010): 430–41.

——. "Greetings from the Cybercaliphate: Some Notes on Homeland Insecurity." *International Affairs* 81, no. 5 (2005): 925–50.

——. "The Perils of Hyper-vigilance: The War on Terrorism and the Surveillance State in South-East Asia." *Intelligence and National Security* 17, no. 4 (2002): 31–54.

——. *Sacred Violence: Political Religion in a Secular Age*. London: Palgrave Macmillan, 2014.

Jones, David Martin, M. L. R. Smith, and John Stone. "Counter-COIN: Counterinsurgency and the Preemption of Strategy." *Studies in Conflict and Terrorism* 35, no. 9 (2012): 597–617.

Juris, Jeffrey S. *Networking Futures: The Movements Against Corporate Globalization*. Durham, NC: Duke University Press, 2008.

Kadvany, John. *Imre Lakatos and the Guises of Reason*. Durham, NC: Duke University Press, 2001.

Kagan, Frederick W., and Kimberly Kagan. "The Patton of Counterinsurgency." *Weekly Standard*, October 3, 2008.

Kagan, Kimberley. *The Surge: A Military History*. New York: Encounter, 2009.

Kahl, Colin H. "COIN of the Realm: Is There a Future for Counterinsurgency?" *Foreign Affairs* 86, no. 6 (2007): 169–76.

Kahn, Herman. *On Escalation: Metaphors and Scenarios*. New York: Praeger, 1965.

Kaldor, Mary. *New and Old Wars: Organized Violence in a Global Era*. Stanford: Stanford University Press, 1999.

Kaplan, Fred. *The Insurgents: David Petraeus and the Plot to Change the American Way of War*. New York: Simon and Schuster, 2013.

Karnow, Stanley. *Vietnam: A History*. London: Pimlico, 1994.

Karpat, Kemal H. *The Politicization of Islam: Reconstructing Faith, States, and Community in the Late Ottoman Empire*. Oxford: Oxford University Press, 1981.

KCL Insurgency Group. "Reviewing UK Army Countering Insurgency." Meeting, June 20, 2007, King's College, London.

Keddie, Nikki R. *An Islamic Response to Imperialism: Political and Religious Writings of Jamal a-Din "al-Afghani."* Berkeley: University of California Press, 1998.

Kedourie, Elie. *Afghani and Adud: An Essay on Religious Unbelief and Political Activism in Modern Islam*. London: Cass, 1966.

Keegan, John. *A History of Warfare*. New York: Vintage, 1994.

Kelly, George Armstrong. *Lost Soldiers: The French Army and Empire in Crisis, 1945–62*. Cambridge, MA: MIT Press, 1965.

Kilcullen, David. *The Accidental Guerrilla: Fighting Small Wars in the Midst of a Big One*. London: Hurst, 2009.

——. "Countering Global Insurgency." *Journal of Strategic Studies* 28, no. 4 (2005): 597–617.

——. *Counterinsurgency*. Oxford: Oxford University Press, 2010.

——. "Counterinsurgency Redux." *Survival* 48, no. 4 (2006): 111–30.

——. "Ethics, Politics, and Non-state Warfare." *Anthropology Today* 23, no. 3 (2007): 20.

——. "Subversion and Counter Subversion in the Campaign Against Terrorism in Europe." *Studies in Conflict and Terrorism* 30, no. 8 (2007): 647–66.

——. "Twenty-Eight Articles: Fundamentals of Company-Level Counterinsurgency." *Small Wars Journal*, March 29, 2006, 1–11. smallwarsjournal.com/documents/28articles.pdf.

Kiszley, Lt. Gen. Sir John. "Learning About Counterinsurgency." *Military Review*, March–April 2007, 5–11.

Kitson, Frank. *Bunch of Five*. London: Faber, 1977.

———. *Gangs and Counter-Gangs*. London: Barrie and Rockliff, 1960.

———. *Low-Intensity Operations: Subversion, Insurgency, and Peacekeeping*. London: Faber, 1971.

———. *Warfare as a Whole*. London: Faber, 1987.

Klein, Naomi. *No Logo*. New York: Picador, 2000.

Krause, Lincoln. "Playing for the Breaks: Insurgent Mistakes." *Parameters* 39, no. 4 (2009): 49–64.

Krepenivich, Andrew F. *The Army and Vietnam*. Baltimore: Johns Hopkins University Press, 1986.

Krieger, Major Mark P. "We the People Are Not the Center of Gravity." *Military Review*, July–August 2007, 96–100.

Labignette, Capt. [no first name given]. "Cas concrete de guerre révolutionnaire." *Revue demilitaire l'information*, no. 281 (February–March 1957): 30–33.

Ladwig, Walter C. "Managing Counterinsurgency: Lessons from Malaya." *Military Review*, May–June 2007, 56–66.

LaFeber, Walter. "The Rise and Fall of Colin Powell." *Political Science Quarterly* 124, no. 1 (2009): 71–93.

Lake, David A., and Robert Powell, eds. *Strategic Choice and International Relations*. Princeton: Princeton University Press, 1999.

Laqueur, Walter. "Terrorism—a Balance Sheet." In Walter Laqueur, ed., *The Terrorism Reader*, 251–67. Philadelphia: Temple University Press, 1978.

———, ed. *The Terrorism Reader*. Philadelphia: Temple University Press, 1978.

Larsonn, Thomas. *The Race to the Top: The Real Story of Globalization*. Washington, D.C.: Cato Institute, 2001.

"Lebanon: The Multinational Force." *Country-data.com*, n.d. http://www.country-data.com/cgi-bin/query/r-8078.htm.

Ledwidge, Frank. *Losing Small Wars: British Military Failure in Iraq and Afghanistan*. New Haven: Yale University Press, 2011.

The Legacy of Lawrence of Arabia. BBC2, Episode 1, January 16, 2010, and Episode 2, January 23, 2010.

Lerner, Daniel. *The Passing of Traditional Society: Modernizing the Middle East*. New York: Free Press, 1958.

Lévy, Bernard-Henri. *Left in Dark Times: A Stand Against the New Barbarism*. New York: Random House, 2008.

Levy, Marion J. *Modernization: Latecomers and Survivors*. New York: Free Press, 1972.

Lewis, Paul. *Guerrillas and Generals: Dirty War in Argentina*. Greenwood, CT: Praeger, 2002.

Lieb, Peter. "Suppressing Insurgencies in Comparison: The German in the Ukraine, 1918, and the British in Mesopotamia." *Small Wars and Insurgencies* 23, nos. 4–5 (2012): 627–47.

Lindblom, Charles. "Political Science in the 1940s and 1950s." *Daedalus* 126, no. 1 (1997): 225–52.

Lipset, Seymour Martin. "Some Social Requisites of Democracy: Economic Development and Political Legitimacy." *American Political Science Review* 53, no. 1 (1959): 69–105.

Lodge, Juliet, ed. *Terrorism: A Challenge to the State.* Oxford: Martin Robertson, 1981.

Lowry, Richard S. *New Dawn: The Battles for Fallujah.* New York: Savas Beatie, 2010.

Luttwak, Edward. "Give War a Chance." *Foreign Affairs* 78, no. 4 (1999): 36–44.

Lynn, John A. "Patterns of Insurgency and Counterinsurgency." *Military Review*, July–August 2005, 22–27.

Mackinlay, John. *Globalisation and Insurgency.* Adelphi Paper no. 352. London: International Institute for Strategic Studies and Oxford University Press, 2002.

——. *The Insurgent Archipelago.* London: Hurst, 2009.

——. "Tackling Bin Laden: Lessons from History." *Observer*, October 28, 2001.

Malkasian, Carter. "The Role of Perceptions and Political Reform in Counterinsurgency: The Case of Western Iraq, 2004–05." *Small Wars and Insurgencies* 17, no. 3 (2006): 367–94.

Manea, Octavian. "Learning from Today's Crisis of Counterinsurgency." *Small Wars Journal*, October 8, 2013. http://smallwarsjournal.com/jrnl/art/learning-from-today's-crisis-of-counterinsurgency.

Mann, Maj. Morgan. "The Power Equation: Using Tribal Politics in Counterinsurgency." *Military Review*, May–June 2007, 104–8.

Mansoor, Peter R. *Baghdad at Sunrise: A Brigade Commander's War in Iraq.* New Haven: Yale University Press, 2009.

——. *Surge: My Journey with General David Petraeus and the Remaking of the Iraq War.* New Haven: Yale University Press, 2013.

Mansoor, Col. Peter R., and Maj. Mark S. Ulrich. "Linking Doctrine to Action: A New Center-of-Gravity Analysis." *Military Review*, September–October 2007, 45–51.

Marchak, Patricia. *God's Assassins: State Terrorism in Argentina in the 1970s.* Montreal: McGill-Queens University Press, 1999.

Markel, Wade. "Draining the Swamp: The British Strategy of Population Control." *Parameters* 36, no. 1 (2006): 35–48.

——. "Winning Our Own Hearts and Minds: Promotion in Wartime." *Military Review*, November–December 2004, 25–30.

Marshall, Alex. "Imperial Nostalgia, the Liberal Lie, and the Perils of Postmodern Counterinsurgency." *Small Wars and Insurgencies* 21, no. 2 (2010): 233–58.

Martinez, Luis. *The Algerian Civil War, 1990–1998.* New York: Columbia University Press, 2000.

Masters, Jonathan, and Zachary Laub. "Al-Qaeda in Iraq (a.k.a. Islamic State in Iraq and Greater Syria)." Council on Foreign Relations, October 29, 2013. http://www.cfr.org/iraq/al-qaeda-iraq-k-islamic-state-iraq-greater-syria/p14811.

McCuen, John J. *The Art of Counter-Revolutionary War: The Strategy of Counter-Insurgency.* London: Faber, 1966. Reprint, St. Petersburg, FL: Hailer, 2005.

McDonald, Henry. *Gunsmoke and Mirrors: How Sinn Féin Dressed Up Defeat as Victory.* Dublin: Gill and Macmillan, 2008.

McDougall, Walter A. *Promised Land, Crusader State: The American Encounter with the World Since 1776.* New York: Houghton Mifflin, 1997.

McFate, Montgomery. "Anthropology and Counterinsurgency: The Strange Story of Their Curious Relationship." *Military Review*, March–April 2005, 24–38.

——. "Building Bridges or Burning Heretics." *Anthropology Today* 23, no. 3 (2007): 21.

——. "Iraq: The Social Context of IEDs." *Military Review*, May–June 2005, 37–40.

——. "The Military Utility of Understanding Adversary Culture." *Joint Forces Quarterly* 38, 3rd quarter (2005): 42–48.

McFate, Montgomery, and Andrea V. Jackson, "The Object of War: Counterinsurgency and the Four Tools of Political Competition." *Military Review*, January–February 2006, 13–16.

——. "An Organizational Solution for DOD's Cultural Knowledge Needs." *Military Review*, July–August 2005, 18–21.

McGreal, Chris, and Jon Boone. "US Launches New Afghan Counterinsurgency Strategy." *Guardian*, September 24, 2009. http://www.guardian.co.uk/world/2009/sep/24/us-adopts-new-afghan-plan.

McGrew, Anthony G. "Conceptualizing Global Politics." In Anthony G. McGrew and Paul G. Lewis, eds., *Global Politics, Globalization, and the Nation-State*, 1–30. Cambridge, UK: Polity, 1992.

McGrew, Anthony G., and Paul G. Lewis, eds. *Global Politics, Globalization and the Nation-State*. Cambridge, UK: Polity, 1992.

McGuffin, John. *The Guinea Pigs*. Harmondsworth, UK: Penguin, 1974.

McInnes, Colin. *Hot War, Cold War: The British Army's Way in Warfare, 1945–95*. London: Brassey's, 1996.

McInnes, Colin, and G. D. Sheffield, eds. *Warfare in the Twentieth Century: Theory and Practice*. London: Unwin Hyman, 1988.

McKnight, Gerard. *The Mind of the Terrorist*. London: Michael Joseph, 1974.

McMaster, H. R. *Dereliction of Duty: Lyndon Johnson, Robert McNamara, the Joint Chiefs of Staff, and the Lies That Led to Vietnam*. New York: HarperCollins, 1997.

McNamara, Robert S. *In Retrospect: The Tragedy and Lessons of Vietnam*. New York: Vintage, 1996.

McStiofain, Séan. *Memoirs of a Revolutionary*. Edinburgh: Cremonesi, 1975.

Melillo, Michael R. "Outfitting a Big-War Military with Small-War Capabilities." *Parameters* 36, no. 3 (2006): 22–35.

Metz, Steven. "Counterinsurgency and American Strategy, Past and Future." *World Politics Review*, January 24, 2012. http://www.worldpoliticsreview.com/articles/11248/counter-insurgency-and-american-strategy-past-and-future.

——. *Rethinking Insurgency*. Carlisle, PA: Strategic Studies Institute, 2007.

Meyer, Christopher. *Getting Our Way: 500 Years of Adventure and Intrigue. The Inside Story of British Diplomacy*. London: Weidenfeld and Nicolson, 2009.

Michaels, Jeffery H., and Matthew Ford. "Bandwagonistas: Rhetorical Re-description, Strategic Choice, and the Politics of Counter-Insurgency." *Small Wars and Insurgencies* 22, no. 2 (2011): 352–84.

Millen, Raymond. "The Hobbesian Notion of Self-Preservation Concerning Human Behavior During an Insurgency." *Parameters* 36, no. 4 (2006–2007): 4–13.

Mills, C. Wright. *The Power Elite*. New York: Oxford University Press, 1956.

Mockaitis, Thomas R. *British Counter-Insurgency, 1919–1960*. London: Macmillan, 1990.

——. *British Counter-Insurgency in the Post-imperial Era*. Manchester, UK: Manchester University Press, 1995.

——. "The Minimum Force Debate: Contemporary Sensibilities Meet Imperial Practice." *Small Wars and Insurgencies* 23, nos. 4–5 (2012): 762–80.

Møller, Bjørn. "The Faces of War." In Håkan Wiberg and Christian P. Scherrer, eds., *Ethnicity and Intra-state Conflict: Types, Causes, and Peace Strategies*, 15–34. Aldershot, UK: Ashgate, 1999.

Moloney, Ed. *A Secret History of the IRA*. London: Penguin, 2002.

Moltke, Helmuth von. *Moltke on the Art of War: Selected Writings*. Edited by Daniel J. Hughes. New York: Presidio, 1993.

Morgenthau, Hans. "Vietnam and the National Interest." In Marvin E. Gettleman, ed., *Vietnam: History, Documents, and Opinions on a Major Crisis*, 391–92. London: Penguin, 1965.

Mueller, John. "The Banality of Ethnic War." *International Security* 25, no. 1 (2000): 42–70.

Murphy, Dan. "One Year After bin Laden's Killing, al-Qaeda Is in Tatters." *Christian Science Monitor*, May 1, 2012.

Myrdal, Gunnar. *Asian Drama: An Inquiry Into the Poverty of Nations*. London: Allen Lane and Penguin, 1968.

Nagl, John. "Constructing the Legacy of Field Manual 3-24." *Joint Forces Quarterly* 58, 3rd quarter (2010): 118–20.

——. "Foreword to the University of Chicago Press Edition." In *The US Army/Marine Corps Counterinsurgency Field Manual*, xii–xx. Chicago: University of Chicago Press, 2007.

——. *Learning to Eat Soup with a Knife: Counterinsurgency Lessons from Malaya and Vietnam*. Chicago: University of Chicago Press, 2002.

——. "Let's Win the Wars We're In." *Joint Forces Quarterly* 52, 1st quarter (2009): 20–26.

——. "Local Security Forces." In Thomas Rid and Thomas Kearney, eds., *Understanding Counterinsurgency: Doctrine, Operations, and Challenges*, 160–70. London: Routledge, 2010.

Nagl, John A., and Brian Burton. "Thinking Globally and Acting Locally: Counterinsurgency Lessons from Modern Wars—a Reply to Smith and Jones." *Journal of Strategic Studies* 33, no. 1 (2010): 123–38.

Naughton, John. "Steven Pinker: Fighting Talk from the Prophet of Peace." *Observer*, October 15, 2011.

Neumann, Peter. *Britain's Long War: British Strategy in the Northern Ireland Conflict, 1969–98*. London: Palgrave Macmillan, 2003.

Neumann, Peter, and M. L. R. Smith. *The Strategy of Terrorism: How It Works and Why It Fails*. London: Routledge, 2008.

Newsinger, John. *British Counter-Insurgency: From Palestine to Northern Ireland*. London: Palgrave, 2002.

——. "From Counter-Insurgency to Internal Security: Northern Ireland, 1962–1992." *Small Wars and Insurgencies* 6, no. 1 (1995): 88–111.

Nooy, Gerd de, ed. *The Clausewitzian Dictum and the Future of Western Military Strategy*. The Hague: Kluwer Law International, 1997.

Norton-Taylor, Richard. "General Hits Out at US Tactics." *Guardian*, April 21, 2004.

Norton-Taylor, Richard, and Jamie Wilson. "US Army in Iraq Institutionally Racist, Claims British Officer." *Guardian*, January 12, 2006.

Oakeshott, Michael. *The Politics of Faith and the Politics of Scepticism*. Edited by Timothy Fuller. New Haven: Yale University Press, 1996.

——. *Rationalism in Politics and Other Essays*. London: Methuen, 1981.

O'Callaghan, Sean. *The Informer*. London: Corgi, 1998.

O'Doherty, Malachi. *The Trouble with Guns: Republican Strategy and the Provisional IRA*. Belfast: Blackstaff, 1998.

Office of the President of the United States. *National Security Strategy*. Washington, D.C.: Office of the President of the United States, 2010.

Ollivant, Douglas. *Countering the New Orthodoxy: Reinterpreting Counterinsurgency in Iraq*. National Security Studies Program Policy Paper. Washington, D.C.: New America Foundation, June 2011. http://www.newamerica.net/sites/newamerica.net/files/policy-docs/Ollivant_Reinterpreting_Counterinsurgency.pdf.

Ollivant, Lt. Col. Douglas A., and Lt. Eric D. Chewing. "Producing Victory: Rethinking Conventional Forces in COIN Operations." *Military Review*, July–August 2006, 50–59.

O'Neill, Bard E. *Insurgency and Terrorism: Inside Modern Revolutionary Warfare*. Dulles, VA: Brassey's, 1990.

"On This Day" (February 26, 1984). *BBC News*, n.d. http://news.bbc.co.uk/onthisday/hi/dates/stories/february/26/newsid_4153000/4153013.stm.

Packer, George. "Knowing the Enemy: Can Social Scientists Redefine the 'War on Terror'?" *New Yorker*, December 18, 2006.

Page, Michael. *Prisons, Peace, and Terrorism: Penal Policy and the Reduction of Terrorism in Northern Ireland, Italy, and the Basque Country, 1968–97*. Basingstoke, UK: Macmillan, 1998.

Paget, Julian. *Counter-Insurgency Campaigning*. London: Faber, 1967.

Paret, Peter. *French Revolutionary Warfare from Indochina to Algeria: The Analysis of a Political and Military Doctrine*. New York: Praeger, 1964.

——, ed. *Makers of Modern Strategy: From Machiavelli to the Nuclear Age*. Oxford: Clarendon Press, 1986.

Parsons, Talcott. *On Institutions and Social Evolution*. Chicago. University of Chicago Press, 1982.

——. *The Social System*. New York: Free Press, 1951.

Patriquin, Capt. Travis. "Using Occam's Razor to Connect the Dots: The Ba'ath Party and the Insurgency in Tal Afar." *Military Review*, January–February 2007, 16–25.

Peters, Ralph. "The New Strategic Trinity." *Parameters* 28, no. 4 (1998–1999): 73–79.

Petraeus, Lt. Gen. David. "Learning Counterinsurgency: Observations from Soldiering in Iraq." *Military Review*, January–February 2006, 2–11.

Pieterse, Jan Nederveen. "Globalization as Hybridization." In Mike Featherstone, Scott Lash, and Roland Robertson, eds., *Global Modernities*, 99–105. London: Sage, 1995.

Pimlott, John, ed. *Guerrilla Warfare*. London: Bison Books, 1985.

Pinker, Steven. *The Better Angels of Our Nature: A History of Violence and Humanity*. London: Penguin, 2011.

Pion-Berlin, David, and George A. Lopez. "Of Victims and Executioners: Argentine State Terror, 1975–1979." *International Studies Quarterly* 35, no. 1 (1991): 63–86.

Popper, Karl. *The Logic of Scientific Discovery*. London: Routledge, 2002.

Porch, Douglas. *Counterinsurgency: Exposing the Myths of the New Way of War*. Cambridge, UK: Cambridge University Press, 2013.

——. "The Dangerous Myth and Dubious Promise of COIN." *Small Wars and Insurgencies* 22, no. 2 (2011): 239–57.

——. "David Galula and the Revival of COIN in the US Military." In Celeste Ward Gventer, David Martin Jones, and M. L. R. Smith, eds., *The New Counterinsurgency Era in Critical Perspective*, 173–98. London: Palgrave Macmillan, 2014.

——. Introduction to Charles E. Callwell, *Small Wars: Their Principles and Practice*, v–xviii. Lincoln: University of Nebraska Press and Bison Books, 1996.

Porter, Patrick. "Shadow Wars: Asymmetric Warfare in the Past and Future." *Security Dialogue* 37, no. 4 (2006): 551–61

Preston, Richard A., Alex Roland, and Sydney F. Wise. *Men in Arms: A History of Warfare and Its Interrelationships with Western Society*. New York: Harcourt Brace Jovanovich, 1991.

Pritchard, James, and M. L. R. Smith. "Thompson in Helmand: Comparing Theory to Practice in British Counter-Insurgency Operations in Afghanistan." *Civil Wars* 12, nos. 1–2 (2010): 65–90.

Pye, Lucian W., and Sidney Verba, eds. *Political Culture and Political Development*. Princeton: Princeton University Press, 1965.

Pyle, Christopher H. *Getting Away with Torture: Secret Government, War Crimes, and Rule of Law*. Washington, D.C.: Potomac Books, 2009.

Qutb, Sayyid. *Milestones*. New York: Mother Mosque Foundation, 1979.

Raphaeli, Nimrod. *Radical Islamist Profiles: Ayman Muhammad Rabi al Zawahiri: The Making of an Arch Terrorist*. Berlin: Middle East Research Institute, 2003.

Record, Jeffrey. "External Assistance: Enabler of Insurgent Success." *Parameters* 36, no. 3 (2006): 36–49.

——. "Why the Strong Lose." *Parameters* 35, no. 4 (2005–2006): 16–31.

Reed, Brian. "A Social Network Approach to Understanding an Insurgency." *Parameters* 37, no. 2 (2007): 19–30.

Reis, Bruno. "The Myth of British Minimum Force in Counterinsurgency Campaigns During Decolonisation (1945–1970)." *Journal of Strategic Studies* 34, no. 2 (2011): 245–79.

Ricks, Thomas, E. *Fiasco: The American Military Adventure in Iraq*. New York: Penguin, 2006.

——. *The Gamble: General David Petraeus and the American Military Adventure in Iraq, 2006–2008*. New York: Penguin, 2009.

Rid, Thomas. "The Nineteenth Century Origins of Counterinsurgency Doctrine." *Journal of Strategic Studies* 33, no. 5 (2010): 727–58.

Rid, Thomas, and Thomas Kearney, eds. *Understanding Counterinsurgency: Doctrine, Operations, and Challenges*. London: Routledge, 2010.

Risen, James. *State of War: The Secret History of the CIA and the Bush Administration*. New York: Free Press, 2007.

Rogers, Paul. *Global Security and the War on Terror: Elite Power and the Illusion of Control*. London: Routledge, 2008.

Rostow, W. W. *Politics and the Stages of Growth*. Cambridge, UK: Cambridge University Press, 1971.

Rovner, Joshua. "The Heroes of COIN." *Orbis* 52, no. 2 (2012): 215–32.

——. "Questions About COIN After Iraq and Afghanistan." In Celeste Ward Gventer, David Martin Jones, and M. L. R. Smith, *The New Counter-Insurgency Era in Critical Perspective*, 299–318. London: Palgrave Macmillan, 2014.

Russell, Alec. "How the West Turned a Blind Eye Despite General's 'Genocide Fax.'" *Daily Telegraph*, April 6, 2004.

Russell, Charles, Leon Banker, and Bowman Miller. "Out-Inventing the Terrorist." In Yonah Alexander, David Carlton, and Paul Wilkinson, eds., *Terrorism: Theory and Practice*, 3–37. Boulder, CO: Westview, 1979.

Rustow, Dankwart A. *A World of Nations: Problems of Political Modernization*. Washington, D.C.: Brookings Institution Press, 1972.

Ryder, Chris. *The RUC: A Force Under Fire*. London: Methuen, 1989.

Sacks, Jonathan. *The Home We Build Together: Recreating Society*. London: Continuum, 2008.

Salt, James, and M. L. R. Smith, "Reassessing Military Assistance to the Civil Powers: Are Traditional British Anti-terrorist Responses Still Effective?" *Low Intensity Conflict and Law Enforcement* 13, no. 3 (2005): 227–49.

Scahill, Jeremy. *Dirty Wars: The World Is a Battlefield*. London: Serpent's Tail, 2013.

Schelling, Thomas C. *Choice and Consequence: Perspectives of an Errant Economist*. Cambridge, MA: Harvard University Press, 1984.

——. *The Strategy of Conflict*. New York: Oxford University Press, 1980.

Selvadurai, S. D., and M. L. R. Smith. "Black Tigers, Bronze Lotus: The Evolution and Dynamics of Sri Lanka's Strategies of Dirty War." *Studies in Conflict and Terrorism* 36, no. 7 (2013): 547–72.

Sepp, Kalev I. "Best Practices in Counterinsurgency." *Military Review*, May–June 2005, 8–12.

Sewall, Sarah. "Introduction to the University of Chicago Press Edition: A Radical Field Manual." In *The US Army/Marine Corps Counterinsurgency Field Manual*, xxi–xlii. Chicago: University of Chicago Press, 2007.

——. "Modernizing US Counterinsurgency Practice: Rethinking Risk and Developing a National Strategy." *Military Review*, September–October 2006, 103–9.

Sheffield, G. D. "*Blitzkrieg* and Attrition: Land Operations in Europe 1914–45." In Colin McInnes and G. D. Sheffield, eds., *Warfare in the Twentieth Century: Theory and Practice*, 51–79. London: Unwin Hyman, 1988.

——. *The Chief: Douglas Haig and the British Army*. London: Aurum, 2011.

Shepherd, William E. *Sayyid Qutb and Islamic Activism*. Leiden: Brill, 1996.

Shils, Edward. *Tradition*. London: Faber and Faber, 1981.

Shirer, William L. *Berlin Diary: The Journal of a Foreign Correspondent, 1934–1941*. Boston: Little Brown, 1941.

Shy, John, and Thomas Collier. "Revolutionary War." In Peter Paret, ed., *Makers of Modern Strategy: From Machiavelli to the Nuclear Age*, 815–59. Oxford: Clarendon Press, 1986.

Simms, Brendan. *Unfinest Hour: Britain and the Destruction of Bosnia.* London: Penguin, 2001.

Singer, J. David, and Melvin Small. *Resort to Arms: International and Civil Wars, 1816–1980.* Beverly Hills, CA: Sage, 1982.

Smith, M. L. R. *Fighting for Ireland? The Military Strategy of the Irish Republican Movement.* London: Routledge, 1995.

——. "Guerrillas in the Mist: Reassessing Strategy and Low Intensity Warfare." *Review of International Studies* 29, no. 1 (2003): 19–37.

——. "Quantum Strategy: The Interior World of War." *Infinity Journal* 3, no. 1 (2012): 10–13.

Smith, M. L. R., and Peter R. Neumann. "Motorman's Long Journey: Changing the Strategic Setting in Northern Ireland." *Contemporary British History* 19, no. 4 (2005): 413–35.

Smith, M. L. R., and Sophie Roberts. "War in the Gray: Exploring the Concept of Dirty War." *Studies in Conflict and Terrorism* 31, no. 5 (2008): 377–98.

Smith, M. L. R., and John Stone. "Explaining Strategic Theory." *Infinity Journal* 1, no. 4 (2011): 27–30.

Smith, Rupert. *The Utility of Force: The Art of War in the Modern World.* London: Allen Lane, 2005.

Smoke, Richard. *War: Controlling Escalation.* Cambridge, MA: Harvard University Press, 1977.

Snyder, Craig A., ed. *Contemporary Security and Strategy.* London: Palgrave Macmillan, 2008.

Sorley, Lewis. *A Better War: The Unexamined Victories and Final Tragedy of America's Last Years in Vietnam.* Orlando, FL: Harcourt, 1999.

Stannard, Matthew B. "Montgomery McFate's Mission." *San Francisco Chronicle,* April 29, 2007.

Stevenson, Jonathan. *"We Wrecked the Place": Contemplating an End to Northern Ireland's Troubles.* New York: Free Press, 1996.

Stone, John. "Escalation and the War on Terror." *Journal of Strategic Studies* 35, no. 5 (2012): 639–61.

——. *Military Strategy: The Politics and Technique of War.* London: Continuum, 2011.

Sullivan, Maj. Michael D. "Leadership in Counterinsurgency: A Tale of Two Leaders." *Military Review,* September–October 2007, 119–23.

Summers, Harry. "A War Is a War Is a War Is a War." In Loren B. Thompson, ed., *Low-Intensity Conflict: The Pattern of Warfare in the Modern World,* 27–45. Lexington, MA: Lexington Books, 1989.

Surridge, Keith. "An Example to Be Followed or a Warning to Be Avoided? The British, Boers, and Guerrilla Warfare, 1900–1902." *Small Wars and Insurgencies* 23, nos. 4–5 (2012): 608–26.

Taber, Robert. *War of the Flea: The Classic Study of Guerrilla Warfare.* New York: L. Stuart, 1965.

Taylor, Peter. *Beating the Terrorists: Interrogation at Omagh, Gough, and Castlereagh.* London: Penguin, 1980.

Terraine, John. *The Smoke and the Fire: Myths and Anti-myths of War, 1861–1945.* London: Sidgwick and Jackson, 1980.

"Text of George Bush's Speech." *Guardian,* September 21, 2001.

Thomas, Jason. "Romancing the COIN." *Small Wars Journal,* March 13, 2012. http://smallwarsjournal.com/jrnl/art/romancing-the-coin.

Thompson, Loren B., ed. *Low-Intensity Conflict: The Pattern of Warfare in the Modern World*. Lexington, MA: Lexington Books, 1989.

Thompson, Robert. *Defeating Communist Insurgency: Experiences from Malaya and Vietnam*. London: Chatto and Windus, 1966.

Thornton, Rod. "The British Army and the Origins of Its Philosophy of Minimum Force." *Small Wars and Insurgencies* 15, no. 1 (2006): 85–106.

——. "'Minimum Force': A Reply to Huw Bennett." *Small Wars and Insurgencies* 20, no. 1 (2009): 215–26.

Till, Geoffrey. "The Evolution of Strategy in the New World Order." In Craig A. Snyder, ed., *Contemporary Security and Strategy*, 147–74. London: Palgrave Macmillan, 2008.

Toase, Francis. Introduction to Robin Corbett, ed., *Guerrilla Warfare from 1939 to the Present Day*, 6–21. London: Guild, 1986.

Tomes, Robert. "Schlock and Blah: Counter-Insurgency Realities in a Rapid Dominance Era." *Small Wars and Insurgencies* 16, no. 1 (2005): 37–56.

Townshend, Charles. *Britain's Civil Wars: Counterinsurgency in the Twentieth Century*. London: Faber & Faber, 1986.

Tressler, David M. *Negotiation in the New Strategic Environment: Lessons from Iraq*. Carlisle, PA: Strategic Studies Institute, 2007.

Trinquier, Roger. *Modern Warfare: A French View of Counterinsurgency*. London: Pall Mall, 1964. Reprint, Westport, CT: Praeger, 2006.

Ucko, David. "Innovation or Inertia? The US Military and the Learning of Counterinsurgency." *Orbis* 52, no. 2 (2008): 290–310.

——. *The New Counterinsurgency Era: Transforming the U.S. Military for Modern Wars*. Washington, D.C.: Georgetown University Press, 2009.

Ucko, David H., and Robert Egnell. *Counterinsurgency in Crisis: Britain and the Challenges of Modern Warfare*. New York: Columbia University Press, 2013.

UK Chief of the General Staff. *Operation Banner: An Analysis of Military Operations in Northern Ireland*. Army Code 71842. London: Ministry of Defence, July 2006.

UK House of Commons, Defence Committee. *Iraq: An Initial Assessment of Post-conflict Operations*. Sixth Report of Session 2004–2005, vol. 1. London: Her Majesty's Stationary Office, 2005.

UK Ministry of Defence. *Stability Operations in Iraq (Op Telic 2-5): An Analysis from a Land Perspective*. London: Ministry of Defence, 2005. http://download.cabledrum.net/wikileaks_archive/file/uk-stbility-operations-in-iraq-2006.pdf.

Urban, Mark. *Big Boys Rules: The Secret Struggle Against the IRA*. London: Faber, 1992.

——. *Task Force Black: The Explosive True Story of the SAS and the Secret War in Iraq*. London: Abacus, 2011.

U.S. Army. *PRT Playbook: Tactics, Techniques, and Procedures*. Fort Leavenworth, KS: Center for Army Lessons Learned, 2007.

The US Army/Marine Corps Counterinsurgency Field Manual. Chicago: University of Chicago Press, 2007.

U.S. Department of the Army, Headquarters. *Counterinsurgency*. FM3-24/MCWP 3-33.5. Washington, D.C.: U.S. Department of the Army, Headquarters, 2006.

U.S. Department of Defense. *Dictionary of Military and Associate Terms*. Washington, D.C.: U.S. Department of Defense, November 8, 2010. http://www.dtic.mil/doctrine/dod_dictionary/data/d/3840.html.

Vacca, W. Alexander, and Mark Davidson, "The Regularity of Regular Warfare." *Parameters* 41, no. 2 (2011): 18–28.

Van Creveld, Martin. *The Transformation of War*. New York: Free Press, 1991.

Van Ishoven, Armand. *The Luftwaffe and the Battle of Britain*. New York: Scribner, 1980.

Voegelin, Eric. *Modernity Without Restraint: Political Religions; The New Science of Politics; and Science, Politics, and Gnosticism*. Vol. 5 of *The Collected Works of Eric Voegelin*. Columbia: University of Missouri Press, 2000.

Võ Nguyên Giáp. *People's War, People's Army: The Viet Cong Insurrection Manual for Underdeveloped Countries*. New York: Praeger, 1962.

Waldman, Thomas. "British 'Post-conflict' Operations: Into the Heart of Strategic Darkness." *Civil Wars* 9, no. 1 (2007): 61–86.

Walker, Jonathan. *Aden Insurgency: The Savage War in South Arabia 1962–1967*. Staplehurst, UK: Spellmount, 2005.

Walter, Barbara F. "Designing Transitions from Civil War: Demobilization, Democratization, and Commitments to Peace." *International Security* 25, no. 1 (1999): 127–55.

Ware, Oscar. "Preparing for an Irregular Future Counterinsurgency." *Small Wars Journal*, July 18, 2013. http://smallwarsjournal.com/jrnl/art/preparing-for-an-irregular-future-counterinsurgency.

White House. "Osama bin Laden Dead: Remarks by the President on Osama bin Laden." May 2, 2011. http://www.whitehouse.gov/blog/2011/05/02/osama-bin-laden-dead.

Whittingham, Daniel. "'Savage Warfare': C. E. Callwell, the Roots of Counter-Insurgency, and the Nineteenth Century Context." *Small Wars and Insurgencies* 23, nos. 4–5 (2012): 591–607.

Wiberg, Håkan, and Christian P. Scherrer, eds. *Ethnicity and Intra-state Conflict: Types, Causes, and Peace Strategies*. Aldershot, UK: Ashgate, 1999.

Wilkinson, Paul. *Terrorism and the Liberal State*. New York: New York University Press, 1986.

Wilkinson, Paul, and A. M. Stewart, eds. *Contemporary Research on Terrorism*. Aberdeen, Scotland: Aberdeen University Press, 1987.

Wilson, Col. Gregory. "Anatomy of a Successful COIN Operation: OEF-Philippines and the Indirect Approach." *Military Review*, November–December 2006, 2–12.

Wipfli, Ralph, and Steven Metz. "COIN of the Realm: US Counterinsurgency Strategy." Colloquium brief, U.S. Army War College and 21st Century Defense Initiative of the Brookings Institution, Strategic Studies Institute, c. 2008. http://www.strategicstudiesinstitute.army.mil/pdffiles/pub846.pdf.

Yarger, Harry R. *Strategic Theory for the 21st Century: The Little Book on Big Strategy*. Carlisle, PA: Strategic Studies Institute, 2006.

Zulaika, Joseba, and William A. Douglass. "The Terrorist Subject: Terrorism Studies and the Absent Subjectivity." *Critical Studies on Terrorism* 1, no. 1 (2008): 27–36.

Index